Praise for *The Holocaust Industry*

"Its courageous attacks on the financial extortions of groups like the W[orld] J[ewish]C[ongress] are of great importance and, one hopes, will have an impact. Its strident tone, attacked by most of the book's hostile critics, strikes me as highly appropriate, especially given the author's careful sourcing of most of his claims."
– Professor William Rubenstein, University of Wales

"These fraudsters need to be unmasked, and Finkelstein believes that he is the man to do it. In 150 short pages he sets out to expose their machinations. If his indictment is a true one, it should prompt prosecutions, sackings, protest. The book shouts scandal. It is a polemic, communicated at maximum volume."
– *The Times*

"Finkelstein has raised some important and uncomfortable issues." – *Jewish Quarterly*

"Into this minefield, through which most have trodden perhaps a little too gingerly, has bust Norman Finkelstein, a Jew and a self-professed iconoclast, heretic and enemy of the American-Jewish establishment – and he is lobbing grenades." –*Spectator*

"A short, sharp, and copiously noted polemic." – *Times Higher Educational Supplement*

"Finkelstein is at his best when he skewers those who would sacralize the Holocaust." – *Los Angeles Times Book Review*

"His basic argument that the memories of the Holocaust are being debased is serious and should be given its due." –*Economist*

"Clever, explosive, sometimes even wryly funny." – *Salon*

"This is, in short, a lucid, provocative and passionate book. Anyone with an open mind and an interest in the subject should ignore the critical brickbats and read what Finkelstein has to say." –*Statesman*

Norman G. Finkelstein taught political theory and the Israel-Palestine conflict for many years. He is the author of many books, which have been translated into more than forty foreign editions, including *What Gandhi Says*; *This Time We Went Too Far*; *Beyond Chutzpah*; *Image and Reality of the Israel-Palestine Conflict*; and *I'll Burn That Bridge When I Get to It*.

THE HOLOCAUST INDUSTRY

REFLECTIONS ON THE EXPLOITATION OF JEWISH SUFFERING

Second Paperback Edition

◆

NORMAN G. FINKELSTEIN

VERSO
London • New York

This paperback edition published by Verso 2024
First published by Verso 2000
© Norman G. Finkelstein 2000, 2001, 2003, 2015, 2024

1 3 5 7 9 10 8 6 4 2

Verso
UK: 6 Meard Street, London W1F 0EG
US: 388 Atlantic Avenue, Brooklyn, NY 11217
versobooks.com

Verso is the imprint of New Left Books

ISBN-13: 978-1-80429-721-6
ISBN-13: 978-1-78168-440-5 (UK EBK)
ISBN-13: 978-1-84467-487-9 (US EBK)

British Library Cataloguing in Publication Data
A catalogue record for this book is available from the British Library

Library of Congress Cataloging-in-Publication Data
A catalog record for this book is available from the Library of Congress

Typeset by SetSystems Ltd, Saffron Walden, Essex
Printed in the UK by CPI Mackays

"It seems to me the Holocaust is being sold – it is not being taught."

Rabbi Arnold Jacob Wolf, Hillel Director, Yale University[1]

---

[1] Michael Berenbaum, *After Tragedy and Triumph* (Cambridge: 1990), 45.

CONTENTS

ACKNOWLEDGMENTS

Colin Robinson of Verso conceived the idea of this book. Roane Carey molded my reflections into a coherent narrative. At every stage in the book's production Noam Chomsky and Shifra Stern provided assistance. Jennifer Loewenstein and Eva Schweitzer criticized various drafts. Rudolph Baldeo provided personal support and encouragement. I am indebted to all of them. In these pages I attempt to represent my parents' legacy. Accordingly, the book is dedicated to my two siblings, Richard and Henry, and my nephew, David.

FOREWORD TO THE SECOND PAPERBACK EDITION

This will almost certainly be my last word on the Holocaust industry. In prior editions of this book I said pretty much everything I wanted for many years to say: it was finally – pardon the cliché – off my chest. On the other hand, I requested of my publishers, and they generously consented, to put out a second paperback edition focusing on the Swiss banks case. My main concern is to provide readers and, especially, future researchers with a clear picture of what happened and a guide to what to look for amid the heaps of disinformation. Regrettably, the trial record cannot be fully trusted. The presiding judge in the case elected – for reasons not divulged but fairly simple to deduce – not to docket crucial documents. In addition, the Claims Resolution Tribunal (CRT), which could have produced an objective assessment of the charges against the Swiss banks, also can't any longer be trusted. Midway in its work and heading towards vindicating the Swiss banks, the CRT was radically revamped by key figures in the Holocaust industry. Its only function now is to protect the blackmailers' reputation. These developments are copiously documented in the new postscript for this edition. Using as my foil an authoritative account of the Holocaust compensation campaign, I present in the new appendix a comprehensive overview of this "double shakedown" of European countries and survivors of the Nazi holocaust. Although I would be most curious to read a refutation by someone from the Holocaust industry of my findings, I suspect – again, for reasons not difficult to discern – that none will be forthcoming. Yet silence, as my late mother used to say, is also an answer.

Apart from an abundance of *ad hominem* slurs, criticism of my book has fallen largely into two categories. Mainstream critics allege that I conjured a "conspiracy theory," while those on the Left ridicule the book as a defense of "the banks." None, so far as I can tell, question my actual findings. Although the explanatory value of conspiracy theories is marginal, this does not mean that, in the real world, individuals and institutions don't strategize and scheme. To believe otherwise is no less naive than to believe that a vast conspiracy manipulates worldly affairs. In *The Wealth of Nations*, Adam Smith observes that capitalists "seldom meet together, even for merriment and diversion, but the conversation ends in a conspiracy against the public, or in some contrivance to raise prices."[1] Does this make Smith's classic a "conspiracy theory"? Indeed, "conspiracy theory" has become scarcely more than a term of abuse to discredit a politically incorrect sequencing of facts: to maintain that powerful American Jewish organizations, institutions and individuals, in league with the

---

[1] Adam Smith, *The Wealth of Nations* (New York: 2000), intro. by Robert Reich, p. 148.

Clinton administration, coordinated their assault on the Swiss banks is thus alleged to be *prima facie* a conspiracy theory (not to mention anti-Semitic); but to maintain that Swiss banks coordinated an assault on Jewish victims of the Nazi holocaust and their heirs can't be called a conspiracy theory.

It is often wondered why I, a person of the Left, would defend Swiss bankers. In fact I subscribe to Bertolt Brecht's credo: "What's robbing a bank compared to owning one?" Yet my concern in the book is not at all with Swiss bankers or, for that matter, German industrialists. Rather, it is restoring the integrity of the historical record and the sanctity of the Jewish people's martyrdom. I deplore the Holocaust industry's corruption of history and memory in the service of an extortion racket. Leftist critics claim that I have made common cause with the Right. They seem not to have noticed the company they're keeping – a repellent gang of well-heeled hoodlums and hucksters as well as egregious apologists for American and Israeli violence. Rather than help expose them, my critics on the Left rant about "the banks," regardless of the facts. It is a sad (but telling) commentary on how little respect for truth and the dead counts in their moral calculus.

Apart from those already acknowledged in prior editions of this book, I would like to thank Michael Alvarez, Camille Goodison, Maren Hackmann and Jason Coronel for their assistance.

Norman G. Finkelstein
April 2003
Chicago

FOREWORD TO THE FIRST PAPERBACK EDITION

The Holocaust Industry evoked considerable reaction internationally after its publication in June 2000. It prompted a national debate and reached the top of the bestseller list in many countries ranging from Brazil, Belgium and the Netherlands to Austria, Germany and Switzerland. Every major British publication devoted at least a full page to the book, while France's *Le Monde* devoted two full pages and an editorial. It was the subject of numerous radio and television programs and several feature-length documentaries. The most intense reaction was in Germany. Nearly 200 journalists packed the press conference for the German translation of the book and a capacity crowd of 1,000 (half as many more were turned away for lack of space) attended a raucous public discussion in Berlin. The German edition sold 130,000 copies within weeks and three volumes bearing on the book were published within months.[1] Currently, *The Holocaust Industry* is scheduled for sixteen translations.

[1] Ernst Piper (ed.), *Gibt es wirklich eine Holocaust-Industrie?* (Munchen: 2001),

In contrast to the deafening roar elsewhere, the initial response in the United States was a deafening silence. No mainstream media outlet would touch the book.[2] The US is the corporate headquarters of the Holocaust industry. A study documenting that chocolate caused cancer would presumably elicit a similar response in Switzerland. When the attention abroad proved impossible to ignore, hysterical commentaries in select venues effectively buried the book. Two in particular deserve notice.

The New York Times serves as the main promotional vehicle of the Holocaust industry. It is primarily responsible for having advanced the careers of Jerzy Kosinski, Daniel Goldhagen, and Elie Wiesel. For frequency of coverage, the Holocaust places a close second to the daily weather report. Typically, *The New York Times Index 1999* listed fully 273 entries for the Holocaust. By comparison, the whole of Africa amounted to 32 entries.[3] The 6 August 2000 issue of *The New York Times Book Review* featured a major review of *The Holocaust Industry* ("A Tale of Two Holocausts") by Omer Bartov, an Israeli military

---

Petra Steinberger (ed.), *Die Finkelstein-Debatte* (Munchen: 2001), Rolf Surmann (ed.), *Das Finkelstein-Alibi* (Koln: 2001).

[2] See Christopher Hitchens, "Dead Souls," in *The Nation* (18–25 September 2000).

[3] According to a Lexis–Nexis search for 1999, more than a quarter of the dispatches of the *Times*'s correspondent in Germany, Roger Cohen, hearkened back to the Holocaust. "Listening to Deutsche Welle [a German radio program]," Raul Hilberg wryly observed, "I experience a totally different Germany than when I'm reading the *New York Times*." (*Berliner Zeitung*, 4 September 2000) Incidentally, when the Nazi extermination was actually unfolding, the *Times* pretty much ignored it (see Deborah Lipstadt, *Beyond Belief* [New York: 1993]).

historian turned Holocaust expert. Ridiculing the notion of Holocaust profiteers as a "novel variation of 'The Protocols of the Elders of Zion,'" Bartov let loose a barrage of invective: "bizarre," "outrageous," "paranoid," "shrill," "strident," "indecent," "juvenile," "self-righteous," "arrogant," "stupid," "smug," "fanatic," and so forth.[4] In a priceless sequel some months later, Bartov suddenly reversed himself. Now he railed against the "growing list of Holocaust profiteers," and put forth as a prime example "Norman Finkelstein's 'The Holocaust Industry.'"[5]

In September 2000, *Commentary* senior editor Gabriel Schoenfeld published a blistering attack entitled "Holocaust Reparations – A Growing Scandal." Retracing the ground covered in the third chapter of this book, Schoenfeld chastised Holocaust profiteers inter alia for "unrestrainedly availing themselves of any method, however unseemly or even disreputable," "wrapping themselves in the rhetoric of a sacred cause," and "stoking the fires of anti-Semitism." Although his bill of indictment precisely echoed *The Holocaust Industry*, Schoenfeld denigrated the book and its author in this and a companion *Commentary* piece[6] as "extremist," "lunatic," "crackpot" and "bizarre." A subsequent

---

[4] Indeed, even the author of *Mein Kampf* fared rather better in the *Times* book review. Although highly critical of Hitler's anti-Semitism, the original *Times* review awarded "this extraordinary man" high marks for "his unification of the Germans, his destruction of Communism, his training of the young, his creation of a Spartan State animated by patriotism, his curbing of parliamentary government, so unsuited to the German character, his protection of the right of private property." (James W. Gerard, "Hitler As He Explains Himself," in *The New York Times Book Review* [15 October 1933])

[5] Omer Bartov, "Did Punch Cards Fuel the Holocaust?" in *Newsday* (25 March 2001).

[6] "Holocaust Reparations: Gabriel Schoenfeld and Critics" (January 2001).

op-ed article for the *Wall Street Journal*, by Schoenfeld again, blasted "The New Holocaust Profiteers" (11 April 2001), concluding that "one of the most serious assaults on memory these days comes not from Holocaust deniers . . . but from literary and legal ambulance chasers." This charge also precisely echoed *The Holocaust Industry*. In gracious acknowledgment, Schoenfeld lumped me with Holocaust deniers as an "obvious crackpot."

To both savage and appropriate a book's findings is no mean achievement. The performances of Bartov and Schoenfeld recall a piece of wisdom imparted by my late mother: "It's not an accident that Jews invented the word *chutzpah*." On an altogether different note, it was my rare good fortune that the undisputed dean of Nazi holocaust scholars, Raul Hilberg, repeatedly lent public support to controversial arguments in *The Holocaust Industry*.[7] Like his scholarship Hilberg's integrity humbles. Perhaps it's not an accident that Jews also invented the word *mensch*.

Norman G. Finkelstein
June 2001
New York City

[7] See the Hilberg interviews posted on *www.NormanFinkelstein.com* under "The Holocaust Industry."

INTRODUCTION

This book is both an anatomy and an indictment of the Holocaust industry. In the pages that follow, I will argue that "The Holocaust" is an ideological representation of the Nazi holocaust.[1] Like most ideologies, it bears a connection, if tenuous, with reality. The Holocaust is not an arbitrary but rather an internally coherent construct. Its central dogmas sustain significant political and class interests. Indeed, The Holocaust has proven to be an indispensable ideological weapon. Through its deployment, one of the world's most formidable military powers, with a horrendous human rights record, has cast itself as a "victim" state, and the most successful ethnic group in the United States has likewise acquired victim status. Considerable dividends accrue from this specious victimhood – in particular, immunity to criticism, however justified. Those enjoying this immunity, I might add, have not escaped the moral corruptions that

[1] In this text, *Nazi holocaust* signals the actual historical event, *The Holocaust* its ideological representation.

typically attend it. From this perspective, Elie Wiesel's performance as official interpreter of The Holocaust is not happenstance. Plainly he did not come to this position on account of his humanitarian commitments or literary talents.[2] Rather, Wiesel plays this leading role because he unerringly articulates the dogmas of, and accordingly sustains the interests underpinning, The Holocaust.

The initial stimulus for this book was Peter Novick's seminal study, *The Holocaust in American Life*, which I reviewed for a British literary journal.[3] In these pages the critical dialogue I entered in with Novick is broadened; hence, the extensive number of references to his study. More a congeries of provocative aperçus than a sustained critique, *The Holocaust in American Life* belongs to the venerable American tradition of muckraking. Yet like most muckrakers, Novick focuses only on the most egregious abuses. Scathing and refreshing as it often is, *The*

---

[2] For Wiesel's shameful record of apologetics on behalf of Israel, see Norman G. Finkelstein and Ruth Bettina Birn, *A Nation on Trial: The Goldhagen Thesis and Historical Truth* (New York: 1998), 91n83, 96n90. His record elsewhere is no better. In a new memoir, *And the Sea Is Never Full* (New York: 1999), Wiesel offers this incredible explanation for his silence on Palestinian suffering: "In spite of considerable pressure, I have refused to take a public stand in the Israeli–Arab conflict" (125). In his finely detailed survey of Holocaust literature, literary critic Irving Howe dispatched Wiesel's vast corpus in one lone paragraph with the faint praise that "Elie Wiesel's first book, *Night*, [is] written simply and without rhetorical indulgence." "There has been nothing worth reading since *Night*," literary critic Alfred Kazin agrees. "Elie is now all actor. He described himself to me as a 'lecturer in anguish.'" (Irving Howe, "Writing and the Holocaust," in *New Republic* [27 October 1986]; Alfred Kazin, *A Lifetime Burning in Every Moment* [New York: 1996], 179)

[3] New York: 1999. Norman Finkelstein, "Uses of the Holocaust," in *London Review of Books* (6 January 2000).

Holocaust in American Life is not a radical critique. Root assumptions go unchallenged. Neither banal nor heretical, the book is pitched to the controversial extreme of the mainstream spectrum. Predictably, it received many, though mixed, notices in the American media.

Novick's central analytical category is "memory." Currently all the rage in the ivory tower, "memory" is surely the most impoverished concept to come down the academic pike in a long time. With the obligatory nod to Maurice Halbwachs, Novick aims to demonstrate how "current concerns" shape "Holocaust memory." Once upon a time, dissenting intellectuals deployed robust political categories such as "power" and "interests," on the one hand, and "ideology," on the other. Today, all that remains is the bland, depoliticized language of "concerns" and "memory." Yet given the evidence Novick adduces, Holocaust memory *is* an ideological construct of vested interests. Although chosen, Holocaust memory, according to Novick, is "more often than not" arbitrary. The choice, he argues, is made not from "calculation of advantages and disadvantages" but rather "without much thought for . . . consequences."[4] The evidence suggests the opposite conclusion.

My original interest in the Nazi holocaust was personal. Both my father and mother were survivors of the Warsaw Ghetto and the Nazi concentration camps. Apart from my parents, every family member on both sides was exterminated by the Nazis. My earliest memory, so to speak, of the Nazi holocaust is my mother glued in front of the television watching the trial of Adolf Eichmann (1961) when I came home from school. Although they had been liberated from the camps

[4] Novick, *The Holocaust*, 3–6.

only sixteen years before the trial, an unbridgeable abyss always separated, in my mind, the parents I knew from *that*. Photographs of my mother's family hung on the living-room wall. (None from my father's family survived the war.) I could never quite make sense of my connection with them, let alone conceive what happened. They were my mother's sisters, brother and parents, not my aunts, uncle or grandparents. I remember reading as a child John Hersey's *The Wall* and Leon Uris's *Mila 18*, both fictionalized accounts of the Warsaw Ghetto. (I still recall my mother complaining that, engrossed in *The Wall*, she missed her subway stop on the way to work.) Try as I did, I couldn't even for a moment make the imaginative leap that would join my parents, in all their ordinariness, with that past. Frankly, I still can't.

The more important point, however, is this. Apart from this phantom presence, I do not remember the Nazi holocaust ever intruding on my childhood. The main reason was that no one outside my family seemed to care about what had happened. My childhood circle of friends read widely, and passionately debated the events of the day. Yet I honestly do not recall a single friend (or parent of a friend) asking a single question about what my mother and father endured. This was not a respectful silence. It was simply indifference. In this light, one cannot but be skeptical of the outpourings of anguish in later decades, after the Holocaust industry was firmly established.

I sometimes think that American Jewry "discovering" the Nazi holocaust was worse than its having been forgotten. True, my parents brooded in private; the suffering they endured was not publicly validated. But wasn't that better than the current crass exploitation of Jewish martyrdom? Before the Nazi holocaust became The Holocaust, only a few scholarly studies such as Raul Hilberg's *The Destruction of the European Jews* and memoirs such as Viktor Frankl's *Man's Search for Meaning* and Ella Lingens-Reiner's *Prisoners of Fear* were published on the subject.[5] But this small collection of gems is better than the shelves upon shelves of shlock that now line libraries and bookstores.

Both my parents, although daily reliving that past until the day each died, lost interest by the end of their lives in The Holocaust as a public spectacle. One of my father's lifelong friends was a former inmate with him in Auschwitz, a seemingly incorruptible left-wing idealist who on principle refused German compensation after the war. Eventually he became a director of the Israeli Holocaust museum, Yad Vashem. Reluctantly and with genuine disappointment, my father finally admitted that even this man had been corrupted by the Holocaust industry, tailoring his beliefs for power and profit. As the rendering of The Holocaust assumed ever more absurd forms, my mother liked to quote (with intentional irony) Henry Ford: "History is bunk." The tales of "Holocaust survivors" – all concentration camp inmates, all heroes of the resistance – were a special source of wry amusement in my home. Long ago John Stuart Mill recognized that truths not subject to continual challenge eventually "cease to have the effect of truth by being exaggerated into falsehood."

My parents often wondered why I would grow so indignant at the falsification and exploitation of the Nazi genocide. The most obvious answer is that it has been used to justify criminal policies of the Israeli

---

[5] Raul Hilberg, *The Destruction of the European Jews* (New York: 1961). Viktor Frankl, *Man's Search for Meaning* (New York: 1959). Ella Lingens-Reiner, *Prisoners of Fear* (London: 1948).

state and US support for these policies. There is a personal motive as well. I do care about the memory of my family's persecution. The current campaign of the Holocaust industry to extort money from Europe in the name of "needy Holocaust victims" has shrunk the moral stature of their martyrdom to that of a Monte Carlo casino. Even apart from these concerns, however, I remain convinced that it is important to preserve – to fight for – the integrity of the historical record. In the final pages of this book I will suggest that in studying the Nazi holocaust we can learn much not just about "the Germans" or "the Gentiles" but about all of us. Yet I think that to do so, to truly *learn* from the Nazi holocaust, its physical dimension must be reduced and its moral dimension expanded. Too many public and private resources have been invested in memorializing the Nazi genocide. Most of the output is worthless, a tribute not to Jewish suffering but to Jewish aggrandizement. The time is long past to open our hearts to the rest of humanity's sufferings. This was the main lesson my mother imparted. I never once heard her say: Do not compare. My mother *always* compared. No doubt historical distinctions must be made. But to make out *moral* distinctions between "our" suffering and "theirs" is itself a moral travesty. "You can't compare any two miserable people," Plato humanely observed, "and say that one is happier than the other." In the face of the sufferings of African-Americans, Vietnamese and Palestinians, my mother's credo always was: We are all holocaust victims.

Norman G. Finkelstein
April 2000
New York City

CHAPTER 1

CAPITALIZING THE HOLOCAUST

In a memorable exchange some years back, Gore Vidal accused Norman Podhoretz, then-editor of the American Jewish Committee publication *Commentary*, of being un-American.[1] The evidence was that Podhoretz attached less importance to the Civil War – "the great single tragic event that continues to give resonance to our Republic" – than to Jewish concerns. Yet Podhoretz was perhaps more American than his accuser. For by then it was the "War Against the Jews," not the "War Between the States," that figured as more central to American cultural life. Most college professors can testify that compared to the Civil War many more undergraduates are able to place the Nazi holocaust in the right century and generally cite the number killed. In fact, the Nazi holocaust is just about the only historical reference that resonates in a university classroom today. Polls show that many more Americans can identify The Holocaust than Pearl Harbor or the atomic bombing of Japan.

[1] Gore Vidal, "The Empire Lovers Strike Back," in *Nation* (22 March 1986).

Until fairly recently, however, the Nazi holocaust barely figured in American life. Between the end of World War II and the late 1960s, only a handful of books and films touched on the subject. There was only one university course offering in the United States on the topic.[2] When Hannah Arendt published *Eichmann in Jerusalem* in 1963, she could draw on only two scholarly studies in the English language – Gerald Reitlinger's *The Final Solution* and Raul Hilberg's *The Destruction of the European Jews*.[3] Hilberg's masterpiece itself just managed to see the light of day. His thesis advisor at Columbia University, the German-Jewish social theorist Franz Neumann, strongly discouraged him from writing on the topic ("It's your funeral"), and no university or mainstream publisher would touch the completed manuscript. When it was finally published, *The Destruction of the European Jews* received only a few, mostly critical, notices.[4]

Not only Americans in general but also American Jews, including

[2] Rochelle G. Saidel, *Never Too Late to Remember* (New York: 1996), 32.

[3] Hannah Arendt, *Eichmann in Jerusalem: A Report on the Banality of Evil*, revised and enlarged edition (New York: 1965), 282. The situation in Germany wasn't much different. For example, Joachim Fest's justly admired biography of Hitler, published in Germany in 1973, devotes just four of 750 pages to the extermination of the Jews and a mere paragraph to Auschwitz and other death camps. (Joachim C. Fest, *Hitler* [New York: 1975], 679–82)

[4] Raul Hilberg, *The Politics of Memory* (Chicago: 1996), 66, 105–37. As with scholarship, the quality of the few films on the Nazi holocaust was, however, quite impressive. Amazingly, Stanley Kramer's *Judgment at Nuremberg* (1961) explicitly refers to Supreme Court Justice Oliver Wendell Holmes's 1927 decision sanctioning sterilization of the "mentally unfit" as a precursor of Nazi eugenics programs; Winston Churchill's praise for Hitler as late as 1938; the arming of Hitler by profiteering American industrialists; and the opportunist postwar acquittal of German industrialists by the American military tribunal.

Jewish intellectuals, paid the Nazi holocaust little heed. In an author-itative 1957 survey, sociologist Nathan Glazer reported that the Nazi Final Solution (as well as Israel) "had remarkably slight effects on the inner life of American Jewry." In a 1961 *Commentary* symposium on "Jewishness and the Younger Intellectuals," only two of thirty-one contributors stressed its impact. Likewise, a 1961 roundtable con-vened by the journal *Judaism* of twenty-one observant American Jews on "My Jewish Affirmation" almost completely ignored the subject.[5] No monuments or tributes marked the Nazi holocaust in the United States. To the contrary, major Jewish organizations opposed such memorialization. The question is, Why?

The standard explanation is that Jews were traumatized by the Nazi holocaust and therefore repressed the memory of it. In fact, there is no evidence to support this conclusion. No doubt some survivors did not then or, for that matter, in later years want to speak about what had happened. Many others, however, very much wanted to speak and, once the occasion availed itself, wouldn't stop speaking.[6] The problem was that Americans didn't want to listen.

The real reason for public silence on the Nazi extermination was the conformist policies of the American Jewish leadership and the political climate of postwar America. In both domestic and inter-national affairs American Jewish elites[7] hewed closely to official US

---

[5] Nathan Glazer, *American Judaism* (Chicago: 1957), 114. Stephen J. Whitfield, "The Holocaust and the American Jewish Intellectual," in *Judaism* (Fall 1979).

[6] For sensitive commentary on these two contrasting types of survivor, see Primo Levi, *The Reawakening*, with a new afterword (New York: 1986), 207.

[7] In this text, *Jewish elites* designates individuals prominent in the organizational and cultural life of the mainstream Jewish community.

policy. Doing so in effect facilitated the traditional goals of assimilation and access to power. With the inception of the Cold War, mainstream Jewish organizations jumped into the fray. American Jewish elites "forgot" the Nazi holocaust because Germany – West Germany by 1949 – became a crucial postwar American ally in the US confrontation with the Soviet Union. Dredging up the past served no useful purpose; in fact it complicated matters.

With minor reservations (soon discarded), major American Jewish organizations quickly fell into line with US support for a rearmed and barely de-Nazified Germany. The American Jewish Committee (AJC), fearful that "any organized opposition of American Jews against the new foreign policy and strategic approach could isolate them in the eyes of the non-Jewish majority and endanger their postwar achievements on the domestic scene," was the first to preach the virtues of realignment. The pro-Zionist World Jewish Congress (WJC) and its American affiliate dropped opposition after signing compensation agreements with Germany in the early 1950s, while the Anti-Defamation League (ADL) was the first major Jewish organization to send an official delegation to Germany, in 1954. Together these organizations collaborated with the Bonn government to contain the "anti-German wave" of Jewish popular sentiment.[8]

The Final Solution was a taboo topic of American Jewish elites for yet another reason. Leftist Jews, who were opposed to the Cold War alignment with Germany against the Soviet Union, would not stop

---

[8] Shlomo Shafir, *Ambiguous Relations: The American Jewish Community and Germany Since 1945* (Detroit: 1999), 88, 98, 100–1, 111, 113, 114, 177, 192, 215, 231, 251.

harping on it. Remembrance of the Nazi holocaust was tagged as a Communist cause. Strapped with the stereotype that conflated Jews with the Left – in fact, Jews did account for a third of the vote for progressive presidential candidate Henry Wallace in 1948 – American Jewish elites did not shrink from sacrificing fellow Jews on the altar of anti-Communism. Offering their files on alleged Jewish subversives to government agencies, the AJC and the ADL actively collaborated in the McCarthy-era witch-hunt. The AJC endorsed the death penalty for the Rosenbergs, while its monthly publication, *Commentary*, editorialized that they weren't *really* Jews.

Fearful of association with the political Left abroad and at home, mainstream Jewish organizations opposed cooperation with anti-Nazi German social-democrats as well as boycotts of German manufactures and public demonstrations against ex-Nazis touring the United States. On the other hand, prominent visiting German dissidents like Protestant pastor Martin Niemöller, who had spent eight years in Nazi concentration camps and was now against the anti-Communist crusade, suffered the obloquy of American Jewish leaders. Anxious to boost their anti-Communist credentials, Jewish elites even enlisted in, and financially sustained, right-wing extremist organizations like the All-American Conference to Combat Communism and turned a blind eye as veterans of the Nazi SS entered the country.[9]

---

[9] Ibid., 98, 106, 123–37, 205, 215–16, 249. Robert Warshaw, "The 'Idealism' of Julius and Ethel Rosenberg," in *Commentary* (November 1953). Was it merely a coincidence that at the same time, mainstream Jewish organizations crucified Hannah Arendt for pointing up the collaboration of aggrandizing Jewish elites during the Nazi era? Recalling the perfidious role of the Jewish Council police force, Yitzhak Zuckerman, a leader of the Warsaw Ghetto

Ever anxious to ingratiate themselves with US ruling elites and dissociate themselves from the Jewish Left, organized American Jewry did invoke the Nazi holocaust in one special context: to denounce the USSR. "Soviet [anti-Jewish] policy opens up opportunities which must not be overlooked," an internal AJC memorandum quoted by Novick gleefully noted, "to reinforce certain aspects of AJC domestic program." Typically, that meant bracketing the Nazi Final Solution with Russian anti-Semitism. "Stalin will succeed where Hitler failed," *Commentary* direly predicted. "He will finally wipe out the Jews of Central and Eastern Europe. . . . The parallel with the policy of Nazi extermination is almost complete." Major American Jewish organizations even denounced Soviet repression in Hungary as "only the first station on the way to a Russian Auschwitz."[10]

~

Everything changed with the June 1967 Arab–Israeli war. By virtually all accounts, it was only after this conflict that The Holocaust became a fixture in American Jewish life.[11] The standard explanation of this

uprising, observed: 'There weren't any 'decent' policemen because decent men took off the uniform and became simple Jews" (*A Surplus of Memory* [Oxford: 1993], 244).

[10] Novick, *The Holocaust*, 98–100. In addition to the Cold War, other factors played an ancillary role in American Jewry's postwar downplaying of the Nazi holocaust – for example, fear of anti-Semitism, and the optimistic, assimilationist American ethos in the 1950s. Novick explores these matters in chapters 4–7 of *The Holocaust*.

[11] Apparently the only one denying this connection is Elie Wiesel, who claims that the emergence of The Holocaust in American life was primarily his doing. (Saidel, *Never Too Late*, 33–4)

transformation is that Israel's extreme isolation and vulnerability during the June war revived memories of the Nazi extermination. In fact, this analysis misrepresents both the reality of Mideast power relations at the time and the nature of the evolving relationship between American Jewish elites and Israel.

Just as mainstream American Jewish organizations downplayed the Nazi holocaust in the years after World War II to conform to the US government's Cold War priorities, so their attitude to Israel kept in step with US policy. From early on, American Jewish elites harbored profound misgivings about a Jewish state. Uppermost was their fear that it would lend credence to the "dual loyalty" charge. As the Cold War intensified, these worries multiplied. Already before the founding of Israel, American Jewish leaders voiced concern that its largely Eastern European, left-wing leadership would join the Soviet camp. Although they eventually embraced the Zionist-led campaign for statehood, American Jewish organizations closely monitored and adjusted to signals from Washington. Indeed, the AJC supported Israel's founding mainly out of fear that a domestic backlash against Jews might ensue if the Jewish DPs in Europe were not quickly settled.[12] Although Israel aligned with the West soon after the state was formed, many Israelis in and out of government retained strong affection for the Soviet Union; predictably, American Jewish leaders kept Israel at arm's length.

From its founding in 1948 through the June 1967 war, Israel did not figure centrally in American strategic planning. As the Palestinian Jewish leadership prepared to declare statehood, President Truman

[12] Menahem Kaufman, *An Ambiguous Partnership* (Jerusalem: 1991), 218, 276–7.

waffled, weighing domestic considerations (the Jewish vote) against State Department alarm (support for a Jewish state would alienate the Arab world). To secure US interests in the Middle East, the Eisenhower Administration balanced support for Israel and for Arab nations, favoring, however, the Arabs.

Intermittent Israeli clashes with the United States over policy issues culminated in the Suez crisis of 1956, when Israel colluded with Britain and France to attack Egypt's nationalist leader, Gamal Abdel Nasser. Although Israel's lightning victory and seizure of the Sinai Peninsula drew general attention to its strategic potential, the United States still counted it as only one among several regional assets. Accordingly, President Eisenhower forced Israel's full, virtually unconditional withdrawal from the Sinai. During the crisis, American Jewish leaders did briefly back Israeli efforts to wrest American concessions, but ultimately, as Arthur Hertzberg recalls, they "preferred to counsel Israel to heed [Eisenhower] rather than oppose the wishes of the leader of the United States."[13]

Except as an occasional object of charity, Israel practically dropped from sight in American Jewish life soon after the founding of the state. In fact, Israel was not important to American Jews. In his 1957 survey, Nathan Glazer reported that Israel "had remarkably slight effects on the inner life of American Jewry."[14] Membership in the Zionist Organ-

---

[13] Arthur Hertzberg, *Jewish Polemics* (New York: 1992), 33; although misleadingly apologetic, cf. Isaac Alteras, "Eisenhower, American Jewry, and Israel," in *American Jewish Archives* (November 1985), and Michael Reiner, "The Reaction of US Jewish Organizations to the Sinai Campaign and Its Aftermath," in *Forum* (Winter 1980–1).

[14] Nathan Glazer, *American Judaism* (Chicago: 1957), 114. Glazer continued:

ization of America dropped from the hundreds of thousands in 1948 to the tens of thousands in the 1960s. Only 1 in 20 American Jews cared to visit Israel before June 1967. In his 1956 reelection, which occurred immediately after he forced Israel's humiliating withdrawal from the Sinai, the already considerable Jewish support for Eisenhower increased. In the early 1960s, Israel even faced a drubbing for the Eichmann kidnaping from sections of elite Jewish opinion like Joseph Proskauer, past president of the AJC, Harvard historian Oscar Handlin and the Jewish-owned *Washington Post*. "The kidnaping of Eichmann," Erich Fromm opined, "is an act of lawlessness of exactly the type of which the Nazis themselves . . . have been guilty."[15]

Across the political spectrum, American Jewish intellectuals proved especially indifferent to Israel's fate. Detailed studies of the left-liberal New York Jewish intellectual scene through the 1960s barely mention Israel.[16] Just before the June war, the AJC sponsored a symposium on "Jewish Identity Here and Now." Only three of the thirty-one "best minds in the Jewish community" even alluded to Israel; two of them did so only to dismiss its relevance.[17] Telling irony: just about the only two public Jewish intellectuals who had forged a bond with Israel before June 1967 were Hannah Arendt and Noam Chomsky.[18]

"Israel has meant almost nothing for American Judaism. . . . [T]he idea that Israel . . . could in any serious way affect Judaism in America . . . is recognized as illusory" (115).

[15] Shafir, *Ambiguous Relations*, 222.

[16] See, for example, Alexander Bloom, *Prodigal Sons* (New York: 1986).

[17] Lucy Dawidowicz and Milton Himmelfarb (eds), *Conference on Jewish Identity Here and Now* (American Jewish Committee: 1967).

[18] After emigrating from Germany in 1933, Arendt became an activist in the

Then came the June war. Impressed by Israel's overwhelming display of force, the United States moved to incorporate it as a strategic asset. (Already before the June war the United States had cautiously tilted toward Israel as the Egyptian and Syrian regimes charted an increasingly independent course in the mid-1960s.) Military and economic assistance began to pour in as Israel turned into a proxy for US power in the Middle East.

For American Jewish elites, Israel's subordination to US power was a windfall. Zionism had sprung from the premise that assimilation was a pipe dream, that Jews would always be perceived as potentially disloyal aliens. To resolve this dilemma, Zionists sought to establish a homeland for the Jews. In fact, Israel's founding exacerbated the problem, at any rate for diaspora Jewry: it gave the charge of dual loyalty institutional expression. Paradoxically, after June 1967, Israel *facilitated* assimilation in the United States: Jews now stood on the front lines defending America – indeed, "Western civilization" – against the retrograde Arab hordes. Whereas before 1967 Israel conjured the bogy of dual loyalty, it now connoted super-loyalty. After all, it was not Americans but Israelis fighting and

---

French Zionist movement; during World War II through Israel's founding, she wrote extensively on Zionism. The son of a prominent American Hebraist, Chomsky was raised in a Zionist home and, shortly after Israel's independence, spent time on a kibbutz. Both the public campaigns vilifying Arendt in the early 1960s and Chomsky in the 1970s were spearheaded by the ADL. (Elisabeth Young-Bruehl, *Hannah Arendt* [New Haven: 1982], 105–8, 138–9, 143–4, 182–4, 223–33, 348; Robert F. Barsky, *Noam Chomsky* [Cambridge: 1997], 9–93; David Barsamian (ed.), *Chronicles of Dissent* [Monroe, ME: 1992], 38)

dying to protect US interests. And unlike the American GIs in Vietnam, Israeli fighters were not being humiliated by Third World upstarts.[19]

Accordingly, American Jewish elites suddenly discovered Israel. After the 1967 war, Israel's military élan could be celebrated because its guns pointed in the right direction – against America's enemies. Its martial prowess might even facilitate entry into the inner sanctums of American power. Previously Jewish elites could only offer a few lists of Jewish subversives; now, they could pose as the natural interlocutors for America's newest strategic asset. From bit players, they could advance to top billing in the Cold War drama. Thus for American Jewry, as well as the United States, Israel became a strategic asset.

In a memoir published just before the June war, Norman Podhoretz giddily recalled attending a state dinner at the White House that "included not a single person who was not visibly and absolutely beside himself with delight to be there."[20] Although already editor of the leading American Jewish periodical, *Commentary*, his memoir includes only one fleeting allusion to Israel. What did Israel have to offer an ambitious American Jew? In a later memoir, Podhoretz remembered that after June 1967 Israel became "the religion of the American Jews."[21] Now a prominent supporter of Israel, Podhoretz could boast not merely of attending a White House dinner but of

[19] For an early prefiguration of my argument, see Hannah Arendt, "Zionism Reconsidered" (1944), in Ron Feldman (ed.), *The Jew as Pariah* (New York: 1978), 159.

[20] *Making It* (New York: 1967), 336.

[21] *Breaking Ranks* (New York: 1979), 335.

meeting tête-à-tête with the President to deliberate on the National Interest.

After the June war, mainstream American Jewish organizations worked full time to firm up the American–Israeli alliance. In the case of the ADL, this included a far-flung domestic surveillance operation with ties to Israeli and South African intelligence.[22] Coverage of Israel in *The New York Times* increased dramatically after June 1967. The 1955 and 1965 entries for Israel in *The New York Times Index* each filled 60 column inches. The entry for Israel in 1975 ran to fully 260 column inches. "When I want to feel better," Wiesel reflected in 1973, "I turn to the Israeli items in *The New York Times*."[23] Like Podhoretz, many mainstream American Jewish intellectuals also suddenly found "religion" after the June war. Novick reports that Lucy Dawidowicz, the doyenne of Holocaust literature, had once been a "sharp critic of Israel." Israel could not demand reparations from Germany, she railed in 1953, while evading responsibility for displaced Palestinians: "Morality cannot be that flexible." Yet almost immediately after the June war, Dawidowicz became a "fervent supporter of Israel," acclaiming it as "the corporate paradigm for the ideal image of the Jew in the modern world."[24]

---

[22] Robert I. Friedman, "The Anti-Defamation League Is Spying on You," in *Village Voice* (11 May 1993). Abdeen Jabara, "The Anti-Defamation League: Civil Rights and Wrongs," in *CovertAction* (Summer 1993). Matt Isaacs, "Spy vs Spite," in *SF Weekly* (2–8 February 2000).

[23] Elie Wiesel, *Against Silence*, selected and edited by Irving Abrahamson (New York: 1984), v. i, 283.

[24] Novick, *The Holocaust*, 147. Lucy S. Dawidowicz, *The Jewish Presence* (New York: 1977), 26.

A favorite posture of the post-1967 born-again Zionists was tacitly to juxtapose their own outspoken support for a supposedly beleaguered Israel against the cravenness of American Jewry during The Holocaust. In fact, they were doing exactly what American Jewish elites had always done: marching in lockstep with American power. The educated classes proved particularly adept at striking heroic poses. Consider the prominent left-liberal social critic Irving Howe. In 1956 the journal Howe edited, *Dissent*, condemned the "combined attack on Egypt" as "immoral." Although truly standing alone, Israel was also taken to task for "cultural chauvinism," a "quasi-messianic sense of manifest destiny," and "an undercurrent of expansionism."[25] After the October 1973 war, when American support for Israel peaked, Howe published a personal manifesto "filled with anxiety so intense" in defense of isolated Israel. The Gentile world, he lamented in a Woody Allen-like parody, was awash with anti-Semitism. Even in Upper Manhattan, he lamented, Israel was "no longer chic": everyone, apart from himself, was allegedly in thrall to Mao, Fanon and Guevara.[26]

As America's strategic asset, Israel was not without critics. Besides the increasing international censure of its refusal to negotiate a settlement with the Arabs in accordance with United Nations resolutions and its truculent support of American global ambitions,[27] Israel had to cope with domestic US dissent as well. In American ruling circles,

[25] "Eruption in the Middle East," in *Dissent* (Winter 1957).

[26] "Israel: Thinking the Unthinkable," in *New York* magazine (24 December 1973).

[27] Norman G. Finkelstein, *Image and Reality of the Israel–Palestine Conflict* (New York: 1995), chaps 5–6.

so-called Arabists maintained that putting all the eggs in the Israel basket while ignoring Arab elites undermined US national interests.

Some argued that Israel's subordination to US power and occupation of neighboring Arab states were not only wrong in principle but also harmful to its own interests. Israel would become increasingly militarized and alienated from the Arab world. For Israel's new American Jewish "supporters," however, such talk bordered on heresy: an independent Israel at peace with its neighbors was worthless; an Israel aligned with currents in the Arab world seeking independence from the United States was a disaster. Only an Israeli Sparta beholden to American power would do, because only then could US Jewish leaders act as the spokesmen for American imperial ambitions. Noam Chomsky has suggested that these "supporters of Israel" should more properly be called "supporters of the moral degeneration and ultimate destruction of Israel."[28]

To protect their strategic asset, American Jewish elites "remembered" The Holocaust.[29] The conventional account is that they did so because, at the time of the June war, they believed Israel to be in mortal danger and were thus gripped by fears of a "second Holocaust." This claim does not withstand scrutiny.

Consider the first Arab–Israeli war. On the eve of independence in 1948, the threat against Palestinian Jews seemed far more ominous. David Ben-Gurion declared that "700,000 Jews" were "pitted against

---

[28] Noam Chomsky, *The Fateful Triangle* (Boston: 1983), 4.

[29] Elie Wiesel's career illuminates the nexus between The Holocaust and the June war. Although he had already published his memoir of Auschwitz, Wiesel won public acclaim only after writing two volumes celebrating Israel's victory. (Wiesel, *And the Sea*, 16)

27 million Arabs – one against forty." The United States joined a UN arms embargo on the region, solidifying a clear edge in weaponry enjoyed by the Arab armies. Fears of another Nazi Final Solution haunted American Jewry. Deploring that the Arab states were now "arming Hitler's henchman, the Mufti, while the United States was enforcing its arms embargo," the AJC anticipated "mass suicide and a complete holocaust in Palestine." Even Secretary of State George Marshall and the CIA openly predicted certain Jewish defeat in the event of war.[30] Although the "stronger side, in fact, won" (historian Benny Morris), it was not a walkover for Israel. During the first months of the war, in early 1948, and especially as independence was declared in May, Israel's chances for survival were put at "fifty-fifty" by Yigael Yadin, Haganah chief of operations. Without a secret Czech arms deal, Israel would likely not have survived.[31] After fighting for a year, Israel suffered 6,000 casualties, one percent of its population. Why, then, did The Holocaust not become a focus of American Jewish life after the 1948 war?

Israel quickly proved to be far less vulnerable in 1967 than in its independence struggle. Israeli and American leaders knew beforehand that Israel would easily prevail in a war with the Arab states. This reality became strikingly obvious as Israel routed its Arab neighbors in a few days. As Novick reports, "There were surprisingly few explicit references to the Holocaust in American Jewish mobilization

---

[30] Kaufman, *Ambiguous Partnership*, 287, 306–7. Steven L. Spiegel, *The Other Arab–Israeli Conflict* (Chicago: 1985), 17, 32.

[31] Benny Morris, *1948 And After* (Oxford: 1990), 14–15. Uri Bialer, *Between East and West* (Cambridge: 1990), 180–1.

on behalf of Israel before the war."[32] The Holocaust industry sprung up only *after* Israel's overwhelming display of military dominance and flourished amid extreme Israeli triumphalism.[33] The standard interpretative framework cannot explain these anomalies.

Israel's shocking initial reverses and substantial casualties during, and increasing international isolation after, the October 1973 Arab–Israeli war – conventional accounts maintain – exacerbated American Jewish fears of Israel's vulnerability. Accordingly, Holocaust memory now moved center stage. Novick typically reports: "Among American Jews . . . the situation of a vulnerable and isolated Israel came to be seen as terrifyingly similar to that of European Jewry thirty years earlier. . . . [T]alk of the Holocaust not only 'took off' in America but became increasing [sic] institutionalized."[34] Yet Israel had edged close to the precipice and, in both relative and absolute terms, suffered many more casualties in the 1948 war than in 1973.

True, except for its alliance with the US, Israel was out of favor internationally after the October 1973 war. Compare, however, the 1956 Suez war. Israel and organized American Jewry alleged that, on the eve of the Sinai invasion, Egypt threatened Israel's very existence, and that a full Israeli withdrawal from Sinai would fatally undermine "Israel's vital interests: her survival as a state."[35] The international

---

[32] Novick, *The Holocaust*, 148.

[33] See, for example, Amnon Kapeliouk, *Israel: la fin des mythes* (Paris: 1975).

[34] Novick, *The Holocaust*, 152.

[35] *Commentary*, "Letter from Israel" (February 1957). Throughout the Suez crisis, *Commentary* repeatedly sounded the warning that Israel's "very survival" was at stake.

community nonetheless stood firm. Recounting his brilliant performance at the UN General Assembly, Abba Eban ruefully recalled,
however, that "having applauded the speech with sustained and
vigorous applause, it had gone on to vote against us by a huge
majority."[36] The United States figured prominently in this consensus.
Not only did Eisenhower force Israel's withdrawal, but US public
support for Israel fell into "frightening decline" (historian Peter
Grose).[37] By contrast, immediately after the 1973 war, the United
States provided Israel with massive military assistance, much greater
than it had in the preceding four years combined, while American
public opinion firmly backed Israel.[38] This was the occasion when
"talk of the Holocaust . . . 'took off' in America," at a time when
Israel was less isolated than it had been in 1956.

In fact, the Holocaust industry did not move center stage because Israel's unexpected setbacks during, and pariah status following,
the October 1973 war prompted memories of the Final Solution.
Rather, Sadat's impressive military showing in the October war
convinced US and Israeli policy elites that a diplomatic settlement
with Egypt, including the return of Egyptian lands seized in June
1967, could no longer be avoided. To increase Israel's negotiating
leverage the Holocaust industry increased production quotas. The
crucial point is that after the 1973 war Israel was not isolated from
the United States: these developments occurred within the framework
of the US–Israeli alliance, which remained fully intact.[39] The historical

[36] Abba Eban, *Personal Witness* (New York: 1992), 272.

[37] Peter Grose, *Israel in the Mind of America* (New York: 1983), 304.

[38] A.F.K. Organski, *The $36 Billion Bargain* (New York: 1990), 163, 48.

[39] Finkelstein, *Image and Reality*, chap. 6.

record strongly suggests that, if Israel had truly been alone after the October war, American Jewish elites would no more have remembered the Nazi holocaust than they did after the 1948 or 1956 war.

Novick provides ancillary explanations that are even less convincing. Quoting religious Jewish scholars, for example, he suggests that "the Six Day War offered a folk theology of 'Holocaust and Redemption.'" The "light" of the June 1967 victory redeemed the "darkness" of the Nazi genocide: "it had given God a second chance." The Holocaust could emerge in American life only after June 1967 because "the extermination of European Jewry attained [an] – if not happy, at least viable – ending." Yet in standard Jewish accounts, not the June war but Israel's founding marked redemption. Why did The Holocaust have to await a *second* redemption? Novick maintains that the "image of Jews as military heroes" in the June war "worked to efface the stereotype of weak and passive victims which . . . previously inhibited Jewish discussion of the Holocaust."[40] Yet for sheer courage, the 1948 war was Israel's finest hour. And Moshe Dayan's "daring" and "brilliant" 100-hour Sinai campaign in 1956 prefigured the swift victory in June 1967. Why, then, did American Jewry require the June war to "efface the stereotype"?

Novick's account of how American Jewish elites came to instrumentalize the Nazi holocaust is not persuasive. Consider these representative passages:

---

[40] Novick, *The Holocaust*, 149–50. Novick cites here the noted Jewish scholar Jacob Neusner.

As American Jewish leaders sought to understand the reasons for Israel's isolation and vulnerability – reasons that might suggest a remedy – the explanation commanding the widest support was that the fading of the memories of Nazism's crimes against the Jews, and the arrival on the scene of a generation ignorant of the Holocaust, had resulted in Israel's losing the support it had once enjoyed.

[W]hile American Jewish organizations could do nothing to alter the recent past in the Middle East, and precious little to affect its future, they *could* work to revive memories of the Holocaust. So the "fading memories" explanation offered an agenda for action. [emphasis in original][41]

Why did the "fading memories" explanation for Israel's post-1967 predicament "command[] the widest support"? Surely this was an improbable explanation. As Novick himself copiously documents, the support Israel initially garnered had little to do with "memories of Nazism's crimes,"[42] and, anyhow, these memories had faded long before Israel lost international support. Why could Jewish elites do "precious little to affect" Israel's future? Surely they controlled a formidable organizational network. Why was "reviv[ing] memories of the Holocaust" the only agenda for action? Why not support the international consensus that called for Israel's withdrawal from the lands occupied in the June war *as well as* a "just and lasting peace" between Israel and its Arab neighbors (UN Resolution 242)?

---

[41] Ibid., 153, 155.
[42] Ibid., 69–77.

A more coherent, if less charitable, explanation is that American Jewish elites remembered the Nazi holocaust before June 1967 only when it was politically expedient. Israel, their new patron, had capitalized on the Nazi holocaust during the Eichmann trial.[43] Given its proven utility, organized American Jewry exploited the Nazi holocaust after the June war. Once ideologically recast, The Holocaust (capitalized as I have previously noted) proved to be the perfect weapon for deflecting criticism of Israel. Exactly how I will illustrate presently. What deserves emphasis here, however, is that for American Jewish elites The Holocaust performed the same function as Israel: another invaluable chip in a high-stakes power game. The avowed concern for Holocaust memory was as contrived as the avowed concern for Israel's fate.[44] Thus, organized American Jewry quickly forgave and forgot Ronald Reagan's demented 1985 declaration at Bitburg cemetery that the German soldiers (including Waffen SS members) buried there were "victims of the Nazis just as surely as the victims in the concentration camps." In 1988, Reagan was honored with the "Humanitarian of the Year" award by one of the most prominent Holocaust institutions, the Simon Wiesenthal Center, for his "staunch support of Israel," and in 1994 with the "Torch of Liberty" award by the pro-Israel ADL.[45]

[43] Tom Segev, *The Seventh Million* (New York: 1993), part VI.

[44] Concern for survivors of the Nazi holocaust was equally contrived: a liability before June 1967, they were silenced; an asset after June 1967, they were sanctified.

[45] *Response* (December 1988). Prominent Holocaust-mongers and Israel-supporters like ADL national director Abraham Foxman, past president of the AJC Morris Abram, and chairman of the Conference of Presidents of Major

The Reverend Jesse Jackson's earlier outburst in 1979 that he was "sick and tired of hearing about the Holocaust" was not so quickly forgiven or forgotten, however. Indeed, the attacks by American Jewish elites on Jackson never let up, although not for his "anti-Semitic remarks" but rather for his "espousal of the Palestinian position" (Seymour Martin Lipset and Earl Raab).[46] In Jackson's case, an additional factor was at work: he represented domestic constituencies with which organized American Jewry had been at loggerheads since the late 1960s. In these conflicts, too, The Holocaust proved to be a potent ideological weapon.

It was not Israel's alleged weakness and isolation, not the fear of a "second Holocaust," but rather its proven strength and strategic alliance with the United States that led Jewish elites to gear up the Holocaust industry after June 1967. However unwittingly, Novick provides the best evidence to support that conclusion. To prove that power considerations, not the Nazi Final Solution, determined American policy toward Israel, he writes: "It was when the Holocaust was freshest in the mind of American leaders – the first twenty-five years after the end of the war – that the United States was *least* supportive

---

American Jewish Organizations Kenneth Bialkin, not to mention Henry Kissinger, all rose to Reagan's defense during the Bitburg visit, while the AJC hosted West German Chancellor Helmut Kohl's loyal foreign minister as the guest of honor at its annual meeting the same week. In like spirit, Michael Berenbaum of the Washington Holocaust Memorial Museum later attributed Reagan's Bitburg trip and statements to "the naive sense of American optimism." (Shafir, *Ambiguous Relations*, 302–4; Berenbaum, *After Tragedy*, 14)

[46] Seymour Martin Lipset and Earl Raab, *Jews and the New American Scene* (Cambridge: 1995), 159.

of Israel. . . . It was not when Israel was perceived as weak and vulnerable, but after it demonstrated its strength, in the Six Day War, that American aid to Israel changed from a trickle to a flood" (emphasis in original).[47] That argument applies with equal force to American Jewish elites.

~

There are also domestic sources of the Holocaust industry. Mainstream interpretations point to the recent emergence of "identity politics," on the one hand, and the "culture of victimization," on the other. In effect, each identity was grounded in a particular history of oppression; Jews accordingly sought their own ethnic identity in the Holocaust.

Yet, among groups decrying their victimization, including Blacks, Latinos, Native Americans, women, gays and lesbians, Jews alone are not disadvantaged in American society. In fact, identity politics and The Holocaust have taken hold among American Jews not because of victim status but because they are *not* victims.

As anti-Semitic barriers quickly fell away after World War II, Jews rose to preeminence in the United States. According to Lipset and Raab, per capita Jewish income is almost double that of non-Jews; sixteen of the forty wealthiest Americans are Jews; 40 percent of American Nobel Prize winners in science and economics are Jewish, as are 20 percent of professors at major universities; and 40 percent of partners in the leading law firms in New York and Washington.

[47] Novick, *The Holocaust*, 166.

The list goes on.[48] Far from constituting an obstacle to success, Jewish identity has become the crown of that success. Just as many Jews kept Israel at arm's length when it constituted a liability and became born-again Zionists when it constituted an asset, so they kept their ethnic identity at arm's length when it constituted a liability and became born-again Jews when it constituted an asset.

Indeed, the secular success story of American Jewry validated a core – perhaps the sole – tenet of their newly acquired identity as Jews. Who could any longer dispute that Jews were a "chosen" people? In *A Certain People: American Jews and Their Lives Today*, Charles Silberman – himself a born-again Jew – typically gushes: "Jews would have been less than human had they eschewed any notion of superiority altogether," and "it is extraordinarily difficult for American Jews to expunge the sense of superiority altogether, however much they may try to suppress it." What an American Jewish child inherits, according to novelist Philip Roth, is "no body of law, no body of learning and no language, and finally, no Lord . . . but a kind of psychology: and the psychology can be translated in three words: 'Jews are better.'"[49] As will be seen presently, The Holocaust was the negative version of their vaunted worldly success: it served to validate Jewish chosenness.

By the 1970s, anti-Semitism was no longer a salient feature of American life. Nonetheless, Jewish leaders started sounding alarm bells that American Jewry was threatened by a virulent "new anti-

---

[48] Lipset and Raab, *Jews*, 26–7.

[49] Charles Silberman, *A Certain People* (New York: 1985), 78, 80, 81.

Semitism."[50] The main exhibits of a prominent ADL study ("for those who have died because they were Jews") included the Broadway show *Jesus Christ Superstar* and a counterculture tabloid that "portrayed Kissinger as a fawning sycophant, coward, bully, flatterer, tyrant, social climber, evil manipulator, insecure snob, unprincipled seeker after power" – in the event, an understatement.[51]

For organized American Jewry, this contrived hysteria over a new anti-Semitism served multiple purposes. It boosted Israel's stock as the refuge of last resort if and when American Jews needed one. Moreover, the fund-raising appeals of Jewish organizations purportedly combating anti-Semitism fell on more receptive ears. "The anti-Semite is in the unhappy position," Sartre once observed, "of having a vital need for the very enemy he wishes to destroy."[52] For these Jewish organizations the reverse is equally true. With anti-Semitism in short supply, a cutthroat rivalry between major Jewish "defense" organizations – in particular, the ADL and the Simon Wiesenthal Center – has erupted in recent years.[53] In the matter of fund-raising, incidentally, the alleged threats confronting Israel serve a similar purpose. Returning from a trip to the United States, the respected Israeli journalist Danny Rubinstein reported: "According to most of

---

[50] Novick, *The Holocaust*, 170–2.

[51] Arnold Forster and Benjamin R. Epstein, *The New Anti-Semitism* (New York: 1974), 107.

[52] Jean-Paul Sartre, *Anti-Semite and Jew* (New York: 1965), 28.

[53] Saidel, *Never Too Late*, 222. Seth Mnookin, "Will NYPD Look to Los Angeles For Latest 'Sensitivity' Training?" in *Forward* (7 January 2000). The article reports that the ADL and Simon Wiesenthal Center are vying for the franchise on programs teaching "tolerance."

the people in the Jewish establishment the important thing is to stress again and again the external dangers that face Israel. . . . The Jewish establishment in America needs Israel only as a victim of cruel Arab attack. For such an Israel one can get support, donors, money. . . . Everybody knows the official tally of the contributions collected in the United Jewish Appeal in America, where the name of Israel is used and about half of the sum goes not to Israel but to the Jewish institutions in America. Is there a greater cynicism?" As we will see, the Holocaust industry's exploitation of "needy Holocaust victims" is the latest and, arguably, ugliest manifestation of this cynicism.[54]

The main ulterior motive for sounding the anti-Semitism alarm bells, however, lay elsewhere. As American Jews enjoyed greater secular success, they moved steadily to the right politically. Although still left-of-center on cultural questions such as sexual morality and abortion, Jews grew increasingly conservative on politics and the economy.[55] Complementing the rightward turn was an inward turn, as Jews, no longer mindful of past allies among the have-nots, increasingly earmarked their resources for Jewish concerns only. This reorientation of American Jewry[56] was clearly evident in growing

[54] Noam Chomsky, *Pirates and Emperors* (New York: 1986), 29–30 (Rubinstein).

[55] For a survey of recent poll data confirming this trend, see Murray Friedman, "Are American Jews Moving to the Right?" in *Commentary* (April 2000). In the 1997 New York City mayoral contest pitting Ruth Messinger, a mainstream Democrat, against Rudolph Giuliani, a law-and-order Republican, for example, fully 75% of the Jewish vote went for Giuliani. Significantly, to vote for Giuliani, Jews had to cross traditional party as well as ethnic lines (Messinger is Jewish).

[56] It seems that the shift was also in part due to the displacement of a cosmopolitan Central European Jewish leadership by arriviste and shtetl-

tensions between Jews and Blacks. Traditionally aligned with black people against caste discrimination in the United States, many Jews broke with the Civil Rights alliance in the late 1960s when, as Jonathan Kaufman reports, "the goals of the civil rights movement were shifting – from demands for political and legal equality to demands for economic equality." "When the civil rights movement moved north, into the neighborhoods of these liberal Jews," Cheryl Greenberg similarly recalls, "the question of integration took on a different tone. With concerns now couched in class rather than racial terms, Jews fled to the suburbs almost as quickly as white Christians to avoid what they perceived as the deterioration of their schools and neighborhoods." The memorable climax was the protracted 1968 New York City teachers' strike, which pitted a largely Jewish professional union against Black community activists fighting for control of failing schools. Accounts of the strike often refer to fringe anti-Semitism. The eruption of Jewish racism – not far below the surface before the strike – is less often remembered. More recently, Jewish publicists and organizations have figured prominently in efforts to dismantle affirmative action programs. In key Supreme Court tests – *DeFunis* (1974) and *Bakke* (1978) – the AJC, ADL, and AJ Congress, apparently reflecting mainstream Jewish sentiment, all filed amicus briefs opposing affirmative action.[57]

---

chauvinist Jews of Eastern European descent like New York City mayor Edward Koch and *New York Times* executive editor A.M. Rosenthal. In this regard it bears notice that the Jewish historians dissenting from Holocaust dogmatism have typically come from Central Europe – for example, Hannah Arendt, Henry Friedlander, Raul Hilberg, and Arno Mayer.

[57] See, e.g., Jack Salzman and Cornel West (eds), *Struggles in the Promised Land*

Moving aggressively to defend their corporate and class interests, Jewish elites branded all opposition to their new conservative policies anti-Semitic. Thus ADL head Nathan Perlmutter maintained that the "real anti-Semitism" in America consisted of policy initiatives "corrosive of Jewish interests," such as affirmative action, cuts in the defense budget, and neo-isolationism, as well as opposition to nuclear power and even Electoral College reform.[58]

In this ideological offensive, The Holocaust came to play a critical role. Most obviously, evoking historic persecution deflected present-day criticism. Jews could even gesture to the "quota system" from which they suffered in the past as a pretext for opposing affirmative action programs. Beyond this, however, the Holocaust framework apprehended anti-Semitism as a strictly irrational Gentile loathing of Jews. It precluded the possibility that animus toward Jews might be grounded in a real conflict of interests (more on this later). Invoking The Holocaust was therefore a ploy to delegitimize all criticism of Jews: such criticism could only spring from pathological hatred.

Just as organized Jewry remembered The Holocaust when Israeli power peaked, so it remembered The Holocaust when American Jewish power peaked. The pretense, however, was that, there and here, Jews faced an imminent "second Holocaust." Thus American Jewish elites could strike heroic poses as they indulged in cowardly bullying. Norman Podhoretz, for example, pointed up the new Jewish

---

(New York: 1997), esp. chaps 6, 8, 9, 14, 15. (Kaufman at 111; Greenberg at 166) To be sure, a vocal minority of Jews dissented from this rightward drift.

[58] Nathan Perlmutter and Ruth Ann Perlmutter, *The Real Anti-Semitism in America* (New York: 1982).

resolve after the June 1967 war to "resist any who would in any way and to any degree and for any reason whatsoever attempt to do us harm. . . . We would from now on stand our ground."[59] Just as Israelis, armed to the teeth by the United States, courageously put unruly Palestinians in their place, so American Jews courageously put unruly Blacks in their place.

Lording it over those least able to defend themselves: that is the real content of organized American Jewry's reclaimed courage.

[59] Novick, *The Holocaust*, 173 (Podhoretz).

CHAPTER 2

HOAXERS, HUCKSTERS, AND HISTORY

"**H**olocaust awareness," the respected Israeli writer Boas Evron observes, is actually "an official, propagandistic indoctrination, a churning out of slogans and a false view of the world, the real aim of which is not at all an understanding of the past, but a manipulation of the present." In and of itself, the Nazi holocaust does not serve any particular political agenda. It can just as easily motivate dissent from as support for Israeli policy. Refracted through an ideological prism, however, "the memory of the Nazi extermination" came to serve – in Evron's words – "as a powerful tool in the hands of the Israeli leadership and Jews abroad."[1] The Nazi holocaust became The Holocaust.

Two central dogmas underpin the Holocaust framework: (1) The Holocaust marks a categorically unique historical event; (2) The Holocaust marks the climax of an irrational, eternal Gentile hatred of

[1] Boas Evron, "Holocaust: The Uses of Disaster," in *Radical America* (July–August 1983), 15.

Jews. Neither of these dogmas figured at all in public discourse before the June 1967 war; and, although they became the centerpieces of Holocaust literature, neither figures at all in genuine scholarship on the Nazi holocaust.[2] On the other hand, both dogmas draw on important strands in Judaism and Zionism.

In the aftermath of World War II, the Nazi holocaust was not cast as a uniquely Jewish – let alone a historically unique – event. Organized American Jewry in particular was at pains to place it in a universalist context. After the June war, however, the Nazi Final Solution was radically reframed. "The first and most important claim that emerged from the 1967 war and became emblematic of American Judaism," Jacob Neusner recalls, was that "the Holocaust . . . was unique, without parallel in human history."[3] In an illuminating essay, historian David Stannard ridicules the "small industry of Holocaust hagiographers arguing for the uniqueness of the Jewish experience with all the energy and ingenuity of theological zealots."[4] The uniqueness dogma, after all, makes no sense.

At the most basic level, every historical event is unique, if merely by virtue of time and location, and every historical event bears distinctive features as well as features in common with other historical events. The anomaly of The Holocaust is that its uniqueness is held to be absolutely decisive. What other historical event, one

---

[2] For the distinction between Holocaust literature and Nazi holocaust scholarship, see Finkelstein and Birn, *Nation*, part one, section 3.

[3] Jacob Neusner (ed.), *Judaism in Cold War America, 1945–1990*, v. ii: *In the Aftermath of the Holocaust* (New York: 1993), viii.

[4] David Stannard, "Uniqueness as Denial," in Alan Rosenbaum (ed.), *Is the Holocaust Unique?* (Boulder: 1996), 193.

might ask, is framed largely for its categorical uniqueness? Typically, distinctive features of The Holocaust are isolated in order to place the event in a category altogether apart. It is never clear, however, why the many common features should be reckoned trivial by comparison.

All Holocaust writers agree that The Holocaust is unique, but few, if any, agree why. Each time an argument for Holocaust uniqueness is empirically refuted, a new argument is adduced in its stead. The results, according to Jean-Michel Chaumont, are multiple, conflicting arguments that annul each other: "Knowledge does not accumulate. Rather, to improve on the former argument, each new one starts from zero."[5] Put otherwise: uniqueness is a given in the Holocaust framework; proving it is the appointed task, and disproving it is equivalent to Holocaust denial. Perhaps the problem lies with the premise, not the proof. Even if The Holocaust were unique, what difference would it make? How would it change our understanding if the Nazi holocaust were not the first but the fourth or fifth in a line of comparable catastrophes?

The most recent entry into the Holocaust uniqueness sweepstakes is Steven Katz's *The Holocaust in Historical Context*. Citing nearly 5,000 titles in the first of a projected three-volume study, Katz surveys the full sweep of human history in order to prove that "the

---

[5] Jean-Michel Chaumont, *La concurrence des victimes* (Paris: 1997), 148–9. Chaumont's dissection of the "Holocaust uniqueness" debate is a tour de force. Yet his central thesis does not persuade, at least for the American scene. According to Chaumont, the Holocaust phenomenon originated in Jewish survivors' belated search for public recognition of past suffering. Yet survivors hardly figured in the initial push to move The Holocaust center stage.

Holocaust is phenomenologically unique by virtue of the fact that never before has a state set out, as a matter of intentional principle and actualized policy, to annihilate physically every man, woman and child belonging to a specific people." Clarifying his thesis, Katz explains: "ϕ is uniquely C. ϕ may share A, B. D, . . . X with ▲ but not C. And again ϕ may share A, B, D, . . . X with all ▲ but not C. Everything essential turns, as it were, on ϕ being uniquely C . . . π lacking C is not ϕ. . . . By definition, no exceptions to this rule are allowed. ▲ sharing A, B, D, . . . X with ϕ may be like ϕ in these and other respects . . . but as regards our definition of uniqueness any or all ▲ lacking C are not ϕ. . . . Of course, in its totality ϕ is more than C, but it is never ϕ without C." Translation: A historical event containing a distinct feature is a distinct historical event. To avoid any confusion, Katz further elucidates that he uses the term *phenomenologically* "in a non-Husserlian, non-Shutzean, non-Schelerian, non-Heideggerian, non-Merleau-Pontyan sense." Translation: The Katz enterprise is phenomenal non-sense.[6] Even if the evidence sustained Katz's central thesis, which it does not, it would only prove that The Holocaust contained a distinct feature. The wonder would be were it otherwise. Chaumont infers that Katz's study is actually "ideology" masquerading as "science," more on which presently.[7]

Only a flea's hop separates the claim of Holocaust uniqueness from the claim that The Holocaust cannot be rationally apprehended. If The Holocaust is unprecedented in history, it must stand above and hence cannot be grasped by history. Indeed, The Holocaust is

[6] Steven T. Katz, *The Holocaust in Historical Context* (Oxford: 1994), 28, 58, 60.
[7] Chaumont, *La concurrence*, 137.

unique because it is inexplicable, and it is inexplicable because it is unique.

Dubbed by Novick the "sacralization of the Holocaust," this mystifications's most practiced purveyor is Elie Wiesel. For Wiesel, Novick rightly observes, The Holocaust is effectively a "mystery" religion. Thus Wiesel intones that the Holocaust "leads into darkness," "negates all answers," "lies outside, if not beyond, history," "defies both knowledge and description," "cannot be explained nor visualized," is "never to be comprehended or transmitted," marks a "destruction of history" and a "mutation on a cosmic scale." Only the survivor-priest (read: only Wiesel) is qualified to divine its mystery. And yet, The Holocaust's mystery, Wiesel avows, is "noncommunicable"; "we cannot even talk about it." Thus, for his standard fee of $25,000 (plus chauffeured limousine), Wiesel lectures that the "secret" of Auschwitz's "truth lies in silence."[8]

Rationally comprehending The Holocaust amounts, in this view, to denying it. For rationality denies The Holocaust's uniqueness and mystery. And to compare The Holocaust with the sufferings of others constitutes, for Wiesel, a "total betrayal of Jewish history."[9] Some years back, the parody of a New York tabloid was headlined: "Michael Jackson, 60 Million Others, Die in Nuclear Holocaust." The letters

[8] Novick, The Holocaust, 200–1, 211–12. Wiesel, Against Silence, v. i, 158, 211, 239, 272, v. ii, 62, 81, 111, 278, 293, 347, 371, v. iii, 153, 243. Elie Wiesel, All Rivers Run to the Sea (New York: 1995), 89. Information on Wiesel's lecture fee provided by Ruth Wheat of the Bnai Brith Lecture Bureau."Words," according to Wiesel, "are a kind of horizontal approach, while silence offers you a vertical approach. You plunge into it." Does Wiesel parachute into his lectures?

[9] Wiesel, Against Silence, v. iii, 146.

page carried an irate protest from Wiesel: "How dare people refer to what happened yesterday as a Holocaust? There was only one Holocaust. . . ." In his new memoir Wiesel, proving that life can also imitate spoof, reprimands Shimon Peres for speaking "without hesitation of 'the two holocausts' of the twentieth century: Auschwitz and Hiroshima. He shouldn't have."[10] A favorite Wiesel tag line declares that "the universality of the Holocaust lies in its uniqueness."[11] But if

[10] Wiesel, *And the Sea*, 95. Compare these news items:

> Ken Livingstone, a former member of the Labour Party who is running for mayor of London as an independent, has incensed Jews in Britain by saying global capitalism has claimed as many victims as World War II. "Every year the international financial system kills more people than World War II, but at least Hitler was mad, you know?" . . . "It's an insult to all those murdered and persecuted by Adolf Hitler," said John Butterfill, a Conservative Member of Parliament. Mr. Butterfill also said Mr. Livingstone's indictment of the global financial system had decidedly anti-Semitic overtones. ("Livingstone's Words Anger Jews," in *International Herald Tribune*, 13 April 2000)

> Cuban President Fidel Castro . . . accused the capitalist system of regularly causing deaths on the scale of World War II by ignoring the needs of the poor. "The images we see of mothers and children in whole regions of Africa under the lash of drought and other catastrophes remind us of the concentration camps of Nazi Germany." Referring to war crimes trials after World War II, the Cuban leader said: "We lack a Nuremberg to judge the economic order imposed upon us, where every three years more men, women and children die of hunger and preventable diseases than died in the Second World War." . . . In New York City, Abraham Foxman, national director of the Anti-Defamation League, said . . . "Poverty is serious, it's painful and maybe deadly, but it's not the Holocaust and it's not concentration camps." (John Rice, "Castro Viciously Attacks Capitalism," in *Associated Press*, 13 April 2000)

[11] Wiesel, *Against Silence*, v. iii, 156, 160, 163, 177.

it is incomparably and incomprehensibly unique, how can The Holocaust have a universal dimension?

The Holocaust uniqueness debate is sterile. Indeed, the claims of
Holocaust uniqueness have come to constitute a form of "intellectual
terrorism" (Chaumont). Those practicing the normal comparative
procedures of scholarly inquiry must first enter a thousand and one
caveats to ward off the accusation of "trivializing The Holocaust."[12]

A subtext of the Holocaust uniqueness claim is that The Holocaust
was uniquely evil. However terrible, the suffering of others simply
does not compare. Proponents of Holocaust uniqueness typically
disclaim this implication, but such demurrals are disingenuous.[13]

The claims of Holocaust uniqueness are intellectually barren and
morally discreditable, yet they persist. The question is, Why? In the
first place, unique suffering confers unique entitlement. The unique
evil of the Holocaust, according to Jacob Neusner, not only sets Jews
apart from others, but also gives Jews a "claim upon those others."

---

[12] Chaumont, *La concurrence*, 156. Chaumont also makes the telling point that
the claim of The Holocaust's incomprehensible evil cannot be reconciled with
the attendant claim that its perpetrators were perfectly normal. (310)

[13] Katz, *The Holocaust*, 19, 22. "The claim that the assertion of the Holocaust's
uniqueness is *not* a form of invidious comparison produces systematic double-
talk," Novick observes. "Does anyone . . . believe that the claim of uniqueness
is anything *other* than a claim for preeminence?" (emphasis in original)
Lamentably, Novick himself indulges such invidious comparing. Thus he
maintains that although morally evasive in an American context, "the repeated
assertion that whatever the United States has done to blacks, Native Americans, Vietnamese, or others pales in comparison to the Holocaust is true."
(*The Holocaust*, 197, 15)

For Edward Alexander, the uniqueness of The Holocaust is "moral capital"; Jews must "claim sovereignty" over this "valuable property."[14]

In effect, Holocaust uniqueness – this "claim" upon others, this "moral capital" – serves as Israel's prize alibi. "The singularity of the Jewish suffering," historian Peter Baldwin suggests, "adds to the moral and emotional claims that Israel can make . . . on other nations."[15] Thus, according to Nathan Glazer, The Holocaust, which pointed to the "peculiar *distinctiveness* of the Jews," gave Jews "the right to consider themselves specially threatened and specially worthy of whatever efforts were necessary for survival."[16] (emphasis in original) To cite one typical example, every account of Israel's decision to develop nuclear weapons evokes the specter of The Holocaust.[17] As if Israel otherwise would not have gone nuclear.

There is another factor at work. The claim of Holocaust uniqueness is a claim of Jewish uniqueness. Not the suffering of Jews but that *Jews* suffered is what made The Holocaust unique. Or: The Holocaust is special because Jews are special. Thus Ismar Schorsch, chancellor of the Jewish Theological Seminary, ridicules the Holocaust uniqueness claim as "a distasteful secular version of chosenness."[18] Vehement as

---

[14] Jacob Neusner, "A 'Holocaust' Primer," 178. Edward Alexander, "Stealing the Holocaust," 15–16, in Neusner, *Aftermath*.

[15] Peter Baldwin (ed.), *Reworking the Past* (Boston: 1990), 21.

[16] Nathan Glazer, *American Judaism*, second edition (Chicago: 1972), 171.

[17] Seymour M. Hersh, *The Samson Option* (New York: 1991), 22. Avner Cohen, *Israel and the Bomb* (New York: 1998), 10, 122, 342.

[18] Ismar Schorsch, "The Holocaust and Jewish Survival," in *Midstream* (January 1981), 39. Chaumont convincingly demonstrates that the claim of Holocaust uniqueness originated in, and only makes coherent sense in the context of, the religious dogma of Jewish chosenness. *La concurrence*, 102–7, 121.

he is about the uniqueness of The Holocaust, Elie Wiesel is no less vehement that Jews are unique. "Everything about us is different." Jews are "ontologically" exceptional.[19] Marking the climax of a millennial Gentile hatred of Jews, The Holocaust attested not only to the unique suffering of Jews but to Jewish uniqueness as well.

During and in the aftermath of World War II, Novick reports, "hardly anyone inside [the US] government – and hardly anyone outside it, Jew or Gentile – would have understood the phrase 'abandonment of the Jews.'" A reversal set in after June 1967. "The world's silence," "the world's indifference," "the abandonment of the Jews": these themes became a staple of "Holocaust discourse."[20]

Appropriating a Zionist tenet, the Holocaust framework cast Hitler's Final Solution as the climax of a millennial Gentile hatred of Jews. The Jews perished because all Gentiles, be it as perpetrators or as passive collaborators, wanted them dead. "The free and 'civilized' world," according to Wiesel, handed the Jews "over to the executioner. There were the killers – the murderers – and there were those who remained silent."[21] The historical evidence for a murderous Gentile impulse is nil. Daniel Goldhagen's ponderous effort to prove one variant of this claim in *Hitler's Willing Executioners* barely rose to the comical.[22] Its political utility, however, is considerable. One might note, incidentally, that the "eternal anti-Semitism" theory in fact gives comfort to the anti-Semite. As Arendt says in *The Origins of*

---

[19] Wiesel, *Against Silence*, v. i, 153. Wiesel, *And the Sea*, 133.

[20] Novick, *The Holocaust*, 59, 158–9.

[21] Wiesel, *And the Sea*, 68.

[22] Daniel Jonah Goldhagen, *Hitler's Willing Executioners* (New York: 1996). For a critique, see Finkelstein and Birn, *Nation*.

Totalitarianism, "that this doctrine was adopted by professional anti-semites is a matter of course; it gives the best possible alibi for all horrors. If it is true that mankind has insisted on murdering Jews for more than two thousand years, then Jew-killing is a normal, and even human, occupation and Jew-hatred is justified beyond the need of argument. The more surprising aspect of this explanation is that it has been adopted by a great many unbiased historians and by an even greater number of Jews."[23]

The Holocaust dogma of eternal Gentile hatred has served both to justify the necessity of a Jewish state and to account for the hostility directed at Israel. The Jewish state is the only safeguard against the next (inevitable) outbreak of homicidal anti-Semitism; conversely, homicidal anti-Semitism is behind every attack or even defensive maneuver against the Jewish state. To account for criticism of Israel, fiction writer Cynthia Ozick had a ready answer: "The world wants to wipe out the Jews . . . the world has always wanted to wipe out the Jews."[24] If all the world wants the Jews dead, truly the wonder is that they are still alive – and, unlike much of humanity, not exactly starving.

This dogma has also conferred total license on Israel: Intent as the Gentiles always are on murdering Jews, Jews have every right to protect themselves, however they see fit. Whatever expedient Jews might resort to, even aggression and torture, constitutes legitimate self-defense. Deploring the "Holocaust lesson" of eternal Gentile

---

[23] Hannah Arendt, *The Origins of Totalitarianism* (New York: 1951), 7.

[24] Cynthia Ozick, "All the World Wants the Jews Dead," in *Esquire* (November 1974).

hatred, Boas Evron observes that it "is really tantamount to a deliberate breeding of paranoia. . . . This mentality . . . condones in advance any inhuman treatment of non-Jews, for the prevailing mythology is that 'all people collaborated with the Nazis in the destruction of Jewry,' hence everything is permissible to Jews in their relationship to other peoples."[25]

In the Holocaust framework, Gentile anti-Semitism is not only ineradicable but also always irrational. Going far beyond classical Zionist, let alone standard scholarly, analyses, Goldhagen construes anti-Semitism as "divorced from actual Jews," "fundamentally *not* a response to any objective evaluation of Jewish action," and "independent of Jews' nature and actions." A Gentile mental pathology, its "host domain" is "the mind." (emphasis in original) Driven by "irrational arguments," the anti-Semite, according to Wiesel, "simply resents the fact that the Jew exists."[26] "Not only does anything Jews do or refrain from doing have nothing to do with anti-Semitism," sociologist John Murray Cuddihy critically observes, "but any *attempt* to explain anti-Semitism by referring to the Jewish contribution to anti-Semitism is itself an instance of anti-Semitism!" (emphasis in original)[27] The point, of course, is not that anti-Semitism is justifiable,

---

[25] Boas Evron, *Jewish State or Israeli Nation* (Bloomington: 1995), 226–7.

[26] Goldhagen, *Hitler's Willing Executioners*, 34–5, 39, 42. Wiesel, *And the Sea*, 48.

[27] John Murray Cuddihy, "The Elephant and the Angels: The Incivil Irritatingness of Jewish Theodicy," in Robert N. Bellah and Frederick E. Greenspahn (eds), *Uncivil Religion* (New York: 1987), 24. In addition to this article, see his "The Holocaust: The Latent Issue in the Uniqueness Debate," in P.F. Gallagher (ed.), *Christians, Jews, and Other Worlds* (Highland Lakes, NJ: 1987).

nor that Jews are to blame for crimes committed against them, but that anti-Semitism develops in a specific historical context with its attendant interplay of interests. "A gifted, well-organized, and largely successful minority can inspire conflicts that derive from objective inter-group tensions," Ismar Schorsch points out, although these conflicts are "often packaged in anti-Semitic stereotypes."[28]

The irrational essence of Gentile anti-Semitism is inferred inductively from the irrational essence of The Holocaust. To wit, Hitler's Final Solution uniquely lacked rationality – it was "evil for its own sake," "purposeless" mass killing; Hitler's Final Solution marked the culmination of Gentile anti-Semitism; therefore Gentile anti-Semitism is essentially irrational. Taken apart or together, these propositions do not withstand even superficial scrutiny.[29] Politically, however, the argument is highly serviceable.

By conferring total blamelessness on Jews, the Holocaust dogma immunizes Israel and American Jewry from legitimate censure. Arab

---

[28] Schorsch, *The Holocaust*, 39. Incidentally, the claim that Jews constitute a "gifted" minority is also, in my view, a "distasteful secular version of chosenness."

[29] Whereas a full exposition of this topic is beyond the scope of the essay, consider just the first proposition. Hitler's war against the Jews, even if irrational (and that itself is a complex issue), would hardly constitute a unique historical occurrence. Recall, for example, the central thesis of Joseph Schumpeter's treatise on imperialism that "non-rational and irrational, purely instinctual inclinations toward war and conquest play a very large role in the history of mankind . . . numberless wars – perhaps the majority of all wars – have been waged without . . . reasoned and reasonable interest." (Joseph Schumpeter, "The Sociology of Imperialism," in Paul Sweezy (ed.), *Imperialism and Social Classes* [New York: 1951], 83)

hostility, African-American hostility: they are "fundamentally *not* a response to any objective evaluation of Jewish action" (Goldhagen).[30] Consider Wiesel on Jewish persecution: "For two thousand years . . . we were always threatened. . . . For what? For no reason." On Arab hostility to Israel: "Because of who we are and what our homeland Israel represents – the heart of our lives, the dream of our dreams – when our enemies try to destroy us, they will do so by trying to destroy Israel." On Black people's hostility to American Jews: "The people who take their inspiration from us do not thank us but attack us. We find ourselves in a very dangerous situation. We are again the scapegoat on all sides. . . . We helped the blacks; we always helped them. . . . I feel sorry for blacks. There is one thing they should learn from us and that is gratitude. No people in the world knows gratitude as we do; we are forever grateful."[31] Ever chastised, ever innocent: this is the burden of being a Jew.[32]

---

[30] Explicitly eschewing the Holocaust framework, Albert S. Lindemann's recent study of anti-Semitism starts from the premise that "whatever the power of myth, not all hostility to Jews, individually or collectively, has been based on fantastic or chimerical visions of them, or on projections unrelated to any palpable reality. As human beings, Jews have been as capable as any other group of provoking hostility in the everyday secular world." (*Esau's Tears* [Cambridge: 1997], xvii)

[31] Wiesel, *Against Silence*, v. i, 255, 384.

[32] Chaumont makes the telling point that this Holocaust dogma effectively renders other crimes more acceptable. Insistence on the Jews' radical innocence – i.e. the absence of any rational motive for persecuting, let alone killing, them – "presupposes a 'normal' status for persecutions and killings in other circumstances, creating a de facto division between unconditionally intolerable crimes and crimes which one must – and hence can – live with." (*La concurrence*, 176)

The Holocaust dogma of eternal Gentile hatred also validates the complementary Holocaust dogma of uniqueness. If The Holocaust marked the climax of a millennial Gentile hatred of the Jews, the persecution of non-Jews in The Holocaust was merely accidental and the persecution of non-Jews in history merely episodic. From every standpoint, then, Jewish suffering during The Holocaust was unique.

Finally, Jewish suffering was unique because the Jews are unique. The Holocaust was unique because it was not rational. Ultimately, its impetus was a most irrational, if all-too-human, passion. The Gentile world hated Jews because of envy, jealousy: *ressentiment*. Anti-Semitism, according to Nathan and Ruth Ann Perlmutter, sprang from "gentile jealousy and resentment of the Jews' besting Christians in the marketplace . . . large numbers of less accomplished gentiles resent smaller numbers of more accomplished Jews."[33] Albeit negatively, The Holocaust thus confirmed the chosenness of Jews. Because Jews are better, or more successful, they suffered the ire of Gentiles, who then murdered them.

In a brief aside, Novick muses "what would talk of the Holocaust be like in America" if Elie Wiesel were not its "principal interpreter"?[34] The answer is not difficult to find: Before June 1967 the universalist message of concentration camp survivor Bruno Bettelheim resonated among American Jews. After the June war, Bettelheim was shunted aside in favor of Wiesel. Wiesel's prominence is a function of his ideological utility. Uniqueness of Jewish suffering/uniqueness of the Jews, ever-guilty Gentiles/ever-innocent Jews, unconditional

---

[33] Perlmutters, *Anti-Semitism*, 36, 40.

[34] Novick, *The Holocaust*, 351n19.

defense of Israel/unconditional defense of Jewish interests: Elie Wiesel *is* The Holocaust.

~

Articulating the key Holocaust dogmas, much of the literature on Hitler's Final Solution is worthless as scholarship. Indeed, the field of Holocaust studies is replete with nonsense, if not sheer fraud. Especially revealing is the cultural milieu that nurtures this Holocaust literature.

The first major Holocaust hoax was *The Painted Bird*, by Polish émigré Jerzy Kosinski.[35] The book was "written in English," Kosinski explained, so that "I could write dispassionately, free from the emotional connotation one's native language always contains." In fact, whatever parts he actually wrote – an unresolved question – were written in Polish. The book was purported to be Kosinski's autobiographical account of his wanderings as a solitary child through rural Poland during World War II. In fact, Kosinski lived with his parents throughout the war. The book's motif is the sadistic sexual tortures perpetrated by the Polish peasantry. Pre-publication readers derided it as a "pornography of violence" and "the product of a mind obsessed with sadomasochistic violence." In fact, Kosinski conjured up almost all the pathological episodes he narrates. The book depicts the Polish peasants he lived with as virulently anti-Semitic. "Beat the Jews," they jeer. "Beat the bastards." In fact, Polish peasants harbored the Kosinski family even though they were fully aware of

---

[35] New York: 1965. I rely on James Park Sloan, *Jerzy Kosinski* (New York: 1996), for background.

their Jewishness and the dire consequences they themselves faced if caught.

In the *New York Times Book Review*, Elie Wiesel acclaimed *The Painted Bird* as "one of the best" indictments of the Nazi era, "written with deep sincerity and sensitivity." Cynthia Ozick later gushed that she "immediately" recognized Kosinski's authenticity as "a Jewish survivor and witness to the Holocaust." Long after Kosinski was exposed as a consummate literary hoaxer, Wiesel continued to heap encomiums on his "remarkable body of work."[36]

The Painted Bird became a basic Holocaust text. It was a best-seller and award-winner, translated into numerous languages, and required reading in high school and college classes. Doing the Holocaust circuit, Kosinski dubbed himself a "cut-rate Elie Wiesel." (Those unable to afford Wiesel's speaking fee – "silence" doesn't come cheap – turned to him.) Finally exposed by an investigative newsweekly,

---

[36] Elie Wiesel, "Everybody's Victim," in *New York Times Book Review* (31 October 1965). Wiesel, *All Rivers*, 335. The Ozick quote is from Sloan, 304–5. Wiesel's admiration of Kosinski does not surprise. Kosinski wanted to analyze the "new language," Wiesel to "forge a new language," of the Holocaust. For Kosinski, "what lies between episodes is both a comment on and something commented upon by the episode." For Wiesel, "the space between any two words is vaster than the distance between heaven and earth." There's a Polish proverb for such profundity: "From empty to vacuum." Both also liberally sprinkled their ruminations with quotes from Albert Camus, the telltale sign of a charlatan. Recalling that Camus once told him, "I envy you for Auschwitz," Wiesel continues: "Camus could not forgive himself for not knowing that majestic event, that mystery of mysteries." (Wiesel, *All Rivers*, 321; Wiesel, *Against Silence*, v. ii., 133)

Kosinski was still stoutly defended by the *New York Times*, which alleged that he was the victim of a Communist plot.[37]

A more recent fraud, Binjamin Wilkomirski's *Fragments*,[38] borrows promiscuously from the Holocaust kitsch of *The Painted Bird*. Like Kosinski, Wilkomirski portrays himself as a solitary child survivor who becomes mute, winds up in an orphanage and only belatedly discovers that he is Jewish. Like *The Painted Bird*, the chief narrative conceit of *Fragments* is the simple, pared-down voice of a child-naif, also allowing time frames and place names to remain vague. Like *The Painted Bird*, each chapter of *Fragments* climaxes in an orgy of violence. Kosinski represented *The Painted Bird* as "the slow unfreezing of the mind"; Wilkomirski represents *Fragments* as "recovered memory."[39]

[37] Geoffrey Stokes and Eliot Fremont-Smith, "Jerzy Kosinski's Tainted Words," in *Village Voice* (22 June 1982). John Corry, "A Case History: 17 Years of Ideological Attack on a Cultural Target," in *New York Times* (7 November 1982). To his credit, Kosinski did undergo a kind of deathbed conversion. In the few years between his exposure and his suicide, Kosinski deplored the Holocaust industry's exclusion of non-Jewish victims. "Many North American Jews tend to perceive it as Shoah, as an exclusively Jewish disaster. . . . But at least half of the world's Romanies (unfairly called Gypsies), some 2.5 million Polish Catholics, millions of Soviet citizens and various nationalities, were also victims of this genocide. . . ." He also paid tribute to the "bravery of the Poles" who "sheltered" him "during the Holocaust" despite his so-called Semitic "looks." (Jerzy Kosinski, *Passing By* [New York: 1992], 165–6, 178–9) Angrily asked at a Holocaust conference what the Poles did to save Jews, Kosinski snapped back: "What did the Jews do to save the Poles?"

[38] New York: 1996. For background to the Wilkomirski hoax, see esp. Elena Lappin, "The Man With Two Heads," in *Granta*, no. 66, and Philip Gourevitch, "Stealing the Holocaust," in *New Yorker* (14 June 1999).

[39] Another important "literary" influence on Wilkomirski is Wiesel. Compare

A hoax cut out of whole cloth, *Fragments* is nevertheless the archetypal Holocaust memoir. It is set first in the concentration camps, where every guard is a crazed, sadistic monster joyfully cracking the skulls of Jewish newborns. Yet, the classic memoirs of the Nazi concentration camps concur with Auschwitz survivor Dr. Ella Lingens-Reiner: "There were few sadists. Not more than five or

---

these passages:

> Wilkomirski: "I saw her wide-open eyes, and all of a sudden I knew: these eyes knew it all, they'd seen everything mine had, they knew infinitely more than anyone else in this country. I knew eyes like this, I'd seen them a thousand times, in the camp and later on. They were Mila's eyes. We children used to tell each other everything with these eyes. She knew it, too; she looked straight through my eyes and into my heart."

> Wiesel: "The eyes – I must tell you about their eyes. I must begin with that, for their eyes precede all else, and everything is comprehended within them. The rest can wait. It will only confirm what you already know. But their eyes – their eyes flame with a kind of irreducible truth, which burns and is not consumed. Shamed into silence before them, you can only bow your head and accept the judgment. Your only wish now is to see the world as they do. A grown man, a man of wisdom and experience, you are suddenly impotent and terribly impoverished. Those eyes remind you of your childhood, your orphan state, cause you to lose all faith in the power of language. Those eyes negate the value of words; they dispose of the need for speech." (*The Jews of Silence* [New York: 1966], 3)

Wiesel rhapsodizes for another page and a half about "the eyes." His literary prowess is matched by his mastery of the dialectic. In one place Wiesel avows, "I believe in collective guilt, unlike many liberals." In another place he avows, "I emphasize that I do not believe in collective guilt." (Wiesel, *Against Silence*, v. ii, 134; Wiesel, *And the Sea*, 152, 235)

ten percent."[40] Ubiquitous German sadism figures prominently, however, in Holocaust literature. Doing double service, it "documents" the unique irrationality of The Holocaust as well as the fanatical anti-Semitism of the perpetrators.

The singularity of *Fragments* lies in its depiction of life not during but after The Holocaust. Adopted by a Swiss family, little Binjamin endures yet new torments. He is trapped in a world of Holocaust deniers. "Forget it – it's a bad dream," his mother screams. "It was only a bad dream. . . . You're not to think about it any more." "Here in this country," he chafes, "everyone keeps saying I'm to forget, and that it never happened, I only dreamed it. But they know all about it!"

Even at school, "the boys point at me and make fists and yell: 'He's raving, there's no such thing. Liar! He's crazy, mad, he's an idiot.'" (An aside: They were right.) Pummeling him, chanting anti-Semitic ditties, all the Gentile children line up against poor Binjamin, while the adults keep taunting, "You're making it up!"

Driven to abject despair, Binjamin reaches a Holocaust epiphany. "The camp's still there – just hidden and well disguised. They've taken off their uniforms and dressed themselves up in nice clothes so as not to be recognized. . . . Just give them the gentlest of hints that maybe, possibly, you're a Jew – and you'll feel it: these are the same people, and I'm sure of it. They can still kill, even out of uniform." More than a homage to Holocaust dogma, *Fragments* is the smoking

---

[40] Bernd Naumann, *Auschwitz* (New York: 1966), 91. See Finkelstein and Birn, *Nation*, 67–8, for extensive documentation.

gun: even in Switzerland – neutral Switzerland – all the Gentiles want to kill the Jews.

Fragments was widely hailed as a classic of Holocaust literature. It was translated into a dozen languages and won the Jewish National Book Award, the *Jewish Quarterly* Prize, and the Prix de Mémoire de la Shoah. Star of documentaries, keynoter at Holocaust conferences and seminars, fund-raiser for the United States Holocaust Memorial Museum, Wilkomirski quickly became a Holocaust poster boy.

Acclaiming *Fragments* a "small masterpiece," Daniel Goldhagen was Wilkomirski's main academic champion. Knowledgeable historians like Raul Hilberg, however, early on pegged *Fragments* as a fraud. Hilberg also posed the right questions after the fraud's exposure: "How did this book pass as a memoir in several publishing houses? How could it have brought Mr. Wilkomirski invitations to the United States Holocaust Memorial Museum as well as recognized universities? How come we have no decent quality control when it comes to evaluating Holocaust material for publication?"[41]

Half-fruitcake, half-mountebank, Wilkomirski, it turns out, spent the entire war in Switzerland. He is not even Jewish. Listen, however, to the Holocaust industry post-mortems:

Arthur Samuelson (publisher): *Fragments* "is a pretty cool book. . . . It's only a fraud if you call it non-fiction. I would then reissue it, in the fiction category. Maybe it's not true – then he's a better writer!"

---

[41] Lappin, 49. Hilberg always asked the right questions. Hence his pariah status in the Holocaust community; see Hilberg, *The Politics of Memory*, passim.

Carol Brown Janeway (editor and translator): "If the charges . . . turn out to be correct, then what's at issue are not empirical facts that can be checked, but spiritual facts that must be pondered. What would be required is soul-checking, and that's an impossibility."

There's more. Israel Gutman is a director of Yad Vashem and a Holocaust lecturer at Hebrew University. He is also a former inmate of Auschwitz. According to Gutman, "it's not that important" whether *Fragments* is a fraud. "Wilkomirski has written a story which he has experienced deeply; that's for sure. . . . He is not a fake. He is someone who lives this story very deeply in his soul. The pain is authentic." So it doesn't matter whether he spent the war in a concentration camp or a Swiss chalet; Wilkomirski is not a fake if his "pain is authentic": thus speaks an Auschwitz survivor turned Holocaust expert. The others deserve contempt; Gutman, just pity.

The New Yorker titled its exposé of the Wilkomirski fraud "Stealing the Holocaust." Yesterday Wilkomirski was feted for his tales of Gentile evil; today he is chastised as yet another evil Gentile. It's *always* the Gentiles' fault. True, Wilkomirski fabricated his Holocaust past, but the larger truth is that the Holocaust industry, built on a fraudulent misappropriation of history for ideological purposes, was primed to celebrate the Wilkomirski fabrication. He was a Holocaust "survivor" waiting to be discovered.

In October 1999, Wilkomirski's German publisher, withdrawing *Fragments* from bookstores, finally acknowledged publicly that he wasn't a Jewish orphan but a Swiss-born man named Bruno Doessekker. Informed that the jig was up, Wilkomirski thundered defiantly,

"I am Binjamin Wilkomirski!" Not until a month later did the American publisher, Schocken, drop *Fragments* from its list.[42]

Consider now Holocaust secondary literature. A telltale sign of this literature is the space given over to the "Arab connection." Although the Mufti of Jerusalem didn't play "any significant part in the Holocaust," Novick reports, the four-volume *Encyclopedia of the Holocaust* (edited by Israel Gutman) gave him a "starring role." The Mufti also gets top billing in Yad Vashem: "The visitor is left to conclude," Tom Segev writes, "that there is much in common between the Nazis' plans to destroy the Jews and the Arabs' enmity to Israel." At an Auschwitz commemoration officiated by clergy representing all religious denominations, Wiesel objected *only* to the presence of a Muslim qadi: "Were we not forgetting . . . Mufti Hajj Amin el-Husseini of Jerusalem, Heinrich Himmler's friend?" Incidentally, if the Mufti figured so centrally in Hitler's Final Solution, the wonder is that Israel didn't bring him to justice like Eichmann. He was living openly right next door in Lebanon after the war.[43]

Especially in the wake of Israel's ill-fated invasion of Lebanon in 1982 and as official Israeli propaganda claims came under withering attack by Israel's "new historians," apologists desperately sought to tar the Arabs with Nazism. Famed historian Bernard Lewis managed to devote a full chapter of his short history of anti-Semitism, and fully three pages of his "brief history of the last 2,000 years" of the Middle

---

[42] "Publisher Drops Holocaust Book," in *New York Times* (3 November 1999). Allan Hall and Laura Williams, "Holocaust Hoaxer?" in *New York Post* (4 November 1999).

[43] Novick, *The Holocaust*, 158. Segev, *Seventh Million*, 425. Wiesel, *And the Sea*, 198.

East, to Arab Nazism. At the liberal extreme of the Holocaust spectrum, Michael Berenbaum of the Washington Holocaust Memorial Museum generously allowed that "the stones thrown by Palestinian youths angered by Israel's presence . . . are not synonymous with the Nazi assault against powerless Jewish civilians."[44]

The most recent Holocaust extravaganza is Daniel Jonah Goldhagen's *Hitler's Willing Executioners*. Every important journal of opinion printed one or more reviews within weeks of its release. *The New York Times* featured multiple notices, acclaiming Goldhagen's book as "one of those rare new works that merit the appellation landmark" (Richard Bernstein). With sales of half a million copies and translations slated for 13 languages, *Hitler's Willing Executioners* was hailed in *Time* magazine as the "most talked about" and second best nonfiction book of the year.[45]

Pointing to the "remarkable research," and "wealth of proof . . . with overwhelming support of documents and facts," Elie Wiesel heralded *Hitler's Willing Executioners* as a "tremendous contribution to the understanding and teaching of the Holocaust." Israel Gutman praised it for "raising anew clearly central questions" that "the main body of Holocaust scholarship" ignored. Nominated for the Holocaust chair at Harvard University, paired with Wiesel in the national media, Goldhagen quickly became a ubiquitous presence on the Holocaust circuit.

---

[44] Bernard Lewis, *Semites and Anti-Semites* (New York: 1986), chap. 6; Bernard Lewis, *The Middle East* (New York: 1995), 348–50. Berenbaum, *After Tragedy*, 84.

[45] *New York Times*, 27 March, 2 April, 3 April 1996. *Time*, 23 December 1996.

The central thesis of Goldhagen's book is standard Holocaust dogma: driven by pathological hatred, the German people leapt at the opportunity Hitler availed them to murder the Jews. Even leading Holocaust writer Yehuda Bauer, a lecturer at the Hebrew University and director of Yad Vashem, has at times embraced this dogma. Reflecting several years ago on the perpetrators' mindset, Bauer wrote: "The Jews were murdered by people who, to a large degree, did not actually hate them. . . . The Germans did not have to hate the Jews in order to kill them." Yet, in a recent review of Goldhagen's book, Bauer maintained the exact opposite: "The most radical type of murderous attitudes dominated from the end of the 1930s onward. . . . [B]y the outbreak of World War II the vast majority of Germans had identified with the regime and its antisemitic policies to such an extent that it was easy to recruit the murderers." Questioned about this discrepancy, Bauer replied: "I cannot see any contradiction between these statements."[46]

Although bearing the apparatus of an academic study, *Hitler's Willing Executioners* amounts to little more than a compendium of sadistic violence. Small wonder that Goldhagen vigorously championed Wilkomirski: *Hitler's Willing Executioners* is *Fragments* plus footnotes. Replete with gross misrepresentations of source material and internal contradictions, *Hitler's Willing Executioners* is devoid of schol-

---

[46] Yehuda Bauer, "Reflections Concerning Holocaust History," in Louis Greenspan and Graeme Nicholson (eds), *Fackenheim* (Toronto: 1993), 164, 169. Yehuda Bauer, "On Perpetrators of the Holocaust and the Public Discourse," in *Jewish Quarterly Review*, no. 87 (1997), 348–50. Norman G. Finkelstein and Yehuda Bauer, "Goldhagen's *Hitler's Willing Executioners*: An Exchange of Views," in *Jewish Quarterly Review*, nos 1–2 (1998), 126.

arly value. In *A Nation on Trial*, Ruth Bettina Birn and this writer documented the shoddiness of Goldhagen's enterprise. The ensuing controversy instructively illuminated the inner workings of the Holocaust industry.

Birn, the world's leading authority on the archives Goldhagen consulted, first published her critical findings in the Cambridge *Historical Journal*. Refusing the journal's invitation for a full rebuttal, Goldhagen instead enlisted a high-powered London law firm to sue Birn and Cambridge University Press for "many serious libels." Demanding an apology, a retraction, and a promise from Birn that she not repeat her criticisms, Goldhagen's lawyers then threatened that "the generation of any publicity on your part as a result of this letter would amount to a further aggravation of damages."[47]

Soon after this writer's equally critical findings were published in *New Left Review*, Metropolitan, an imprint of Henry Holt, agreed to publish both essays as a book. In a front-page story, the *Forward* warned that Metropolitan was "preparing to bring out a book by Norman Finkelstein, a notorious ideological opponent of the State of Israel." The *Forward* acts as the main enforcer of "Holocaust correctness" in the United States.

Alleging that "Finkelstein's glaring bias and audacious statements . . . are irreversibly tainted by his anti-Zionist stance," ADL head

---

[47] For background and the next paragraphs, see Charles Glass, "Hitler's (un)willing executioners," in *New Statesman* (23 January 1998), Laura Shapiro, "A Battle Over the Holocaust," in *Newsweek* (23 March 1998), and Tibor Krausz, "The Goldhagen Wars," in *Jerusalem Report* (3 August 1998). For these and related items, cf. *www.NormanFinkelstein.com* (with a link to Goldhagen's web site).

Abraham Foxman called on Holt to drop publication of the book: "The issue . . . is not whether Goldhagen's thesis is right or wrong but what is 'legitimate criticism' and what goes beyond the pale." "Whether Goldhagen's thesis is right or wrong," Metropolitan associate publisher Sara Bershtel replied, "is precisely the issue."

Leon Wieseltier, literary editor of the pro-Israel *New Republic*, intervened personally with Holt president Michael Naumann. "You don't know who Finkelstein is. He's poison, he's a disgusting self-hating Jew, he's something you find under a rock." Pronouncing Holt's decision a "disgrace," Elan Steinberg, executive director of the World Jewish Congress, opined, "If they want to be garbagemen they should wear sanitation uniforms."

"I have never experienced," Naumann later recalled, "a similar attempt of interested parties to publicly cast a shadow over an upcoming publication." The prominent Israeli historian and journalist, Tom Segev, observed in *Haaretz* that the campaign verged on "cultural terrorism."

As chief historian of the War Crimes and Crimes Against Humanity Section of the Canadian Department of Justice, Birn next came under attack from Canadian Jewish organizations. Claiming that I was "anathema to the vast majority of Jews on this continent," the Canadian Jewish Congress denounced Birn's collaboration in the book. Exerting pressure through her employer, the CJC filed a protest with the Justice Department. This complaint, joined to a CJC-backed report calling Birn "a member of the perpetrator race" (she is German-born), prompted an official investigation of her.

Even after the book's publication, the ad hominem assaults did not let up. Goldhagen alleged that Birn, who has made the prosecution of

Nazi war criminals her life's work, was a purveyor of anti-Semitism, and that I was of the opinion that Nazism's victims, including my own family, deserved to die.[48] Goldhagen's colleagues at the Harvard Center for European Studies, Stanley Hoffmann and Charles Maier, publicly lined up behind him.[49]

Calling the charges of censorship a "canard," *The New Republic* maintained that "there is a difference between censorship and upholding standards." *A Nation on Trial* received endorsements from the leading historians on the Nazi holocaust, including Raul Hilberg, Christopher Browning and Ian Kershaw. These same scholars uniformly dismissed Goldhagen's book; Hilberg called it "worthless." Standards, indeed.

Consider, finally, the pattern: Wiesel and Gutman supported Goldhagen; Wiesel supported Kosinski; Gutman and Goldhagen supported Wilkomirski. Connect the players: this is Holocaust literature.

---

[48] Daniel Jonah Goldhagen, "Daniel Jonah Goldhagen Comments on Birn," in *German Politics and Society* (Summer 1998), 88, 91n2. Daniel Jonah Goldhagen, "The New Discourse of Avoidance," n25 (*www.Goldhagen.com/nda2html*)

[49] Hoffmann was Goldhagen's advisor for the dissertation that became *Hitler's Willing Executioners*. Yet, in an egregious breach of academic protocol, he not only wrote a glowing review of Goldhagen's book for *Foreign Affairs* but also denounced *A Nation on Trial* as "shocking" in a second review for the same journal. (*Foreign Affairs*, May/June 1996 and July/August 1998) Maier posted a lengthy intervention on the H-German web site (*www2.h-net.msu.edu*). Ultimately, the only "aspects of this unfolding situation" that Maier found "really distasteful and reprehensible" were the criticisms of Goldhagen. Thus he lent "support to a subsequent finding of malice" in Goldhagen's lawsuit against Birn and deplored my argumentation as "fanciful and inflammatory speculation." (23 November 1997)

All the hype notwithstanding, there is no evidence that Holocaust deniers exert any more influence in the United States than the flat-earth society does. Given the nonsense churned out daily by the Holocaust industry, the wonder is that there are so *few* skeptics. The motive behind the claim of widespread Holocaust denial is not hard to find. In a society saturated with The Holocaust, how else to justify yet more museums, books, curricula, films and programs than to conjure up the bogy of Holocaust denial? Thus Deborah Lipstadt's acclaimed book, *Denying the Holocaust*,[50] as well as the results of an ineptly worded American Jewish Committee poll alleging pervasive Holocaust denial,[51] were released just as the Washington Holocaust Memorial Museum opened.

Denying the Holocaust is an updated version of the "new anti-

---

[50] New York: 1994. Lipstadt occupies the Holocaust chair at Emory University and was recently appointed to the United States Holocaust Memorial Council.

[51] Employing a double negative, the AJC poll practically invited confusion: "Does it seem possible or does it seem impossible to you that the Nazi extermination of the Jews never happened?" Twenty-two percent of respondents answered "It seems possible." In subsequent polls, which rephrased the question straightforwardly, Holocaust denial approached zero. A recent AJC survey of 11 countries found that, notwithstanding pervasive right-wing extremists' claims to the contrary, "few people denied the Holocaust." (Jennifer Golub and Renae Cohen, *What Do Americans Know About the Holocaust?* [The American Jewish Committee: 1993]; "Holocaust Deniers Unconvincing – Surveys," in *Jerusalem Post* [4 February 2000]) Yet in Congressional testimony regarding "anti-Semitism in Europe," David Harris of the AJC highlighted the salience of Holocaust denial in the European Right without once mentioning the AJC's own finding that this denial finds virtually no resonance among the general public. (Hearings before the Foreign Relations Committee, United States Senate, 5 April 2000)

Semitism" tracts. To document widespread Holocaust denial, Lipstadt cites a handful of crank publications. Her *pièce de résistance* is Arthur Butz, a nonentity who teaches electrical engineering at Northwestern University and who published his book *The Hoax of the Twentieth Century* with an obscure press. Lipstadt entitles the chapter on him "Entering the Mainstream." Were it not for the likes of Lipstadt, no one would ever have heard of Arthur Butz.

In fact, the one truly mainstream holocaust denier is Bernard Lewis. A French court even convicted Lewis of denying genocide. But Lewis denied the Turkish genocide of Armenians during World War I, not the Nazi genocide of Jews, and Lewis is pro-Israel.[52] Accordingly, this instance of holocaust denial raises no hackles in the United States. Turkey is an Israeli ally, extenuating matters even further. Mention of an Armenian genocide is therefore taboo. Elie Wiesel and Rabbi Arthur Hertzberg as well as the AJC and Yad Vashem withdrew from an international conference on genocide in Tel Aviv because the academic sponsors, against Israeli government urging, included sessions on the Armenian case. Wiesel also sought, unilaterally, to abort the conference and, according to Yehuda Bauer, personally lobbied others not to attend.[53] Acting at Israel's behest,

---

[52] See "France Fines Historian Over Armenian Denial," in *Boston Globe* (22 June 1995), and "Bernard Lewis and the Armenians," in *Counterpunch* (16–31 December 1997).

[53] Israel Charny, "The Conference Crisis. The Turks, Armenians and the Jews," in *The Book of the International Conference on the Holocaust and Genocide. Book One: The Conference Program and Crisis* (Tel Aviv: 1982). Israel Amrani, "A Little Help for Friends," in *Haaretz* (20 April 1990) (Bauer). In Wiesel's bizarre account, he resigned as conference chair in order "not to offend our

the US Holocaust Council practically eliminated mention of the Armenians in the Washington Holocaust Memorial Museum, and Jewish lobbyists in Congress blocked a day of remembrance for the Armenian genocide.[54]

To question a survivor's testimony, to denounce the role of Jewish collaborators, to suggest that Germans suffered during the bombing of Dresden or that any state except Germany committed crimes in World War II – this is all evidence, according to Lipstadt, of Holocaust denial.[55] And to suggest that Wiesel has profited from the Holocaust industry, or even to question him, amounts to Holocaust denial.[56]

The most "insidious" forms of Holocaust denial, Lipstadt suggests, are "immoral equivalencies": that is, denying the uniqueness of The Holocaust.[57] This argument has intriguing implications. Daniel Goldhagen argues that Serbian actions in Kosovo "are, in their essence, different from those of Nazi Germany only in scale."[58] That would make Goldhagen "in essence" a Holocaust denier. Indeed, across the political spectrum, Israeli commentators compared Serbia's actions in

---

Armenian guests." Presumably he also attempted to abort the conference and urged others against attending out of courtesy to the Armenians. (Wiesel, *And the Sea*, 92)

[54] Edward T. Linenthal, *Preserving Memory* (New York: 1995), 228ff., 263, 312–13.

[55] Lipstadt, *Denying*, 6, 12, 22, 89–90.

[56] Wiesel, *All Rivers*, 333, 336.

[57] Lipstadt, *Denying*, chapter 11.

[58] "A New Serbia," in *New Republic* (17 May 1999).

Kosovo with Israeli actions in 1948 against the Palestinians.[59] By Goldhagen's reckoning, then, Israel committed a Holocaust. Not even Palestinians claim that anymore.

Not all revisionist literature – however scurrilous the politics or motivations of its practitioners – is totally useless. Lipstadt brands David Irving "one of the most dangerous spokespersons for Holocaust denial" (he recently lost a libel suit in England against her for these and other assertions). But Irving, notorious as an admirer of Hitler and sympathizer with German national socialism, has nevertheless, as Gordon Craig points out, made an "indispensable" contribution to our knowledge of World War II. Both Arno Mayer, in his important study of the Nazi holocaust, and Raul Hilberg cite Holocaust denial publications. "If these people want to speak, let them," Hilberg observes. "It only leads those of us who do research to re-examine what we might have considered as obvious. And that's useful for us."[60]

~

[59] See, for example, Meron Benvenisti, "Seeking Tragedy," in *Haaretz* (16 April 1999), Zeev Chafets, "What Undergraduate Clinton Has Forgotten," in *Jerusalem Report* (10 May 1999), and Gideon Levi, "Kosovo: It is Here," in *Haaretz* (4 April 1999). (Benvenisti limits the Serbian comparison to Israeli actions after May 1948.)

[60] Arno Mayer, *Why Did the Heavens Not Darken?* (New York: 1988). Christopher Hitchens, "Hitler's Ghost," in *Vanity Fair* (June 1996) (Hilberg). For a balanced assessment of Irving, see Gordon A. Craig, "The Devil in the Details," in *New York Review of Books* (19 September 1996). Rightly dismissing Irving's claims on the Nazi holocaust as "obtuse and quickly discredited," Craig nonetheless continues: "He knows more about National Socialism than

Annual Days of Remembrance of the Holocaust are a national event. All 50 states sponsor commemorations, often in state legislative chambers. The Association of Holocaust Organizations lists over 100 Holocaust institutions in the United States. Seven major Holocaust museums dot the American landscape. The centerpiece of this memorialization is the United States Holocaust Memorial Museum in Washington.

The first question is why we even have a federally mandated and funded Holocaust museum in the nation's capitol. Its presence on the Washington Mall is particularly incongruous in the absence of a museum commemorating crimes in the course of American history. Imagine the wailing accusations of hypocrisy here were Germany to build a national museum in Berlin to commemorate not the Nazi genocide but American slavery or the extermination of the Native Americans.[61]

---

most professional scholars in his field, and students of the years 1933–1945 owe more than they are always willing to admit to his energy as a researcher and to the scope and vigor of his publications. . . . His book *Hitler's War . . .* remains the best study we have of the German side of the Second World War and, as such, indispensable for all students of that conflict. . . . Such people as David Irving, then, have an indispensable part in the historical enterprise, and we dare not disregard their views."

[61] For the abortive attempts between 1984 and 1994 to build a national African-American museum on the Washington Mall, see Fath Davis Ruffins, "Culture Wars Won and Lost, Part II: The National African-American Museum Project," in *Radical History Review* (Winter 1998). The Congressional initiative was finally killed by Senator Jesse Helms of North Carolina. The Washington Holocaust museum's annual budget is $50 million, of which $30 million is federally subsidized.

It "tries meticulously to refrain from any attempt at indoctrination," the Holocaust museum's designer wrote, "from any manipulation of impressions or emotions." Yet from conception through completion, the museum was mired in politics.[62] With a reelection campaign looming, Jimmy Carter initiated the project to placate Jewish contributors and voters, galled by the President's recognition of the "legitimate rights" of Palestinians. The chairman of the Conference of Presidents of Major American Jewish Organizations, Rabbi Alexander Schindler, deplored Carter's recognition of Palestinian humanity as a "shocking" initiative. Carter announced plans for the museum while Prime Minister Menachem Begin was visiting Washington and in the midst of a bruising Congressional battle over the Administration's proposed sale of weaponry to Saudi Arabia. Other political issues also emerge in the museum. It mutes the Christian background to European anti-Semitism so as not to offend a powerful constituency. It downplays the discriminatory US immigration quotas before the war, exaggerates the US role in liberating the concentration camps, and silently passes over the massive US recruitment of Nazi war criminals at the war's end. The Museum's overarching message is that "we" couldn't even conceive, let alone commit, such evil deeds. The Holocaust "cuts against the grain of the American ethos," Michael Berenbaum observes in the companion book to the museum. "We see in [its] perpetration a violation of every essential American value." The Holocaust museum signals the Zionist lesson that Israel was the

---

[62] For background, see Linenthal, *Preserving Memory*, Saidel, *Never Too Late*, esp. chaps 7, 15, and Tim Cole, *Selling the Holocaust* (New York: 1999), chap. 6.

"appropriate answer to Nazism" with the closing scenes of Jewish survivors struggling to enter Palestine.[63]

The politicization begins even before one crosses the museum's threshold. It is situated on Raoul Wallenberg Place. Wallenberg, a Swedish diplomat, is honored because he rescued thousands of Jews and ended up in a Soviet prison. Fellow Swede Count Folke Bernadotte is not honored because, although he too rescued thousands of Jews, former Israeli Prime Minister Yitzak Shamir ordered his assassination for being too "pro-Arab."[64]

The crux of Holocaust museum politics, however, bears on *whom* to memorialize. Were Jews the only victims of The Holocaust, or did others who perished because of Nazi persecution also count as

---

[63] Michael Berenbaum, *The World Must Know* (New York: 1993), 2, 214. Omer Bartov, *Murder In Our Midst* (Oxford: 1996), 180.

[64] For details, see Kati Marton, *A Death in Jerusalem* (New York: 1994), chap. 9. In his memoir Wiesel recalls the "legendary 'terrorist' past" of Bernadotte's actual assassin, Yehoshua Cohen. Note the inverted commas around terrorist. (Wiesel, *And the Sea*, 58) The New York City Holocaust Museum, although no less mired in politics (both Mayor Ed Koch and Governor Mario Cuomo were courting Jewish votes and money), was also from early on a plaything of local Jewish developers and financiers. At one point, developers sought to downplay "Holocaust" in the museum's name for fear that it would depress property values in the adjacent luxury housing complex. Wags quipped that the complex should be named "Treblinka Towers," and the surrounding streets "Auschwitz Avenue" and "Birkenau Boulevard." The museum solicited funds from J. Peter Grace despite revelations of his association with a convicted Nazi war criminal, and it organized a gala at The Hot Rod – "The New York Holocaust Memorial Commission invites you to Rock and Roll the Night Away." (Saidel, *Never Too Late*, 8, 121, 132, 145, 158, 161, 191, 240)

victims?[65] During the museum's planning stages, Elie Wiesel (along with Yehuda Bauer of Yad Vashem) led the offensive to commemorate Jews alone. Deferred to as the "undisputed expert on the Holocaust period," Wiesel tenaciously argued for the preeminence of Jewish victimhood. "As always, they began with Jews," he typically intoned. "As always, they did not stop with Jews alone."[66] Yet not Jews but Communists were the first political victims, and not Jews but the handicapped were the first genocidal victims, of Nazism.[67]

Justifying preemption of the Gypsy genocide posed the main challenge to the Holocaust Museum. The Nazis systematically

[65] Novick dubs this the "6 million" versus "11 million" controversy. The 5 million figure for non-Jewish civilian deaths apparently originated with famed "Nazi-hunter" Simon Wiesenthal. Noting that it "makes no historical sense," Novick writes, "Five million is either much too low (for all non-Jewish civilians killed by the Third Reich) or much too high (for non-Jewish groups targeted, like Jews, for murder)." He hastens to add, however, that "what's at stake, of course, is not numbers as such, but what we mean, what we're referring to, when we talk of 'the Holocaust.'" Strangely, after entering this caveat, Novick supports commemorating only Jews because the 6 million figure "describes something specific and determinate," while the 11 million figure "is unacceptably mushy." (Novick, The Holocaust, 214–26)

[66] Wiesel, Against Silence, v. iii. 162, 166.

[67] For the handicapped as Nazism's first genocidal victims, see esp. Henry Friedlander, The Origins of Nazi Genocide (Chapel Hill: 1995). According to Leon Wieseltier, the non-Jews who perished at Auschwitz "died a death invented for the Jews . . . victims of a 'solution' designed for others" (Leon Wieseltier, "At Auschwitz Decency Dies Again," in New York Times [3 September 1989]). Yet, as numerous scholarly studies show, it was the death invented for handicapped Germans that was then inflicted on Jews; in addition to Friedlander's study, see, for example, Michael Burleigh, Death and Deliverance (Cambridge: 1994).

murdered as many as a half-million Gypsies, with proportional losses roughly equal to the Jewish genocide.[68] Holocaust writers like Yehuda Bauer maintained that the Gypsies did not fall victim to the same genocidal onslaught as Jews. Respected holocaust historians like Henry Friedlander and Raul Hilberg, however, have argued that they did.[69]

Multiple motives lurked behind the museum's marginalizing of the Gypsy genocide. First: one simply couldn't compare the loss of Gypsy and Jewish life. Ridiculing the call for Gypsy representation on the US Holocaust Memorial Council as "cockamamie," executive director Rabbi Seymour Siegel doubted whether Gypsies even "existed" as a people: "There should be some recognition or acknowledgment of the gypsy people . . . if there is such a thing." He did allow, however, that "there was a suffering element under the Nazis." Edward Linenthal recalls the Gypsy representatives' "deep suspicion" of the council, "fueled by clear evidence that some council members viewed

---

[68] See Guenter Lewy, *The Nazi Persecution of the Gypsies* (Oxford: 2000), 221–2, for various estimates of Gypsies killed.

[69] Friedlander, *Origins*: "Alongside Jews, the Nazis murdered the European Gypsies. Defined as a 'dark-skinned' racial group, Gypsy men, women and children could not escape their fate as victims of Nazi genocide. . . . [T]he Nazi regime systematically murdered only three groups of human beings: the handicapped, Jews, and Gypsies" (xii–xiii). (Apart from being a first-rate historian, Friedlander is also a former Auschwitz inmate.) Raul Hilberg, *The Destruction of the European Jews* (New York: 1985) (in three volumes), v. iii, 999–1000. With his usual veracity, Wiesel claims disappointment in his memoir that the Holocaust Memorial Council, which he chaired, didn't include a Gypsy representative – as if he had been powerless to nominate one. (Wiesel, *And the Sea*, 211)

Rom participation in the museum the way a family deals with unwelcome, embarrassing relatives."[70]

Second: acknowledging the Gypsy genocide meant the loss of an exclusive Jewish franchise over The Holocaust, with a commensurate loss of Jewish "moral capital." Third: if the Nazis persecuted Gypsies and Jews alike, the dogma that The Holocaust marked the climax of a millennial Gentile hatred of Jews was clearly untenable. Likewise, if Gentile envy spurred the Jewish genocide, did envy also spur the Gypsy genocide? In the museum's permanent exhibition, non-Jewish victims of Nazism receive only token recognition.[71]

Finally, the Holocaust museum's political agenda has also been shaped by the Israel–Palestine conflict. Before serving as the museum's director, Walter Reich wrote a paean to Joan Peters's fraudulent *From Time Immemorial*, which claimed that Palestine was literally empty before Zionist colonization.[72] Under State Department pressure, Reich was forced to resign after refusing to invite Yasir Arafat, now a compliant American ally, to visit the museum. Offered a sub-director's position, Holocaust theologian John Roth was then badgered into resigning because of past criticism of Israel. Repudiating a

[70] Linenthal, *Preserving Memory*, 241–6, 315.

[71] Although the New York City Holocaust Museum's "particularistic Jewish bent" (Saidel) was even more pronounced – non-Jewish victims of Nazism early on received notice that it was "for Jews only" – Yehuda Bauer flew into a rage at the Commission's mere hint that the Holocaust encompassed more than Jewish losses. "Unless this is immediately and radically changed," Bauer threatened in a letter to Commission members, "I shall take every opportunity to . . . attack this outrageous design from every public platform I have." (Saidel, *Never Too Late*, 125–6, 129, 212, 221, 224–5)

[72] For background, see Finkelstein, *Image and Reality*, chap. 2.

book the museum originally endorsed because it included a chapter by Benny Morris, a prominent Israeli historian critical of Israel, Miles Lerman, the museum's chairman, avowed, "To put this museum on the opposite side of Israel – it's inconceivable."[73]

In the wake of Israel's appalling attacks against Lebanon in 1996, climaxing in the massacre of more than a hundred civilians at Qana, *Haaretz* columnist Ari Shavit observed that Israel could act with impunity because "we have the Anti-Defamation League . . . and Yad Vashem and the Holocaust Museum."[74]

[73] "ZOA Criticizes Holocaust Museum's Hiring of Professor Who Compared Israel to Nazis," in *Israel Wire* (5 June 1998). Neal M. Sher, "Sweep the Holocaust Museum Clean," in *Jewish World Review* (22 June 1998). "Scoundrel Time," in *PS – The Intelligent Guide to Jewish Affairs* (21 August 1998). Daniel Kurtzman, "Holocaust Museum Taps One of Its Own for Top Spot," in *Jewish Telegraphic Agency* (5 March 1999). Ira Stoll, "Holocaust Museum Acknowledges a Mistake," in *Forward* (13 August 1999).

[74] Noam Chomsky, *World Orders Old and New* (New York: 1996), 293–4 (Shavit).

CHAPTER 3

THE DOUBLE SHAKEDOWN

CHAPTER 7

THE DOUBLE SHADOW

The term "Holocaust survivor" originally designated those who suffered the unique trauma of the Jewish ghettos, concentration camps and slave labor camps, often in sequence. The figure for these Holocaust survivors at war's end is generally put at some 100,000.[1] The number of living survivors cannot be more than a quarter of this figure now. Because enduring the camps became a crown of martyrdom, many Jews who spent the war elsewhere represented themselves as camp survivors. Another strong motive behind this misrepresentation, however, was material. The postwar German government provided compensation to Jews who had been in ghettos or camps. Many Jews fabricated their pasts to meet this eligibility requirement.[2] "If everyone who claims to be a survivor actually is one," my mother used to exclaim, "who did Hitler kill?"

[1] Henry Friedlander, "Darkness and Dawn in 1945: The Nazis, the Allies, and the Survivors," in *US Holocaust Memorial Museum, 1945 – the Year of Liberation* (Washington: 1995), 11–35.

[2] See, for example, Segev, *Seventh Million*, 248.

Indeed, many scholars have cast doubt on the reliability of survivor testimony. "A great percentage of the mistakes I discovered in my own work," Hilberg recalls, "could be attributed to testimonies." Even within the Holocaust industry, Deborah Lipstadt, for example, wryly observes that Holocaust survivors frequently maintain they were personally examined by Josef Mengele at Auschwitz.[3]

Apart from the frailties of memory, some Holocaust survivor testimony may be suspect for additional reasons. Because survivors are now revered as secular saints, one doesn't dare question them. Preposterous statements pass without comment. Elie Wiesel reminisces in his acclaimed memoir that, recently liberated from Buchenwald and only eighteen years old, "I read *The Critique of Pure Reason* – don't laugh! – in Yiddish." Leaving aside Wiesel's acknowledgment that at the time "I was wholly ignorant of Yiddish grammar," *The Critique of Pure Reason* was never translated into Yiddish. Wiesel also remembers in intricate detail a "mysterious Talmudic scholar" who "mastered Hungarian in two weeks, just to surprise me." Wiesel tells a Jewish weekly that he "often gets hoarse or loses his voice" as he silently reads his books to himself "aloud, inwardly." And to a *New York Times* reporter, he recalls that he was once hit by a taxi in Times Square. "I flew an entire block. I was hit at 45th Street and Broadway, and the ambulance picked me up at 44th." "The truth I present is unvarnished," Wiesel sighs, "I cannot do otherwise."[4]

---

[3] Lappin, *Man With Two Heads*, 48. D.D. Guttenplan, "The Holocaust on Trial," in *Atlantic Monthly* (February 2000), 62 (but cf. text above, where Lipstadt equates doubting a survivor's testimony with Holocaust denial).

[4] Wiesel, *All Rivers*, 121–30, 139, 163–4, 201–2, 336. *Jewish Week*, 17 September 1999. *New York Times*, 5 March 1997.

In recent years, "Holocaust survivor" has been redefined to designate not only those who endured but also those who managed to evade the Nazis. It includes, for example, more than 100,000 Polish Jews who found refuge in the Soviet Union after the Nazi invasion of Poland. However, "those who had lived in Russia had not been treated differently than citizens of the country," historian Leonard Dinnerstein observes, while "the survivors of the concentration camps looked like the living dead."[5] One contributor to a Holocaust web site maintained that, although he spent the war in Tel Aviv, he was a Holocaust survivor because his grandmother died in Auschwitz. To judge by Israel Gutman, Wilkomirski is a Holocaust survivor because his "pain is authentic." The Israeli Prime Minister's office recently put the number of "living Holocaust survivors" at nearly a million. The main motive behind this inflationary revision is again not hard to find. It is difficult to press massive new claims for reparations if only a handful of Holocaust survivors are still alive. In fact, Wilkomirski's main accomplices were, in one way or another, tapped into the Holocaust reparations network. His childhood friend from Auschwitz, "little Laura," collected money from a Swiss Holocaust fund although in reality she was an American-born frequenter of satanic cults. His chief Israeli sponsors were active in or subsidized by organizations involved in Holocaust compensation.[6]

The reparations issue provides unique insight into the Holocaust industry. As we have seen, aligning with the United States in the

---

[5] Leonard Dinnerstein, *America and the Survivors of the Holocaust* (New York: 1982), 24.

[6] Daniel Ganzfried, "Binjamin Wilkomirski und die verwandelte Polin," in *Weltwoche* (4 November 1999).

Cold War, Germany was quickly rehabilitated and the Nazi holocaust forgotten. Nonetheless, in the early 1950s Germany entered into negotiations with Jewish institutions and signed indemnification agreements. With little if any external pressure, it has paid out to date some $60 billion.

Compare first the American record. Some 4–5 million men, women and children died as a result of the US wars in Indochina. After the American withdrawal, a historian recalls, Vietnam desperately needed aid. "In the South, 9,000 out of 15,000 hamlets, 25 million acres of farmland, 12 million acres of forest were destroyed, and 1.5 million farm animals had been killed; there were an estimated 200,000 prostitutes, 879,000 orphans, 181,000 disabled people, and 1 million widows; all six of the industrial cities in the North had been badly damaged, as were provincial and district towns, and 4,000 out of 5,800 agricultural communes." Refusing, however, to pay any reparations, President Carter explained that "the destruction was mutual." Declaring that he saw no need for "any apologies, certainly, for the war itself," President Clinton's Defense Secretary, William Cohen, similarly opined: "Both nations were scarred by this. They have their scars from the war. We certainly have ours."[7]

The German government sought to compensate Jewish victims with three different agreements signed in 1952. Individual claimants received payments according to the terms of the Law on Indemnification (*Bundesentschädigungsgesetz*). A separate agreement with Israel subsidized the absorption and rehabilitation of several hundred thou-

---

[7] Marilyn B. Young, *The Vietnam Wars* (New York: 1991), 301–2. "Cohen: US Not Sorry for Vietnam War," in *Associated Press* (11 March 2000).

sand Jewish refugees. The German government also negotiated at the same time a financial settlement with the Conference on Jewish Material Claims Against Germany, an umbrella of all major Jewish organizations including the American Jewish Committee, American Jewish Congress, Bnai Brith, the Joint Distribution Committee, and so forth. The Claims Conference was supposed to use the monies, $10 million annually for twelve years, or about a billion dollars in current values, for Jewish victims of Nazi persecution who had fallen through the cracks in the compensation process.[8] My mother was a case in point. A survivor of the Warsaw Ghetto, Majdanek concentration camp and slave labor camps at Czestochowa and Skarszysko-Kamiena, she received only $3,500 in compensation from the German government. Other Jewish victims (and many who in fact were not victims), however, received lifetime pensions from Germany eventually totaling hundreds of thousands of dollars. The monies given to the Claims Conference were earmarked for those Jewish victims who had received only minimal compensation.

Indeed, the German government sought to make explicit in the agreement with the Claims Conference that the monies would go solely to Jewish survivors, strictly defined, who had been unfairly or inadequately compensated by German courts. The Conference expressed outrage that its good faith was doubted. After reaching agreement, the Conference issued a press release underlining that the monies would be used for "Jewish persecutees of the Nazi regime for

---

[8] For background, see esp. Nana Sagi, *German Reparations* (New York: 1986), and Ronald W. Zweig, *German Reparations and the Jewish World* (Boulder: 1987). Both volumes are official histories commissioned by the Claims Conference.

whom the existing and proposed legislation cannot provide a remedy." The final accord called on the Conference to use the monies "for the relief, rehabilitation and resettlement of Jewish victims."

The Claims Conference promptly annulled the agreement. In a flagrant breach of its letter and spirit, the Conference earmarked the monies not for the rehabilitation of Jewish victims but rather for the rehabilitation of Jewish *communities*. Indeed, a guiding principle of the Claims Conference prohibited use of monies for "direct allocations to individuals." In a classic instance of looking after one's own, however, the Conference provided exemptions for two categories of victims: rabbis and "outstanding Jewish leaders" received individual payments. The constituent organizations of the Claims Conference used the bulk of the monies to finance various pet projects. Whatever benefits (if any) the actual Jewish victims received were indirect or incidental.[9] Large sums were circuitously channeled to Jewish communities in the Arab world and facilitated Jewish emigration from Eastern Europe.[10]

---

[9] In reply to a question recently put by German Parliament member Martin Hohmann (CDU), the German government acknowledged (albeit in extremely convoluted language) that only about 15 percent of the monies given to the Claims Conference actually benefited Jewish victims of Nazi persecution. (personal communication, 23 February 2000)

[10] In his official history, Ronald Zweig explicitly acknowledges that the Claims Conference violated the agreement's terms: "The influx of Conference funds allowed the Joint [Distribution Committee] to continue programs in Europe it would otherwise have terminated, and to undertake programs it would otherwise not have considered because of lack of funds. But the most significant change in the JDC budget resulting from reparations payments was the allocation for the Moslem countries, where the Joint's activities increased by an average of 68 percent during the first three years of Conference

They also subsidized cultural undertakings such as Holocaust museums and university chairs in Holocaust studies, as well as a Yad Vashem showboat pensioning "righteous Gentiles."

More recently, the Claims Conference sought to appropriate for itself denationalized Jewish properties in the former East Germany worth hundreds of millions of dollars that rightfully belonged to living Jewish heirs. As the Conference came under attack by defrauded Jews for this and other abuses, Rabbi Arthur Hertzberg cast a plague on both sides, sneering that "it's not about justice, it's a fight for money."[11] When Germans or Swiss refuse to pay compensation, the heavens cannot contain the righteous indignation of organized American Jewry. But when Jewish elites rob Jewish survivors, no ethical issues arise: it's just about money.

Although my late mother received only $3,500 in compensation, others involved in the reparations process have made out quite well.

---

allocations. Despite the formal restrictions on the use of the reparation funds in the agreement with Germany, the money was used where the needs were the greatest. Moses Leavitt [senior Claims Conference officer] . . . observed: 'Our budget was based on priority of needs in and outside of Israel, the Moslem countries, all included. . . . We did not consider the Conference fund as anything but a part of a general fund placed at our disposal in order to meet the area of Jewish needs for which we were responsible, the area of greatest priority'" (German Reparations, 74).

[11] See for example Lorraine Adams, "The Reckoning," in Washington Post Magazine (20 April 1997), Netty C. Gross, "The Old Boys Club," and "After Years of Stonewalling, the Claims Conference Changes Policy," in Jerusalem Report (15 May 1997, 16 August 1997), Rebecca Spence, "Holocaust Insurance Team Racking Up Millions in Expenses as Survivors Wait," in Forward (30 July 1999), and Verena Dobnik, "Oscar Hammerstein's Cousin Sues German Bank Over Holocaust Assets," in AP Online (20 November 1998) (Hertzberg).

The reported annual salary of Saul Kagan, long-time Executive Secretary of the Claims Conference, is $105,000. Between stints at the Conference, Kagan was convicted of 33 counts of willfully misapplying funds and credit while heading a New York bank. (The conviction was overturned only after multiple appeals.) Alfonse D'Amato, the ex-Senator from New York, mediates Holocaust lawsuits against German and Austrian banks for $350 per hour plus expenses. For the first 6 months of his labors, he took in $103,000. Earlier Wiesel publicly praised D'Amato for his "sensitivity to Jewish suffering." Lawrence Eagleburger, Secretary of State under President Bush, earns an annual salary of $300,000 as chair of the International Commission On Holocaust-Era Insurance Claims. "Whatever he's being paid," Elan Steinberg of the World Jewish Congress opined, "it is an absolute bargain." Kagan rings up in 12 days, Eagleburger in 4 days, and D'Amato in 10 hours what my mother received for suffering six years of Nazi persecution.[12]

The award for most enterprising Holocaust huckster, however, must surely go to Kenneth Bialkin. For decades a prominent US Jewish leader, he headed the ADL and chaired the Conference of Presidents of Major American Jewish Organizations. Currently, Bialkin represents the Generali insurance company *against* the Eagleburger Commission for a reported "high sum of money."[13]

~

[12] Greg B. Smith, "Federal Judge OKs Holocaust Accord," in *Daily News* (7 January 2000). Janny Scott, "Jews Tell of Holocaust Deposits," in *New York Times* (17 October 1996). Saul Kagan read a draft of this section on the Claims Conference. The final version incorporates all his factual corrections.

[13] Elli Wohlgelernter, "Lawyers and the Holocaust," in *Jerusalem Post* (6 July 1999).

In recent years, the Holocaust industry has become an outright extortion racket. Purporting to represent all of world Jewry, living and dead, it is laying claim to Holocaust-era Jewish assets throughout Europe. Fittingly dubbed the "last chapter of The Holocaust," this double shakedown of European countries as well as legitimate Jewish claimants first targeted Switzerland. I will first review the allegations against the Swiss. I will then turn to the evidence, demonstrating that many of the charges were not only based on deceit but apply even more accurately to those issuing them than to their targets.

Commemorating the 50th anniversary of the end of World War II, Switzerland's president formally apologized in May 1995 for denying Jews refuge during the Nazi holocaust.[14] About the same time, discussion reopened on the long-simmering question of Jewish assets deposited in Swiss accounts before and during the war. In a widely reported story, an Israeli journalist cited a document – misread, as it turned out – proving that Swiss banks still held Holocaust-era Jewish accounts worth billions of dollars.[15]

The World Jewish Congress, a moribund organization until its campaign denouncing Kurt Waldheim as a war criminal, leapt at this

---

[14] For background to this section, see Tom Bower, *Nazi Gold* (New York: 1998), Itamar Levin, *The Last Deposit* (Westport, Conn.: 1999), Gregg J. Rickman, *Swiss Banks and Jewish Souls* (New Brunswick, NJ: 1999), Isabel Vincent, *Hitler's Silent Partners* (New York: 1997), Jean Ziegler, *The Swiss, the Gold and the Dead* (New York: 1997). Although suffering from a pronounced anti-Swiss bias, these books contain much useful information.

[15] Levin, *Last Deposit*, chaps 6–7. For the erroneous Israeli report (although he doesn't mention it, Levin was the author), see Hans J. Halbheer, "To Our American Friends," in *American Swiss Foundation Occasional Papers* (n.d.).

new opportunity to flex its muscle. Early on it was understood that Switzerland was easy prey. Few would sympathize with rich Swiss bankers as against "needy Holocaust survivors." But more importantly, Swiss banks were highly vulnerable to economic pressures from the United States.[16]

In late 1995, Edgar Bronfman, president of the WJC and the son of a Jewish Claims Conference official, and Rabbi Israel Singer, the secretary-general of the WJC and a real estate tycoon, met with the Swiss bankers.[17] Bronfman, heir to the Seagram liquor fortune (his personal wealth is estimated at $3 billion), would later modestly inform the Senate Banking Committee that he spoke "on behalf of the Jewish people" as well as "the 6 million, those who cannot speak for themselves."[18] The Swiss bankers declared that they could locate only 775 unclaimed dormant accounts, worth a total of $32 million. They

[16] Thirteen branches of six Swiss banks operated in the United States. Swiss banks loaned American businesses $38 billion in 1994, and managed hundreds of billions of dollars in investments in American stocks and banks for their clients.

[17] In 1992, the WJC spawned a new organization, the World Jewish Restitution Organization (WJRO), which claimed legal jurisdiction over the assets of Holocaust survivors, living and dead. Headed by Bronfman, the WJRO is formally an umbrella of Jewish organizations modeled on the Jewish Claims Conference.

[18] Hearings before the Committee on Banking, Housing, and Urban Affairs, United States Senate, 23 April 1996. Bronfman's defense of "Jewish interests" is highly selective. He is a major business associate of the right-wing German media mogul Leo Kirch, notorious in recent years for trying to fire a German newspaper editor who supported a Supreme Court decision barring Christian crosses in public schools. (www.Seagram.com/company_info/history/main.html; Oliver Gehrs, "Einfluss aus der Dose," in Tagesspiegel [12 September 1995])

offered this sum as a basis for negotiations with the WJC, which refused it as inadequate. In December 1995, Bronfman teamed up with Senator D'Amato. His poll ratings at a nadir and a Senate race not far off, D'Amato savored this occasion to boost his standing in the Jewish community, with its crucial votes and wealthy political donors. Before the Swiss were finally brought to their knees, the WJC, working with the gamut of Holocaust institutions (including the US Holocaust Memorial Museum and the Simon Wiesenthal Center), had mobilized the entire US political establishment. From President Clinton, who buried the hatchet with D'Amato (the Whitewater hearings were still going on) to lend support, through eleven agencies of the federal government as well as the House and Senate, down to state and local governments across the country, bipartisan pressures were brought to bear as one public official after another lined up to denounce the perfidious Swiss.

Using the House and Senate banking committees as a springboard, the Holocaust industry orchestrated a shameless campaign of vilification. With an infinitely compliant and credulous press ready to give banner headlines to any Holocaust-related story, however preposterous, the smear campaign proved unstoppable. Gregg Rickman, D'Amato's chief legislative aide, boasts in his account that the Swiss bankers were forced "into the court of public opinion where we controlled the agenda. The bankers were on our turf and conveniently, we were judge, jury, and executioner." Tom Bower, a main researcher in the anti-Swiss campaign, dubs the D'Amato call for hearings a "euphemism for a public trial or a kangaroo court."[19]

---

[19] Rickman, *Swiss Banks*, 50–1. Bower, *Nazi Gold*, 299–300.

The "mouthpiece" of the anti-Swiss juggernaut was WJC executive director Elan Steinberg. His main function was dispensing disinformation. "Terror by embarrassment," according to Bower, "was Steinberg's weapon, as he uttered a string of accusations designed to cause discomfort and shock. OSS reports, often based on rumor and uncorroborated sources and disregarded for years by historians as hearsay, suddenly assumed uncritical credibility and widespread publicity." "The last thing the banks need is negative publicity," Rabbi Singer explained. "We will do it until the banks say, 'Enough. We want a compromise.'" Anxious to share the limelight, Rabbi Marvin Hier, Dean of the Simon Wiesenthal Center, spectacularly alleged that the Swiss incarcerated refugee Jews in "slave-labor camps." (With wife and son on the payroll, Hier runs the Simon Wiesenthal Center as a family business; together the Hiers drew a salary of $520,000 in 1995. The Center is renowned for its "Dachau-meets-Disneyland" museum exhibits and "the successful use of sensationalistic scare tactics for fund-raising.") "In light of the media barrage of mixing truth and assumption, fact and fiction," Itamar Levin concludes, "it is easy to understand why many Swiss believe their country was the victim of an international conspiracy of some kind."[20]

---

[20] Bower, *Nazi Gold*, 295 ("mouthpiece"), 306–7; cf. 319. Alan Morris Schom, "The Unwanted Guests, Swiss Forced Labor Camps, 1940–1944," A Report Prepared for the Simon Wiesenthal Center, January 1998. (Schom states these were "in reality slave-labor camps.") Levin, *Last Deposit*, 158, 188. For a sober treatment of the Swiss refugee camps, see Ken Newman (ed.), *Swiss Wartime Work Camps: A Collection of Eyewitness Testimonies, 1940–1945* (Zurich: 1999), and International Commission of Experts, Switzerland – Second World War, *Switzerland and Refugees in the Nazi Era* (Bern: 1999), chap. 4.4.4. Saidel,

The campaign rapidly degenerated into a libel of the Swiss people. Bower, in a study supported by D'Amato's office and the Simon Wiesenthal Center, typically reports that "a country whose citizens . . . boasted to their neighbors about their enviable wealth, was quite knowingly profiting from blood money"; that "the apparently respectable citizens of the world's most peaceful nation . . . committed an unprecedented theft"; that "dishonesty was a cultural code that individual Swiss had mastered to protect the nation's image and prosperity"; that the Swiss were "instinctively attracted to healthy profits" (only the Swiss?); that "self-interest was the supreme guide for all of Switzerland's banks" (only Switzerland's banks?); that "Switzerland's small breed of bankers had become greedier and more immoral than most"; that "concealment and deception were practiced arts among Swiss diplomats" (only Swiss diplomats?); that "apologies and resignations were not common in Switzerland's political tradition" (unlike our own?); that "Swiss greed was unique"; that the "Swiss character" combined "simplicity and duplicity," and "behind the appearance of civility was a layer of obstinacy, and beyond that was solid egotistical incomprehension of anyone else's opinion"; that the Swiss were "not just a peculiarly charmless people who had produced no artists, no heroes since William Tell and no statesmen, but were dishonest Nazi collaborators who had profited from genocide," and on and on. Rickman points to this "deeper truth" about the Swiss: "Down deep, perhaps deeper than they thought, a latent arrogance about

---

Never Too Late, 222–3 ("Dachau", "sensationalistic"). Yossi Klein Halevi, "Who Owns the Memory?" in *Jerusalem Report* (25 February 1993). Wiesenthal rents out his name to the Center for $90,000 annually.

themselves and against others existed in their very makeup. Try as they did, they could not hide their upbringing."[21] Many of these slurs are remarkably like the slurs cast against Jews by anti-Semites.

The main charge was that there had been, in the words of Bower's subtitle, "a fifty-year Swiss-Nazi conspiracy to steal billions from Europe's Jews and Holocaust survivors." In what has become a mantra of the Holocaust restitution racket, this constituted "the greatest robbery in the history of mankind." For the Holocaust industry, all matters Jewish belong in a separate, superlative category – *the* worst, *the* greatest. . . .

The Holocaust industry first alleged that Swiss banks had systematically denied legitimate heirs of Holocaust victims access to dormant accounts worth between $7 billion and $20 billion. "For the past 50 years," *Time* reported in a cover story, a "standing order" of the Swiss banks "has been to stall and stonewall when Holocaust survivors ask about their dead relatives' accounts." Recalling the secrecy legislation enacted by Swiss banks in 1934 partly to prevent a Nazi shakedown of Jewish depositors, D'Amato lectured the House Banking Committee: "Isn't it ironic that the very system that encouraged people to come and open accounts, the secrecy was then used to deny the people themselves, and their heirs, their legacy, their right? It was perverted, distorted, twisted."

Bower breathlessly recounts the discovery of one key piece of evidence of Swiss perfidy against Holocaust victims: "Luck and diligence provided a nugget that confirmed the validity of Bronfman's

[21] Bower, *Nazi Gold*, xi, xv, 8, 9, 42, 44, 56, 84, 100, 150, 219, 304. Rickman, *Swiss Banks*, 219.

complaint. An intelligence report from Switzerland in July 1945 stated that Jacques Salmanovitz, the owner of the Société Générale de Surveillance, a notary and trust company in Geneva with links to the Balkan countries, possessed a list of 182 Jewish clients who had entrusted 8.4 million Swiss francs and about $90,000 to the notary pending their arrival from the Balkans. The report added that Jews had still not claimed their possessions. Rickman and D'Amato were ecstatic." In his own account, Rickman likewise brandishes this "proof of Swiss criminality." Neither, however, mentions in this specific context that Salmanovitz was Jewish. (The actual validity of these claims will be discussed below.)[22]

In late 1996 a parade of elderly Jewish women and one man delivered moving testimony before the Congressional banking committees on the malfeasance of the Swiss bankers. Yet almost none of these witnesses, according to Itamar Levin, an editor of Israel's main business newspaper, "had real proof of the existence of assets in Swiss banks." To enhance the theatrical effect of this testimony, D'Amato called Elie Wiesel to bear witness. In testimony later widely quoted, Wiesel expressed shock – shock! – at the revelation that the perpetrators of the Holocaust sought to plunder Jews before killing them: "In the beginning we thought the final solution was motivated by poisoned ideology alone. Now we know that they didn't simply want to kill Jews, as horrible as this may sound, they wanted Jewish

[22] Thomas Sancton, "A Painful History," in *Time*, 24 February 1997. Hearings before the Committee on Banking and Financial Services, House of Representatives, 25 June 1997. Bower, *Nazi Gold*, 301–2. Rickman, *Swiss Banks*, 48. Levin is equally silent on Salmanovitz being a Jew (cf. 5, 129, 135).

money. Each day we learn more about that tragedy. Is there no limit
to pain? No limit to the outrage?" Of course, Nazi plunder of the
Jews is hardly news; a large part of Raul Hilberg's seminal study, *The
Destruction of the European Jews*, published in 1961, is devoted to the
Nazi expropriation of the Jews.[23]

It was also claimed that the Swiss bankers filched the deposits of
Holocaust victims and methodically destroyed vital records to cover
their tracks, and that only Jews suffered all these abominations.
Assailing the Swiss at one hearing, Senator Barbara Boxer declared:
"This Committee will not stand for two-faced behavior on the part of
the Swiss banks. Don't tell the world that you are searching when
you are shredding."[24]

Alas, the "propaganda value" (Bower) of elderly Jewish claimants
testifying to Swiss perfidy quickly exhausted itself. The Holocaust
industry accordingly sought out a new exposé. The media frenzy
fixed on the Swiss purchase of gold that the Nazis looted from the
central treasuries of Europe during the war. Although billed as a
startling revelation, it was in fact old news. The author of a standard
study on the subject, Arthur Smith, told the House hearing: "I have
listened all morning and this afternoon to things that, to a large
extent, in outline, were known for a number of years; and I am
surprised about the fact that much of it is presented as new and

---

[23] Levin, *Last Deposit*, 60. Hearings before the Committee on Banking and
Financial Services, House of Representatives, 11 December 1996 (quoting
Wiesel's 16 October 1996 Senate Banking Committee testimony). Raul
Hilberg, *The Destruction of the European Jews* (New York: 1961), chap. 5.

[24] Hearings before the Committee on Banking, Housing, and Urban Affairs,
United States Senate, 6 May 1997.

sensational." The point of the hearings, however, was not to inform but, in journalist Isabel Vincent's words, "to create sensational stories." If enough mud was flung, it was reasonably assumed, Switzerland would give in.[25]

The one truly novel allegation was that the Swiss knowingly trafficked in "victim gold." That is, they purchased vast quantities of gold which the Nazis had resmelted into bars after stripping down concentration- and death-camp victims. The WJC, Bower reports, "needed an emotive issue to link the Holocaust and Switzerland." This new revelation of Swiss treachery was accordingly treated as a godsend. "Few images," Bower continues, "were more searing than the methodical extraction in the extermination camps of gold dental fillings from the mouths of Jewish corpses dragged from the gas chambers." "The facts are very, very distressing," D'Amato mournfully intoned at a House hearing, "because they talk about taking and the plundering of assets from homes, from national banks, from the death camps, gold watches and bracelets and eyeglasses frames and the fillings from people's teeth."[26]

Apart from blocking access to Holocaust accounts and purchas-

---

[25] Hearings before the Committee on Banking and Financial Services, House of Representatives, 11 December 1996. Smith complained to the press that the documents he had unearthed long before were being touted by D'Amato as new discoveries. In a bizarre defense, Rickman, who mobilized a massive contingent of researchers through the US Holocaust museum for the Congressional hearings, replies: "While I knew about Smith's book, I made a point of not reading it so that I could not be accused of using 'his' documents" (113). Vincent, *Silent Partners*, 240.

[26] Bower, *Nazi Gold*, 307. Hearings before the Committee on Banking and Financial Services, House of Representatives, 25 June 1997.

ing looted gold, the Swiss also stood accused of conspiring with Poland and Hungary to defraud Jews. The charge was that monies in unclaimed Swiss accounts belonging to Polish and Hungarian nationals (many but not all Jewish) were used by Switzerland as compensation for Swiss properties nationalized by these governments. Rickman refers to this as a "startling revelation, one that would knock the socks off the Swiss and create a firestorm." But the facts were already widely known and reported in American law journals in the early 1950s. And, for all the media ballyhoo, the total sums involved ultimately came to less than a million dollars in current values.[27]

Already prior to the first Senate hearing on the dormant accounts in April 1996, the Swiss banks had agreed to establish an investigative committee and abide by its findings. Composed of six members, three each from the World Jewish Restitution Organization and the Swiss Bankers Association, and headed by Paul Volcker, former chairman of the US Federal Reserve Bank, the "independent committee of eminent persons" was formally charged in a May 1996 "Memorandum of Understanding." In addition, the Swiss government appointed in December 1996 an "independent commission of experts," chaired by Professor Jean-François Bergier and including prominent Israeli holo-

---

[27] Rickman, *Swiss Banks*, 77. For the definitive treatment of this topic, see Peter Hug and Marc Perrenoud, *Assets in Switzerland of Victims of Nazism and the Compensation Agreements with East Bloc Countries* (Bern: 1997). For early discussion in the United States, see Seymour J. Rubin and Abba P. Schwartz, "Refugees and Reparations," in *Law and Contemporary Problems* (Duke University School of Law: 1951), 283.

caust scholar Saul Friedländer, to investigate Switzerland's gold trade with Germany during World War II.

Before these bodies could even commence work, however, the Holocaust industry pressed for a financial settlement with Switzerland. The Swiss protested that any settlement should naturally await the commissions' findings; otherwise, it constituted "extortion and blackmail." Playing its ever-winning card, the WJC anguished over the plight of "needy Holocaust survivors." "My problem is the timing," Bronfman told the House Banking Committee in December 1996, "and I have all of these Holocaust survivors that I am worried about." One wonders why the anguished billionaire couldn't himself temporarily relieve their plight. Dismissing one Swiss settlement offer of $250 million, Bronfman sniffed: "Don't do any favors. I'll give the money myself." He didn't. Switzerland, however, agreed in February 1997 to establish a $200 million "Special Fund for Needy Victims of the Holocaust" to tide over "persons who need help or support in special ways" until the commissions completed their work. (The fund was still solvent when the Bergier and Volcker commissions issued their reports.) The pressures from the Holocaust industry for a final settlement, however, did not relent; rather, they continued to mount. Renewed Swiss pleas that a settlement should await the commissions' findings – it was the WJC, after all, that originally called for this moral reckoning – still fell on deaf ears. In fact, the Holocaust industry stood only to lose from these findings: if just a few Holocaust-era accounts belonging to Jews were found, the case against the Swiss banks would lose credibility; and if even a large number were found, it would mainly be the legitimate claimants who were compensated, not the Jewish organizations. Another mantra of the

Holocaust industry is that compensation "is about truth and justice, not about money." "It's not about money," the Swiss now quipped. "It's about more money."[28]

Beyond whipping up public hysteria, the Holocaust industry coordinated a two-pronged strategy to "terrorize" (Bower) the Swiss into submission: class-action lawsuits and an economic boycott. The first class-action lawsuit was filed in early October 1996 by Edward Fagan and Robert Swift on behalf of Gizella Weisshaus (her father spoke about monies deposited in Switzerland before his death in Auschwitz, but the banks rebuffed her postwar inquiries) and "others similarly situated" for $20 billion. A few weeks later the Simon Wiesenthal Center, enlisting attorneys Michael Hausfeld and Melvyn Weiss, filed a second class-action lawsuit, and in January 1997 the World Council of Orthodox Jewish Communities initiated yet a third one. All three suits were filed before Judge Edward Korman, a US District Court judge in Brooklyn, who consolidated them. At least one party to the case, Toronto-based attorney Sergio Karas, deplored this tactic: "The class-action suits have done nothing but provoke mass hysteria and Swiss-bashing. They're just perpetuating the myth about Jewish lawyers who just want money." Paul Volcker opposed the class-action

---

[28] Levin, *Last Deposit*, 93, 186. Hearings before the Committee on Banking and Financial Services, House of Representatives, 11 December 1996. Rickman, *Swiss Banks*, 218. Bower, *Nazi Gold*, 318, 323. A week after establishing the Special Fund, Switzerland's president, "terrified of unremitting hostility in America" (Bower), announced the creation of a $5 billion Solidarity Foundation "to reduce poverty, despair, and violence" globally. The foundation's approval, however, required a national referendum, and domestic opposition quickly surfaced. Its fate remains uncertain.

suits on the grounds that they "will impair our work, potentially to the point of ineffectiveness" – for the Holocaust industry an irrelevant concern, if not an added incentive.[29]

The main weapon used to break Swiss resistance, however, was the economic boycott. "Now the battle will be much dirtier," Avraham Burg, chair of the Jewish Agency and Israel's point man in the Swiss banking case, warned in January 1997. "Until now we have held back international Jewish pressure." Already in January 1996 the WJC had begun plotting the boycott. Bronfman and Singer contacted New York City Comptroller Alan Hevesi (whose father had been a prominent AJC official) and New York State Comptroller Carl McCall. Between them, the two comptrollers invest billions of dollars in pension funds. Hevesi also presided over the US Comptrollers Association, which invested $30 trillion in pension funds. In late January Singer strategized with Governor George Pataki of New York as well as with D'Amato and Bronfman at his daughter's wedding. "Look what kind of man I am," the Rabbi mused, "doing business at my daughter's wedding."[30]

In February 1996 Hevesi and McCall wrote the Swiss banks threatening sanctions. In October Governor Pataki publicly lent his support. During the next several months local and state governments in New York, New Jersey, Rhode Island and Illinois all tabled resolutions threatening an economic boycott unless the Swiss banks came clean. In May 1997 the city of Los Angeles, withdrawing

---

[29] Bower, *Nazi Gold*, 315. Vincent, *Silent Partners*, 211. Rickman, *Swiss Banks*, 184 (Volcker).

[30] Levin, *Last Deposit*, 187–8, 125.

hundreds of millions of dollars in pension funds from a Swiss bank, imposed the first sanctions. Hevesi quickly followed suit with sanctions in New York. California, Massachusetts, and Illinois joined in within days.

"I want $3 billion or northward," Bronfman proclaimed in December 1997, "in order to end it all, the class-action suits, the Volcker process and the rest." Meanwhile, D'Amato and New York State banking officials sought to block the newly formed United Bank of Switzerland (a merger of major Swiss banks) from operating in the United States. "If the Swiss are going to keep digging their heels in, then I'll have to ask all US shareholders to suspend their dealings with the Swiss," Bronfman warned in March 1998. "It's coming to a point where it has to resolve itself or it has to be total war." In April the Swiss started buckling under the pressure, but still resisted abject surrender. (Through 1997 the Swiss reportedly spent $500 million to fend off the Holocaust industry attacks.) "There's a virulent cancer throughout the Swiss society," Melvyn Weiss, one of the class-action lawyers, lamented. "We gave them an opportunity to get rid of it with a massive dose of radiation at a cost that is very small and they've turned it down." In June the Swiss banks put forth a "final offer" of $600 million. ADL head Abraham Foxman, shocked by *Swiss* arrogance, could barely contain his rage: "This ultimatum is an insult to the memory of the victims, their survivors and to those in the Jewish community who in good faith reached to the Swiss to work together to resolve this most difficult matter."[31]

In July 1998 Hevesi and McCall threatened stiff new sanctions.

---

[31] Levin, *Last Deposit*, 218. Rickman, *Swiss Banks*, 214, 223, 221.

New Jersey, Pennsylvania, Connecticut, Florida, Michigan, and California joined in within days. In mid-August the Swiss finally caved in. In a class-action settlement mediated by Judge Korman, the Swiss agreed to pay $1.25 billion. "The aim of the additional payment," a Swiss banks press release read, "is to avert the threat of sanctions as well as long and costly court proceedings."[32]

"You have been a true pioneer in this saga," Israeli Prime Minister Benjamin Netanyahu congratulated D'Amato. "The result is not only an achievement in material terms but a moral victory and a triumph of the spirit."[33] Pity he didn't say "the will."

The $1.25 billion settlement with Switzerland covered basically three classes – claimants to dormant Swiss accounts, refugees denied Swiss asylum, and victims of slave labor which Swiss benefited from.[34] For all the righteous indignation about the "perfidious Swiss," however, the comparable American record is, on all these counts, just as bad, if not worse. I will return presently to the matter of dormant US accounts. Like Switzerland, the US denied entry to Jewish refugees fleeing Nazism before and during World War II. Yet the American government hasn't seen fit to compensate, say, Jewish

---

[32] Rickman, *Swiss Banks*, 231.

[33] Ibid. Rickman fittingly entitled this chapter of his account, "Boycotts and Diktats."

[34] For the complete text of the "Class Action Settlement Agreement," see Independent Committee of Eminent Persons, *Report on Dormant Accounts of Victims of Nazi Persecution in Swiss Banks* (Bern: 1999), Appendix O. In addition to the $200 million Special Fund and the $1.25 billion class-action settlement, the Holocaust industry finagled another $70 million from the United States and its allies during a 1997 London conference on the Swiss gold.

refugees aboard the ill-fated ship *St. Louis*. Imagine the reaction if the thousands of Central American and Haitian refugees who were denied asylum after fleeing US-sponsored death squads sought compensation here. And, although dwarfed in size and resources by the United States, Switzerland admitted just as many Jewish refugees as the US (approximately 20,000) during the Nazi holocaust.[35]

The only means to atone for past sins, American politicians lectured Switzerland, was providing material compensation. Stuart Eizenstat, Undersecretary for Commerce and Clinton's Special Envoy for Property Restitution, deemed Swiss compensation to Jewry "an important litmus test of this generation's willingness to face the past and to rectify the wrongs of the past." Although they couldn't be "held responsible for what took place years ago," D'Amato acknowledged during the same Senate hearing, the Swiss still had "a duty of accountability and of attempting to do what is right at this point in time." Publicly endorsing the WJC's compensation demands, President Clinton likewise reflected that "we must confront and, as best

---

[35] For US policy on Jewish refugees during these years, see David S. Wyman, *Paper Walls* (New York: 1985), and *The Abandonment of the Jews* (New York: 1984). For Swiss policy, see Independent Commission of Experts, Switzerland – Second World War, *Switzerland and Refugees in the Nazi Era* (Bern: 1999). A similar mix of factors – economic downturn, xenophobia, anti-Semitism, and, later, security – accounted for the restrictive American and Swiss quotas. Recalling the "hypocrisy in the speeches by other nations, especially the United States which was completely uninterested in liberalizing its immigration laws," the Independent Commission, although harshly critical of Switzerland, reports that its refugee policy was "like the governments of most other states." (42, 263) I found no mention of this point in the extensive US media coverage of the Commission's critical findings.

we can, right the terrible injustice of the past." "History does not have a statute of limitations," chairman James Leach said during the House Banking Committee hearings, and "the past must never be forgotten." "It should be made clear," bipartisan Congressional leaders wrote in a letter to the Secretary of State, that the "response on this restitution matter will be seen as a test of respect for basic human rights and the rule of law." And in an address to the Swiss Parliament, Secretary of State Madeleine Albright explained that the economic benefits accruing to the Swiss from withheld Jewish accounts "were passed along to subsequent generations and that is why the world now looks to the people of Switzerland, not to assume responsibility for actions taken by their forebears, but to be generous in doing what can be done at this point to right past wrongs."[36] Noble sentiments all, but nowhere to be heard – unless they are being actively ridiculed – when it comes to African-American compensation for slavery.[37]

[36] Hearings before the Committee on Banking, Housing, and Urban Affairs, United States Senate, 15 May 1997 (Eizenstat and D'Amato). Hearings before the Committee on Banking, Housing, and Urban Affairs, United States Senate, 23 April 1996 (Bronfman, quoting Clinton and letter of Congressional leaders). Hearings before the Committee on Banking and Financial Services, House of Representatives, 11 December 1996 (Leach). Hearings before the Committee on Banking and Financial Services, House of Representatives, 25 June 1997 (Leach). Rickman, *Swiss Banks*, 204 (Albright).

[37] The only discordant note during the multiple Congressional hearings on Holocaust compensation was sounded by Congresswoman Maxine Waters of California. While registering "1000 percent" support "to get justice for all of the victims of the Holocaust," Waters also questioned "how to take this format and use it to deal with slave labor of my ancestors here in the United States. It's very strange to sit here . . . without wondering what I could be doing . . . to acknowledge slave labor in the United States. . . . Reparations

It remains unclear how "needy Holocaust survivors" will fare in the final settlement. Gizella Weisshaus, the first claimant of a dormant Swiss account to sue, has discharged her attorney, Edward Fagan, bitterly charging that he used her. Still, Fagan's bill to the court totaled $4 million in fees. Total attorney fee demands run to $15 million, with "many" billing at a rate of $600 per hour. One lawyer is asking $2,400 for reading Tom Bower's book, *Nazi Gold*. "Jewish groups and survivors," New York's *Jewish Week* reported, "are taking off the gloves as they vie for a share of the Swiss banks' $1.25 billion Holocaust-era settlement." Plaintiffs and survivors maintain that all the money should go directly to them. Jewish organizations, however, are demanding a piece of the action. Denouncing the aggrandizement

---

in the African-American community have been basically condemned as a radical idea, and many of those . . . who tried so hard to get this issue before the Congress have literally been ridiculed." Specifically she proposed that government agencies directed to achieving Holocaust compensation be directed as well to achieving compensation for "domestic slave labor." "The gentle lady raises an extraordinarily profound subject," James Leach of the House Banking Committee replied, "and the Chair will take it under advisement. . . . The profoundness of the issue you raise in an American historical setting as well as in the human rights setting is deep." The issue will undoubtedly be deposited deep in the Committee's memory hole. (Hearings before the Committee on Banking and Financial Services, House of Representatives, 9 February 2000) Randall Robinson, who is currently leading a campaign to compensate African-Americans for slavery, juxtaposed the US government's "silence" on this theft "even as the US Undersecretary of State, Stuart Eizenstat, labored to make 16 German companies compensate Jews used as slave laborers during the Nazi era." (Randall Robinson, "Compensate the Forgotten Victims of America's Slavery Holocaust," in *Los Angeles Times* [11 February 2000]; cf. Randall Robinson, *The Debt* [New York: 2000], 245)

of the Jewish organizations, Greta Beer, a key Congressional witness against the Swiss banks, beseeched Judge Korman's court that "I don't want to be crushed underfoot like a little insect." Its solicitude for "needy Holocaust survivors" notwithstanding, the WJC wants nearly half the Swiss monies earmarked for Jewish organizations and "Holocaust education." The Simon Wiesenthal Center maintains that if "worthy" Jewish organizations receive monies, "a portion should go to Jewish educational centers." As they "angle" for a bigger share of the loot, Reform and Orthodox organizations each claim that the 6 million dead would have preferred their branch of Judaism as financial beneficiary. Meanwhile, the Holocaust industry forced Switzerland into a settlement because time was allegedly of the essence: "needy Holocaust survivors are dying every day." Once the Swiss signed away the money, however, the urgency miraculously passed. More than a year after the settlement was reached there was still no distribution plan. By the time the money is finally divvied out all the "needy Holocaust survivors" will probably be dead. In fact, as of December 1999, less than half of the $200 million "Special Fund for Needy Victims of the Holocaust" established in February 1997 had been distributed to actual victims. After lawyers' fees have been paid, the Swiss monies will then flow into the coffers of "worthy" Jewish organizations.[38]

---

[38] Philip Lentz, "Reparation Woes," in *Crain's* (15–21 November 1999). Michael Shapiro, "Lawyers in Swiss Bank Settlement Submit Bill, Outraging Jewish Groups," in *Jewish Telegraphic Agency* (23 November 1999). Rebecca Spence, "Hearings on Legal Fees in Swiss Bank Case," in *Forward* (26 November 1999). James Bone, "Holocaust Survivors Protest Over Legal Fee," in *The Times* (London) (1 December 1999). Devlin Barrett, "Holocaust Assets," in *New*

"No settlement can possibly be defended," Burt Neuborne, a New York University law professor and member of the class-action legal team, wrote in the *New York Times*, "if it allows the Holocaust to stand as a profit-making enterprise for the Swiss banks." Edgar Bronfman movingly testified before the House Banking Committee that the Swiss should not "be allowed to make a profit from the ashes of the Holocaust." On the other hand, Bronfman recently acknowledged that the WJC treasury has amassed no less than "roughly $7 billion" in compensation monies.[39]

The authoritative reports on the Swiss banks have meanwhile been published. One can now judge whether in fact there was, as Bower claims, a "fifty-year Swiss-Nazi conspiracy to steal billions from Europe's Jews and Holocaust survivors."

In July 1998 the Independent (Bergier) Commission of Experts issued its report, *Switzerland and Gold Transactions in the Second World War*.[40] The Commission confirmed that Swiss banks purchased gold

---

York Post (2 December 1999). Stewart Ain, "Religious Strife Erupts In Swiss Money Fight," in *Jewish Week* (14 January 2000) ("angle"). Adam Dickter, "Discord in the Court," in *Jewish Week* (21 January 2000). Swiss Fund for Needy Victims of the Holocaust/Shoa, "Overview on Finances, Payments and Pending Applications" (30 November 1999). Holocaust survivors in Israel never received any of the Special Fund monies earmarked for them; see Yair Sheleg, "Surviving Israeli Bureaucracy," in *Haaretz* (6 February 2000).

[39] Burt Neuborne, "Totaling the Sum of Swiss Guilt," in *New York Times* (24 June 1998). Hearings before the Committee on Banking and Financial Services, House of Representatives, 11 December 1996. "Holocaust-Konferenz in Stockholm," in *Frankfurter Allgemeine Zeitung* (26 January 2000) (Bronfman).

[40] Independent Commission of Experts, Switzerland – Second World War, *Switzerland and Gold Transactions in the Second World War, Interim Report* (Bern: 1998).

from Nazi Germany, worth about $4 billion in current values, knowing that it had been plundered from the central banks of occupied Europe. Throughout the hearings on Capitol Hill, members of Congress expressed shock that Swiss banks had trafficked in looted assets and, even worse, still indulged these egregious practices. Deploring the fact that corrupt politicians deposit their ill-gotten gains in Swiss banks, one Congressman called on Switzerland to finally enact legislation against "this secret movement of money by . . . people of political prominence or leadership, of people looting their treasury." Bewailing the "number of international, high profile corrupt government officials and businesspeople who have found sanctuary for their substantial wealth in Swiss banks," another Congressman wondered aloud whether "the Swiss banking system is accommodating this generation's thugs, and the countries they represent, in . . . ways that sanctuary was given to the Nazi regime 55 years ago?"[41] Truly the problem warrants concern. Annually an estimated $100–$200 billion arising from political corruption is sent across borders worldwide and deposited in private banks. The Congressional banking committee reprimands would have carried more weight, however, if fully half

---

[41] Hearings before the Committee on Banking and Financial Services, House of Representatives, 11 December 1996. Called as an expert witness, University of North Carolina historian Gerhard L. Weinberg sanctimoniously testified that the "position of the Swiss Government at the time and in the immediate postwar years was always that looting is legal," and that "priority number one" of the Swiss banks was "making as much money as possible . . . and to do so regardless of the legalities, morality and decency or anything else." (Hearings before the Committee on Banking and Financial Services, House of Representatives, 25 June 1997)

this "illegal flight capital" weren't deposited in American banks with the complete sanction of US law.[42] Recent beneficiaries of this legal US "sanctuary" include Raul Salinas de Gortari, the brother of Mexico's former president, and the family of former Nigerian dictator General Sani Abacha. "The gold looted by Adolf Hitler and his henchmen," Jean Ziegler, a Swiss parliamentarian fiercely critical of the Swiss banks, observes, "does not differ in essence from the blood money" now held in the private Swiss accounts of Third World dictators. "Millions of men, women, and children were driven to their deaths by Hitler's licensed thieves," and "hundreds of thousands of children die annually of disease and malnutrition" in the Third World because "tyrants despoiled their countries with the aid of Swiss financial sharks."[43] And with the aid of American financial sharks as well. I leave to one side the even more important point that many of these tyrants were installed and maintained by US power and authorized by the United States to despoil their countries.

On the specific question of the Nazi holocaust, the Independent Commission concluded that the Swiss banks did purchase "bars containing gold looted by Nazi criminals from the victims of work camps and extermination camps." They didn't, however, knowingly do so: "there is no indication that the decision-makers at the Swiss central bank knew that bars containing such gold were being shipped to Switzerland by the Reichsbank." The Commission put the value of

[42] Raymond W. Baker, "The Biggest Loophole in the Free-Market System," in *Washington Quarterly* (Autumn 1999). Although not sanctioned by US law, much of the $500 billion–$1 trillion annually "laundered" from the drug trade is also "safely deposited into US banks." (ibid.)

[43] Ziegler, *The Swiss*, xii; cf. 19, 265.

"victim gold" unwittingly purchased by Switzerland at $134,428, or about $1 million in current values. This figure includes "victim gold" stripped from Jewish as well as non-Jewish camp inmates.[44]

In December 1999 the Independent (Volcker) Committee of Eminent Persons issued its *Report on Dormant Accounts of Victims of Nazi Persecution in Swiss Banks*.[45] The *Report* documents the findings of an exhaustive audit that lasted three years and cost no less than $500 million.[46] Its central finding on the "treatment of dormant accounts of victims of Nazi persecution" merits extended quotation:

[F]or victims of Nazi persecution there was no evidence of systematic discrimination, obstruction of access, misappropriation, or violation of document retention requirements of Swiss law. However, the Report also criticizes the actions of some banks in their treatment of the accounts of victims of Nazi persecution. The word "some" in the preceding sentence needs to be emphasized since the criticized actions refer mainly to those of specific banks in their handling of individual accounts of victims of Nazi persecution in the context of an investigation of 254 banks covering a period of about 60 years. For the criticized actions, the Report also recognizes that there were mitigating circumstances for the conduct of the banks involved in these activities. The Report acknowledges, moreover, that there is ample evidence of

---

[44] *Switzerland and Gold Transactions in the Second World War*, IV, 48.

[45] Independent Committee of Eminent Persons, *Report on Dormant Accounts of Victims of Nazi Persecution in Swiss Banks* (Bern: 1999). (hereafter *Report*)

[46] The "external cost" of the audit was put at $200 million. (*Report*, p. 4, paragraph 17) The cost to the Swiss banks was put at another $300 million. (Swiss Federal Banking Commission, press release, 6 December 1999)

many cases in which banks actively sought out missing account holders or their heirs, including Holocaust victims, and paid account balances of dormant accounts to the proper parties.

The paragraph mildly concludes that "the Committee believes the criticized actions are of sufficient importance that it is desirable to document in this section the things that did go wrong so that it is possible to learn from the past rather than repeat its mistakes."[47]

The *Report* also found that, although the Committee couldn't track down all the bank records for the "Relevant Period" (1933–45), destruction of records without detection "would be difficult, if not impossible," and that "in fact, no evidence of systematic destruction of account records for the purpose of concealing past behavior has been found." It concludes that the percentage of records recovered (60 percent) was "truly extraordinary" and "truly remarkable," especially given that Swiss law does not require retention of records beyond 10 years.[48]

Yet, compare the *New York Times*'s rendering of the Volcker Committee findings. Under an editorial headline, "The Deceptions of Swiss Banks,"[49] the *Times* reported that the Committee found "no conclusive evidence" that Swiss banks mishandled dormant Jewish

---

[47] *Report*, Annex 5, p. 81, paragraph 1 (cf. Part I, pp. 13–15, paragraphs 41–9).

[48] *Report:* Part I, p. 6, paragraph 22 ("no evidence"); Part I, p. 6, paragraph 23 (banking laws and percentage); Annex 4, p. 58, paragraph 5 ("truly extraordinary") and Annex 5, p. 81, paragraph 3 ("truly remarkable") (cf. Part I, p. 15, paragraph 47, Part I, p. 17, paragraph 58, Annex 7, p. 107, paragraphs 3, 9)

[49] "The Deceptions of Swiss Banks," in *New York Times* (7 December 1999).

accounts. Yet the *Report* categorically stated "no evidence." The *Times* goes on to state that the Committee "found that Swiss banks had somehow managed to lose track of a shockingly large number of these accounts." Yet the *Report* found that the Swiss preserved records of a "truly extraordinary," "truly remarkable" number. Finally, the *Times* reports that, according to the Committee, "many banks had cruelly and deceptively turned away family members trying to recover lost assets." In fact, the *Report* emphasizes that only "some" banks misbehaved and that there were "mitigating circumstances" in these cases, and it points out as well the "many cases" in which banks actively sought out legitimate claimants.

The *Report* does fault the Swiss banks for not being "straightforward and forthright" in prior audits of dormant Holocaust-era accounts. Nonetheless, it seems to credit the shortfall in these audits more to technical factors than malfeasance.[50] The *Report* identifies 54,000 accounts with a "probable or possible relationship with victims of Nazi persecution." But it judges that only in the case of half this number – 25,000 – was the likelihood significant enough to warrant publication of account names. The estimated current value of 10,000 of these accounts for which some information was available runs to $170–$260

---

[50] *Report*, Annex 5, p. 81, paragraph 2. *Report*, Annex 5, pp. 87–8, paragraph 27: "There are a variety of explanations for the substantial under-reporting in the early surveys, but some of the main causes can be attributed to the Swiss banks' use of narrow definitions of 'dormant' accounts; their exclusion of certain types of accounts from their searches or inadequate research; their failure to investigate accounts under certain minimum balances; or their failure to consider account holders to be victims of Nazi violence or persecution unless relatives made such claims at the bank."

million. It proved impossible to estimate the current value of the remaining accounts.[51] The total value of actual dormant Holocaust-era accounts will likely climb much higher than the $32 million originally estimated by the Swiss banks, but will still fall staggeringly short of the $7–$20 billion claimed by the WJC. In subsequent Congressional testimony, Volcker observed that the number of Swiss accounts "probably or possibly" related to Holocaust victims was "many times as large as that emerging from previous Swiss investigations." However, he continued: "I emphasize the words 'probably or possibly' because, except in a relatively few cases, after more than half a century, we were not able to identify with certainty an irrefutable relationship between victims and account holders."[52]

The most explosive finding of the Volcker Committee went unreported in the American media. Alongside Switzerland, the Com-

---

[51] *Report*, p. 10, paragraph 30 ("possible or probable"); p. 20, paragraphs 73–5 (significant probability for 25,000 accounts). *Report*, Annex 4, pp. 65–7, paragraphs 20–6, and p. 72, paragraphs 40–3 (current values). In accordance with the *Report* recommendation, the Swiss Federal Banking Commission agreed in March 2000 to publish the 25,000 account names. ("Swiss Federal Banking Commission Follows Volcker Recommendations," press release, 30 March 2000)

[52] Hearings before the Committee on Banking and Financial Services, House of Representatives, 9 February 2000 (quoted from Volcker's prepared testimony). Compare the caveats entered by the Swiss Federal Banking Commission that "all indications on possible current values of accounts identified are essentially based on assumptions and projections," and that "only in the case of about 1,200 accounts . . . has actual evidence be [sic] found, supported by contemporary in-house banking sources, that the account owners were actually victims of the Holocaust." (press release, 6 December 1999)

mittee observes, the US was *also* a primary safe haven for transferable Jewish assets in Europe:

> The anticipation of war and economic distress, as well as the persecution of Jews and other minorities by the Nazis prior to and during World War II, caused many people, including the victims of this persecution, to move their assets to countries deemed to provide safe havens (importantly including the United States and the United Kingdom). . . . In view of neutral Switzerland's borders with Axis and Axis-occupied countries, Swiss banks and other Swiss financial intermediaries were also recipients of a portion of the assets in search of safety.

An important appendix lists the "favored destinations" of Jewish transferable assets in Europe. The main stated destinations were the US and Switzerland. (Great Britain came in a "low third" as a stated destination.)[53]

The obvious question is, What happened to the dormant Holocaust-era accounts in *American* banks? The House Banking Committee did call one expert witness to testify on this issue. Seymour Rubin, currently a professor at American University, served as deputy chief of the US delegation in the Swiss negotiations after World War II. Under the auspices of American Jewish organizations Rubin also worked during the 1950s with a "group of experts on Jewish communal life in Europe" to identify dormant Holocaust-era accounts

---

[53] *Report*, p. 2, paragraph 8 (cf. p. 23, paragraph 92). *Report*, Appendix S, p. A-134; for a more precise breakdown, cf. pp. A-135ff.

in US banks. In his House testimony Rubin stated that, after a most superficial and rudimentary audit of just New York banks, the value of these accounts was put at $6 million. Jewish organizations requested this sum for "needy survivors" from Congress (abandoned dormant accounts in the US are transferred to the state under the doctrine of escheat). Rubin then recalled:

> [T]he initial estimate of $6 million was rejected by potential Congressional sponsors of the necessary legislation and a limit of $3 million was used in the original draft legislation. . . . In the event, the $3 million figure was slashed in Committee hearings to $1 million. Legislative action further reduced the amount to $500,000. Even that amount was opposed by the Bureau of the Budget, which proposed a limit of $250,000. The legislation however passed with the $500,000.

"The United States," Rubin concluded, "took only very limited measures to identify heirless assets in the United States, and made available . . . a mere $500,000, in contrast to the $32,000,000 acknowledged by Swiss banks even prior to the Volcker inquiry."[54] In other words, *the US record is much worse than the Swiss record.* It bears emphasis that, apart from a fleeting remark by Eizenstat, there was no other mention of the dormant US accounts during the House and Senate banking committee hearings devoted to the Swiss

---

[54] Hearings before the Committee on Banking and Financial Services, House of Representatives, 25 June 1997 (quoted from Rubin's prepared testimony). (For background, see Seymour J. Rubin and Abba P. Schwartz, "Refugees and Reparations," in *Law and Contemporary Problems* [Duke University School of Law: 1951], 286–9.)

banks. Moreover, although Rubin plays a pivotal role in the many secondary accounts of the Swiss banks affair – Bower devotes scores of pages to this "crusader in the State Department" – none mention his House testimony. During the House hearing Rubin also expressed "a certain amount of skepticism with respect to the large amounts [in dormant Swiss accounts] which are being talked about." Needless to say, Rubin's precise insights on this matter were also studiously ignored.

Where was the Congressional hue and cry over "perfidious" American bankers? One member after another of the Senate and House banking committees clamored for the Swiss to "finally pay up." None, however, called on the US to do so. Rather, a House Banking Committee member shamelessly averred – with Bronfman agreeing – that "only" Switzerland "has failed to show the courage to confront its own history."[55] Unsurprisingly, the Holocaust industry didn't launch a campaign to investigate US banks. An audit of our banks on the scale of the Swiss audit would cost American taxpayers not millions but billions of dollars.[56] By the time it was completed American Jews would be seeking asylum in Munich. Courage has its limits.

Already in the late 1940s, when the US was pressing Switzerland to identify dormant Jewish accounts, the Swiss protested that

---

[55] Hearings before the Committee on Banking and Financial Services, House of Representatives, 25 June 1997.

[56] Switzerland's population stood at 4 million for the "Relevant Period" of 1933–45 as compared to the US population of over 130 million. Every Swiss bank account opened, closed or dormant during these years was audited by the Volcker committee.

Americans should first attend to their own backyard.[57] In mid-1997 New York Governor Pataki announced the creation of a State Commission on the Recovery Of Holocaust Victims' Assets to process claims against Swiss banks. Unimpressed, the Swiss suggested that the commission might more usefully process claims against US and Israeli banks.[58] Indeed Bower recalls that Israeli bankers had "refused to release lists of dormant accounts of Jews" after the 1948 war, and recently it has been reported that "unlike countries in Europe, Israel's banks and Zionist organizations are resisting pressure to set up independent commissions to establish how much property and how many dormant accounts were held by Holocaust survivors, and how the owners can be located" (*Financial Times*). (European Jews purchased plots of land and opened bank accounts in Palestine during the British Mandate to support the Zionist enterprise or prepare for future immigration.) In October 1998, the WJC and WJRO "reached a decision in principle to refrain from dealing with the subject of assets in Israel of Holocaust victims on the ground that responsibility for this lay with the Israeli government" (*Haaretz*). The writ of these Jewish organizations thus runs to Switzerland but not to the Jewish state. The most sensational charge leveled against the Swiss banks was that they required death certificates from the heirs of Nazi holocaust victims. Israeli banks have also demanded such documentation. One searches in vain, however, for denunciations of the "perfidious Israelis." To demonstrate that "no moral equivalence can be drawn

---

[57] Levin, *Last Deposit*, 23. Bower, *Nazi Gold*, 256. Bower deems this Swiss demand "unanswerable rhetoric." Unanswerable no doubt, but why rhetoric?

[58] Rickman, *Swiss Banks*, 194–5.

between banks in Israel and Switzerland," the *New York Times* quoted a former Israeli legislator: "Here it was negligence at best; in Switzerland it was a crime."[59] Comment is superfluous.

In May 1998 a Presidential Advisory Commission on Holocaust Assets in the United States was charged by Congress with "conducting original research on the fate of assets taken from victims of the Holocaust that came into the possession of the U.S. Federal government" and "advising the President on policies that should be adopted to make restitution to the rightful owners of stolen property or their heirs." "The Commission's work demonstrates irrefutably," Commission chair Bronfman declared, "that we in the United States are willing to hold ourselves to the same high standard of truth about Holocaust assets to which we have held other nations." Yet a presidential advisory commission with a total budget of $6 million is rather different from a comprehensive $500 million external audit of a nation's entire banking system with unfettered access to all bank records.[60] To dispel any lingering doubts that the US stood in the forefront of efforts to restore Holocaust-era stolen Jewish assets, James Leach, chairman of the House Banking Committee, proudly

---

[59] Bower, *Nazi Gold*, 350–1. Akiva Eldar, "UK: Israel Didn't Hand Over Compensation to Survivors," in *Haaretz* (21 February 2000). Judy Dempsey, "Jews Find It Hard to Reclaim Wartime Property In Israel," in *Financial Times* (1 April 2000). Jack Katzenell, "Israel Has WWII Assets," in *Associated Press* (13 April 2000). Joel Greenberg, "Hunt for Holocaust Victims' Property Turns in New Direction: Toward Israel," in *New York Times* (15 April 2000). Akiva Eldar, "People and Politics," in *Haaretz* (27 April 2000).

[60] For information on the Commission, see *www.pcha.gov* (Bronfman quoted from a 21 November 1999 Commission press release).

announced in February 2000 that a North Carolina museum had returned one painting to an Austrian family. "It underscores United States accountability . . . and I think that is something that this Committee ought to stress."[61]

For the Holocaust industry, the Swiss banks affair – like the postwar torments endured by Swiss Holocaust "survivor" Binjamin Wilkomirski – was yet further proof of an ineradicable and irrational Gentile malice. The affair pointed up the gross insensitivity of even a "liberal democratic, European country," Itamar Levin concludes, to "those who carried the physical and emotional scars of the worst crime in history." An April 1997 Tel Aviv University study reported "an unmistakable rise" in Swiss anti-Semitism. Yet this ominous development couldn't possibly be connected with the Holocaust industry's shakedown of Switzerland. "Jews do not make anti-Semitism," Bronfman sniffed. "Anti-Semites make anti-Semitism."[62]

Material compensation for the Holocaust "is the greatest moral test facing Europe at the end of the twentieth century," Itamar Levin maintains. "This will be the real test of the Continent's treatment of the Jewish people."[63] Indeed, emboldened by its success in shaking down the Swiss, the Holocaust industry moved quickly to "test" the rest of Europe. The next stop was Germany.

After the Holocaust industry settled with Switzerland in August 1998, it deployed the same winning strategy against Germany in

[61] Hearings before the Committee on Banking and Financial Services, House of Representatives, 9 February 2000.

[62] Levin, *Last Deposit*, 223, 204. "Swiss Defensive About WWII Role," in *Associated Press* (15 March 2000). *Time* (24 February 1997) (Bronfman).

[63] Levin, *Last Deposit*, 224.

September. The same three legal teams (Hausfeld–Weiss, Fagan–Swift, and the World Council of Orthodox Jewish Communities) initiated class-action lawsuits against German private industry, demanding no less than $20 billion in compensation. Brandishing the threat of an economic boycott, New York City Comptroller Hevesi began to "monitor" the negotiations in April 1999. The House Banking Committee held hearings in September. Congresswoman Carolyn Maloney declared that "the passage of time must not be an excuse for unjust enrichment" (at any rate, from Jewish slave labor – African-American slave labor is another story) while Committee chairman Leach, reading from the same old script, intoned that "history has no statute of limitations." German companies doing business in the United States, Stuart Eizenstat told the Committee, "value their good will here, and will want to continue the kind of good citizenship in the US and Germany that they've always displayed." Forgoing diplomatic niceties, Congressman Rick Lazio bluntly urged the Committee "to focus on the private sector German companies, in particular, those who do business in the US."[64] To whip up public hysteria against Germany, the Holocaust industry took out multiple full-page newspaper advertisements in October. The awful truth did not suffice; all the Holocaust hot buttons were pressed. An ad denouncing the German pharmaceutical corporation Bayer dragged in Josef Mengele, although the evidence that Bayer "directed" his murderous experiments was nil. Recognizing that the Holocaust juggernaut was irresistible, the Germans caved in to a substantial monetary settlement by year's end.

[64] Hearings before the Committee on Banking and Financial Services, House of Representatives, 14 September 1999.

The Times of London credited this capitulation to the "Holocash" campaign in the United States. "We could not have reached agreement," Eizenstat later told the House Banking Committee, "without the personal involvement and leadership of President Clinton . . . as well as other senior officials" in the US government.[65]

The Holocaust industry charged that Germany had a "moral and legal obligation" to compensate former Jewish slave laborers. "These slave laborers deserve a small measure of justice," Eizenstat pleaded, "in the few years remaining in their lives." Yet, as indicated above, it is simply untrue that they hadn't received any compensation. Jewish slave laborers were covered under the original agreements with Germany compensating concentration camp inmates. The German government indemnified former Jewish slave laborers for "deprivation of liberty" and for "harm to life and limb." Only wages withheld were not formally compensated. Those who sustained enduring injuries

---

[65] Yair Sheleg, "Not Even Minimum Wage," in *Haaretz* (6 October 1999). William Drozdiak, "Germans Up Offer to Nazis' Slave Laborers," in *Washington Post* (18 November 1999). Burt Herman, "Nazi Labor Talks End Without Pact," in *Forward* (20 November 1999). "Bayer's Biggest Headache," in *New York Times* (5 October 1999). Jan Cienski, "Wartime Slave-Labour Survivors' Ads Hit Back," in *National Post* (7 October 1999). Edmund L. Andrews, "Germans To Set Up $5.1 Billion Fund For Nazis' Slaves," in *New York Times* (15 December 1999). Edmund L. Andrews, "Germany Accepts $5.1 billion Accord to End Claims of Nazi Slave Workers," in *New York Times* (18 December 1999). Allan Hall, "Slave Labour List Names 255 German Companies," in *The Times* (London) (9 December 1999). Hearings before the Committee on Banking and Financial Services, House of Representatives, 9 February 2000 (quoted from Eizenstat's prepared testimony).

each received a substantial lifetime pension.[66] Germany also endowed the Jewish Claims Conference with approximately a billion dollars in current values for those Jewish ex-camp inmates who received minimum compensation. As indicated earlier, the Claims Conference, violating the agreement with Germany, used the monies instead for various pet projects. It justified this (mis)use of German compensation on the grounds that "even before the funds from Germany had become available . . . the needs of the 'needy' victims of Nazism had already been largely met."[67] Still, fifty years later the Holocaust industry was demanding money for "needy Holocaust victims" who had been living in poverty because the Germans allegedly never compensated them.

What constitutes "fair" compensation for former Jewish slave laborers is plainly an unanswerable question. One can, however, say this: According to the terms of the new settlement, Jewish former slave laborers are each supposed to receive about $7,500. If the Claims Conference had properly distributed the original German monies, many more former Jewish slave laborers would have received much more much sooner.

Whether "needy Holocaust victims" will ever see any of the new German monies is an open question. The Claims Conference wants a

---

[66] Sagi, *German Reparations*, 161. Probably a quarter of the Jewish slave laborers received such a pension, my late father (an Auschwitz inmate) among them. In fact, the Claims Conference's figure in the current negotiations for Jewish slave laborers still alive is based on those already receiving pensions and compensation from Germany! (German Parliament, 92nd session, 15 March 2000)

[67] Zweig, *German Reparations and the Jewish World*, 98; cf. 25.

large chunk set aside as its own "Special Fund." According to the *Jerusalem Report*, the Conference has "plenty to gain by ensuring that the survivors get nothing." Israeli Knesset member Michael Kleiner (Herut) lambasted the Conference as a "Judenrat, carrying on the Nazis' work in different ways." It's a "dishonest body, conducting itself with professional secrecy, and tainted by ugly public and moral corruption," he charged, "a body of darkness that is maltreating Jewish Holocaust survivors and their heirs, while it sits on a huge pile of money belonging to private individuals, but is doing everything to inherit [the money] while they are still alive."[68] Meanwhile, Stuart Eizenstat, testifying before the House Banking Committee, continued to heap praise on the "transparent process that the Jewish Material Claims Conference has had over the last 40-some-odd years." For sheer cynicism, however, Rabbi Israel Singer ranked without peer. In addition to his secretary-general post at the World Jewish Congress, Singer has served as vice-president of the Claims Conference and was chief negotiator in the German slave-labor talks. He piously reiterated to the House Banking Committee after the Swiss and German settlements that "it would be a shame" if the Holocaust compensation monies were "paid to heirs rather than survivors." "We don't want

---

[68] Conference on Jewish Material Claims Against Germany, "Position Paper – Slave Labor. Proposed Remembrance and Responsibility Fund" (15 June 1999). Netty C. Gross, "$5.1-Billion Slave Labor Deal Could Yield Little Cash For Jewish Claimants," in *Jerusalem Report* (31 January 2000). Zvi Lavi, "Kleiner (Herut): Germany Claims Conference Has Become Judenrat, Carrying on Nazi Ways," in *Globes* (24 February 2000). Yair Sheleg, "MK Kleiner: The Claims Conference Does Not Transfer Indemnifications to Shoah Survivors," in *Haaretz* (24 February 2000).

that money paid to heirs. We want that money to be paid to victims."
Yet, *Haaretz* reports that Singer has been the main proponent of using
Holocaust compensation monies "to meet the needs of the entire
Jewish people, and not just those Jews who were fortunate enough to
survive the Holocaust and live into old age."[69]

In a US Holocaust Memorial Museum publication, Henry Friedlander, the respected Nazi holocaust historian and ex-Auschwitz inmate,
sketched this numerical picture at war's end:

> If there were about 715,000 prisoners in the camps at the start of
> 1945, and at least one third — that is, about 238,000 — perished
> during spring 1945, we can assume that at most 475,000 prisoners
> survived. As Jews had been systematically murdered, and only those
> chosen for labor — in Auschwitz about 15 percent — had even a chance
> to survive, we must assume that Jews made up no more than 20
> percent of the concentration camp population.

"We can thus estimate," he concluded, "that the number of Jewish
survivors numbered no more than 100,000." Friedlander's figure for
surviving Jewish slave laborers at war's end, incidentally, is at the
high end among scholars. In an authoritative study, Leonard Dinnerstein reported: "Sixty thousand Jews . . . walked out of the concentration camps. Within a week more than 20,000 of them had died."[70]

---

[69] Hearings before the Committee on Banking and Financial Services, House of
Representatives, 9 February 2000. Yair Sheleg, "Staking a Claim to Jewish
Claims," in *Haaretz* (31 March 2000).

[70] Henry Friedlander, "Darkness and Dawn in 1945: The Nazis, the Allies, and
the Survivors," in *US Holocaust Memorial Museum, 1945 — The Year of Liberation*

In a May 1999 State Department briefing, Stuart Eizenstat, citing the figure of "groups representing them," put the total number of slave laborers, Jewish and non-Jewish, still alive at "perhaps 70–90,000."[71] Eizenstat was Chief US Envoy in the German slave-labor negotiations and worked closely with the Claims Conference.[72] This would put the total number of still living Jewish slave laborers at 14,000–18,000 (20 percent of 70–90,000). Yet, as it entered into negotiations with Germany, the Holocaust industry demanded compensation for 135,000 still living former Jewish slave laborers. The total number of still living former slave laborers, Jewish and non-Jewish, was put at 250,000.[73] In other words, the number of former Jewish slave laborers still alive increased nearly tenfold from May 1999, and the ratio between living Jewish and non-Jewish slave laborers drastically shifted. In fact, to believe the Holocaust industry, more former Jewish slave laborers are alive today than a

---

(Washington: 1995), 11–35. Dinnerstein, *America and the Survivors of the Holocaust*, 28. Israeli historian Shlomo Shafir reports "the estimate of Jewish survivors at the end of the war in Europe vary from 50,000 to 70,000" (*Ambiguous Relations*, 384n1). Friedlander's total figure for surviving slave laborers, Jewish and non-Jewish, is standard; see Benjamin Ferencz, *Less Than Slaves* (Cambridge: 1979) – "approximately half a million persons were found more or less alive in the camps that were liberated by the Allied armies" (xvii; cf. 240n5).

71 Stuart Eizenstat, Undersecretary of State for Economic, Business and Agricultural Affairs, Chief US Envoy in German Slave-Labor Negotiations, State Department Briefing, 12 May 1999.

72 See Eizenstat's "remarks" at the Conference on Jewish Material Claims Against Germany and Austria Annual Meeting (New York: 14 July 1999).

73 Toby Axelrod, "$5.2 Billion Slave-Labor Deal Only the Start," in *Jewish Bulletin* (12 December 1999; citing *Jewish Telegraphic Agency*).

half-century ago. "What a tangled web we weave," Sir Walter Scott wrote, "when first we practice to deceive."

As the Holocaust industry plays with numbers to boost its compensation claims, anti-Semites gleefully mock the "Jew liars" who even "huckster" their dead. In juggling these numbers the Holocaust industry, however unintentionally, whitewashes Nazism. Raul Hilberg, the leading authority on the Nazi holocaust, puts the figure for Jews murdered at 5.1 million.[74] Yet, if 135,000 former Jewish slave laborers are still alive today, some 600,000 must have survived the war. That's at least a half-million more than standard estimates. One would then have to deduct this half-million from the 5.1 million figure of those killed. Not only does the "6 Million" figure become more untenable but the numbers of the Holocaust industry are rapidly approaching those of Holocaust deniers. Consider that Nazi leader Heinrich Himmler put the total camp population in January 1945 at a little over 700,000 and that, according to Friedlander, about one-third this number was killed off by May. Yet if Jews constituted only 20 percent of the surviving camp population and, as the Holocaust industry implies, 600,000 Jewish inmates survived the war, then fully 3 million inmates in total must have survived. By the Holocaust industry's reckoning, concentration camp conditions couldn't have been harsh at all; in fact, one must suppose a remarkably high fertility and remarkably low mortality rate.[75]

---

[74] Hilberg, The Destruction (1985), v. iii, Appendix B.

[75] In an interview with Die Berliner Zeitung, I cast doubt on the Claims Conference's 135,000 figure, citing Friedlander. The Claims Conference curtly stated in its rebuttal that the 135,000 figure was "based on the best and most trustworthy sources and is therefore correct." Not one of these alleged

The standard claim is that the Final Solution was a uniquely efficient, assembly-line, industrial extermination.[76] But if, as the Holocaust industry suggests, many hundreds of thousands of Jews survived, the Final Solution couldn't have been so efficient after all. It must have been a haphazard affair – exactly what Holocaust deniers argue. *Les extrêmes se touchent*.

In a recent interview Raul Hilberg underscored that numbers do matter in comprehending the Nazi holocaust. Indeed, the Claims Conference's revised figures radically call into question its own understanding. According to the Claims Conference's "position paper" on slave labor in its negotiations with Germany: "Slave labor was one of the three main methods used by the Nazis to murder Jews – the others being shooting and gassing. One of the purposes of slave labor was to work the individuals to death. . . . The term slave is an imprecise word in this context. In general slave masters have an interest to preserve the life and condition of their slaves. However,

---

sources, however, was identified. ("Die Ausbeutung jüdischen Leidens," in *Berliner Zeitung*, 29–30 January 2000; "Gegendarstellung der Jewish Claims Conference," in *Berliner Zeitung*, 1 February 2000) Replying to my criticisms in an interview with *Der Tagesspiegel*, the Claims Conference maintained that some 700,000 Jewish slave laborers survived the war, 350,000–400,000 on the territory of the Reich and 300,000 in concentration camps elsewhere. Pressed to supply scholarly sources, the Claims Conference indignantly refused. Suffice to say that these figures bear no resemblance to any known scholarship on the topic. (Eva Schweitzer, "Entschaedigung für Zwangsarbeiter," in *Tagesspiegel*, 6 March 2000)

[76] "Never before in history," Hilberg has observed, "had people been killed on an assembly-line basis." (*Destruction*, v. iii, 863). The classic treatment of this topic is Zygmunt Bauman's *Modernity and the Holocaust*.

the Nazi plan for the 'slaves' was that their work potential be utilized and then the 'slaves' should be exterminated." Apart from Holocaust deniers, no one has yet disputed that Nazism consigned slave laborers to this horrific fate. How can one reconcile these established facts, however, with the claim that many hundreds of thousands of Jewish slave laborers survived the camps? Hasn't the Claims Conference breached the wall separating the ghastly truth about the Nazi holocaust from Holocaust denial?[77]

In a full-page *New York Times* advertisement, Holocaust industry luminaries such as Elie Wiesel, Rabbi Marvin Hier, and Steven T. Katz condemned "Syria's Denial of the Holocaust." The text decried an editorial in an official Syrian government newspaper that claimed Israel "invents stories about the Holocaust" in order to "receive more money from Germany and other Western establishments." Regrettably, the Syrian charge is true. Yet the irony, lost on both the Syrian government and the signatories to the ad, is that these stories themselves of many hundreds of thousands of survivors constitute a form of Holocaust denial.[78]

---

[77] Guttenplan, "Holocaust on Trial." (Hilberg) Conference on Jewish Material Claims Against Germany, "Position Paper – Slave Labor," 15 June 1999.

[78] "We Condemn Syria's Denial of the Holocaust," in *New York Times* (9 February 2000). To document "increased anti-Semitism" in Europe, David Harris of the AJC pointed to relatively strong survey support for the statement that "Jews are exploiting the memory of the Nazi extermination of the Jews for their own purposes." He also adduced the "extremely negative way that some German papers reported on the Jewish Claims Conference . . . during the recent negotiations over compensation for slave and forced labor. Numerous stories depicted the Claims Conference itself and the mostly Jewish lawyers as greedy and self-serving, and a bizarre discussion ensued in mainstream

The shakedown of Switzerland and Germany has been only a prelude to the grand finale: the shakedown of Eastern Europe. With the collapse of the Soviet bloc, alluring prospects opened up in the former heartland of European Jewry. Cloaking itself in the sanctimonious mantle of "needy Holocaust victims," the Holocaust industry has sought to extort billions of dollars from these already impoverished countries. Pursuing this end with reckless and ruthless abandon, it has become the main fomenter of anti-Semitism in Europe.

The Holocaust industry has positioned itself as the sole legitimate claimant to all the communal and private assets of those who perished during the Nazi holocaust. "It has been agreed with the Government of Israel," Edgar Bronfman told the House Banking Committee, "that heirless assets should accrue to the World Jewish Restitution Organization." Using this "mandate," the Holocaust industry has called on former Soviet-bloc countries to hand over all prewar Jewish properties or come up with monetary compensation.[79] Unlike in the case of

---

newspapers about whether there are as many Jewish survivors as cited by the Claims Conference." (Hearings before the Foreign Relations Committee, United States Senate, 5 April 2000) In fact, I found it nearly impossible to raise this matter in Germany. Although the taboo was finally broken by the liberal German daily *Die Berliner Zeitung*, the courage displayed by its editor, Martin Sueskind, and US correspondent, Stefan Elfenbein, found only a faint echo in the German media, in large part owing to the legal threats and moral blackmail of the Claims Conference as well as the general German reluctance to openly criticize Jews.

[79] Hearings before the Committee on Banking and Financial Services, House of Representatives, 11 December 1996. J.D. Bindenagel (ed.), *Proceedings, Washington Conference on Holocaust-Era Assets: 30 November–3 December 1998* (US Government Printing Office: Washington, DC), 687, 700–1, 706.

Switzerland and Germany, however, it makes these demands away from the glare of publicity. Public opinion has so far not been averse to the blackmailing of Swiss bankers and German industrialists, but it might look less kindly on the blackmailing of starving Polish peasants. Jews who lost family members during the Nazi holocaust might also take a jaundiced view of the WJRO's machinations. Claiming to be the legitimate heir of those who perished in order to appropriate their assets could easily be mistaken for grave-robbery. On the other hand, the Holocaust industry doesn't need a mobilized public opinion. With the support of key US officials, it can easily break the feeble resistance of already prostrate nations.

"It is important to recognize that our efforts at communal property restitution," Stuart Eizenstat told a House committee, "are integral to the rebirth and renewal of Jewish life" in Eastern Europe. Allegedly to "promote the revival" of Jewish life in Poland, the World Jewish Restitution Organization is demanding title over the 6,000 prewar communal Jewish properties, including those currently being used as hospitals and schools. The prewar Jewish population of Poland stood at 3.5 million; the current population is several thousand. Does reviving Jewish life really require one synagogue or school building per Polish Jew? The organization is also laying claim to hundreds of thousands of parcels of Polish land valued in the many tens of billions of dollars. "Polish officials fear," *Jewish Week* reports, that the demand "could bankrupt the nation." When Poland's Parliament proposed limits on compensation to avert insolvency, Elan Steinberg of the WJC denounced the legislation as "fundamentally an anti-American act."[80]

[80] Hearings before International Relations Committee, House of Representatives,

Tightening the screws on Poland, Holocaust industry attorneys filed a class-action lawsuit in Judge Korman's court to compensate "aging and dying Holocaust survivors." The complaint charged that the postwar Polish governments "continued during the last fifty-four years" a genocidal "expulsion to extinction" policy against Jews. New York City Council members jumped in with a unanimous resolution calling on Poland "to pass comprehensive legislation providing for the complete restitution of Holocaust assets," while 57 members of Congress (led by Congressman Anthony Weiner of New York) dispatched a letter to the Polish Parliament demanding "comprehensive legislation that would return 100% of all property and assets seized during the Holocaust." "As the people involved are getting older and older every day," the letter said, "time is running out to compensate those wronged."[81]

---

6 August 1998. Bindenagel, *Washington Conference on Holocaust-Era Assets*, 433. Joan Gralia, "Poland Tries to Get Holocaust Lawsuit Dismissed," in *Reuters* (23 December 1999). Eric J. Greenberg, "Polish Restitution Plan Slammed," in *Jewish Week* (14 January 2000). "Poland Limits WWII Compensation Plan," in *Newsday* (6 January 2000).

[81] *Theo Garb et al. v. Republic of Poland* (United States District Court, Eastern District of New York, June 18, 1999). (The class-action lawsuit was brought by Edward E. Klein and Mel Urbach, the latter a veteran of the Swiss and German settlements. An "amended complaint" submitted on 2 March 2000 was joined by many more lawyers but omits some of the more colorful charges against the postwar Polish governments.) "Dear Leads NYC Council in Call to Polish Government to Make Restitution to Victims of Holocaust Era Property Seizure," in *News From Council Member Noach Dear* (29 November 1999). (The textual quote is from the actual resolution, No. 1072, adopted on 23 November 1999.) "[Anthony D.] Weiner Urges Polish Government To Repatriate Holocaust Claims," US House of Representatives (press release, 14

Testifying before the Senate Banking Committee, Stuart Eizenstat deplored the lax pace of evictions in Eastern Europe: "A variety of problems have arisen in the return of properties. For example, in some countries, when persons or communities have attempted to reclaim properties, they have been asked, sometimes required . . . to allow current tenants to remain for a lengthy period of time at rent-controlled rates."[82] The delinquency of Belarus particularly exercised Eizenstat. Belarus is "very, very far" behind in handing over prewar Jewish properties, he told the House International Relations Committee.[83] The average monthly income of a Belarussian is $100.

To force submission from recalcitrant governments, the Holocaust industry wields the bludgeon of US sanctions. Eizenstat urged Congress to "elevate" Holocaust compensation, put it "high on the list" of requirements for those East European countries that are seeking entry into the OECD, the WTO, the European Union, NATO, and the Council of Europe: "They will listen if you speak. . . . They will get the hint." Israel Singer of the WJC called on Congress to "continue looking at the shopping list" in order to "check" that every country pays up. "It is extremely important that the countries involved in the issue understand," Congressman Benjamin Gilman of the House International Relations Committee said, "that their response . . . is one of several standards by which the United States assesses its

October 1999). (The textual quotes are from the press release and actual letter, dated 13 October 1999.)

[82] Hearings before the Committee on Banking, Housing, and Urban Affairs, United States Senate, 23 April 1996.

[83] Hearings before the International Relations Committee, House of Representatives, 6 August 1998.

bilateral relationship." Avraham Hirschson, chairman of Israel's Knesset Committee on Restitution and Israel's representative on the World Jewish Restitution Organization, paid tribute to Congressional complicity in the shakedown. Recalling his "fights" with the Romanian Prime Minister, Hirschson testified: "But I ask one remark, in the middle of the fighting, and it changed that atmosphere. I told him, you know, in two days I am going to be in a hearing here in Congress. What do you want me to tell them in the hearing? Whole atmosphere was changed." The World Jewish Congress has "created an entire Holocaust industry," a lawyer for survivors warns, and is "guilty of promoting . . . a very ugly resurgence of anti-Semitism in Europe."[84]

"Were it not for the United States of America," Eizenstat aptly observed in his paean to Congress, "very few, if any, of these activities would be ongoing today." To justify the pressures exerted on Eastern Europe, he explained that a hallmark of "Western" morality is to "return or pay compensation for communal and private property wrongfully appropriated." For the "new democracies" in Eastern Europe, meeting this standard "would be commensurate with their passage from totalitarianism to democratic states." Eizenstat is a senior US government official and a prominent supporter of Israel. Yet, judging by the respective claims of Native Americans and Palestinians, neither the US nor Israel has yet made the transition.[85]

---

[84] Hearings before the International Relations Committee, House of Representatives, 6 August 1998. Isabel Vincent, "Who Will Reap the Nazi-Era Reparations?" in *National Post* (20 February 1999).

[85] Hearings before the International Relations Committee, House of Representatives, 6 August 1998. Currently an honorary vice-president of the American

In his House testimony, Hirschson conjured the melancholy spectacle of aging "needy Holocaust victims" from Poland "coming to me to my office in the Knesset each day . . . begging to get back what belongs to them . . . to get back the houses they left, to get back the stores they left." Meanwhile, the Holocaust industry wages battle on a second front. Repudiating the specious mandate of the World Jewish Restitution Organization, local Jewish communities in Eastern Europe have staked out their own claims on heirless Jewish assets. To benefit from such a claim, however, a Jew must formally adhere to the local Jewish community. The hoped-for revival of Jewish life is thus coming to pass as Eastern European Jews parlay their newly discovered roots into a cut of the Holocaust booty.[86]

The Holocaust industry boasts of earmarking compensation monies for charitable Jewish causes. "While charity is a noble cause," a lawyer representing the actual victims observes, "it is wrong to perform it with other people's money." One favorite cause is "Holocaust education" – the "greatest legacy of our efforts," according to Eizenstat. Hirschson is also founder of an organization called "March of the Living," a centerpiece of Holocaust education and a major beneficiary of compensation monies. In this Zionist-inspired spectacle with a cast of thousands, Jewish youth from around the world converge on the

---

Jewish Committee, Eizenstat was the first chairman of the AJC's Institute on American Jewish–Israeli Relations.

[86] Hearings before the International Relations Committee, House of Representatives, 6 August 1998. Marilyn Henry, "Whose Claim Is It Anyway?" in *Jerusalem Post* (4 July 1997). Bindenagel, *Washington Conference on Holocaust-Era Assets*, 705. Editorial, "Jewish Property Belongs to Jews," in *Haaretz* (26 October 1999).

death camps in Poland for first-hand instruction in Gentile wickedness before being flown off to Israel for salvation. The *Jerusalem Report* captures this Holocaust kitsch moment on the March: " 'I'm so scared, I can't go on, I want to be in Israel already,' repeats a young Connecticut woman over and over. Her body is shaking. . . . Suddenly her friend pulls out a large Israeli flag. She wraps it around the two of them and they move on." An Israeli flag: don't leave home without it.[87]

Speaking at the Washington Conference on Holocaust-Era Assets, David Harris of the AJC waxed eloquent on the "profound impact" pilgrimages to Nazi death camps have on Jewish youth. The *Forward* took note of an episode particularly fraught with pathos. Under the headline "Israeli Teens Frolic With Strippers After Auschwitz Visit," the newspaper explained that, according to experts, the kibbutz students "hired strippers to release the troubling emotions raised by the trip." These same torments apparently racked Jewish students on a US Holocaust Memorial Museum field trip who, according to the *Forward*, "were running around and having a wonderful time and feeling each other up and whatever."[88] Who can doubt the wisdom of

[87] Sergio Karas, "Unsettled Accounts," in *Globe and Mail* (1 September 1998). Stuart Eizenstat, "Remarks," Conference on Jewish Material Claims Against Germany and Austria Annual Meeting (New York: 14 July 1999). Tom Sawicki, "6,000 Witnesses," in *Jerusalem Report* (5 May 1994).

[88] Bindenagel, *Washington Conference on Holocaust-Era Assets*, 146. Michael Arnold, "Israeli Teens Frolic With Strippers After Auschwitz Visit," in *Forward* (26 November 1999). Manhattan Congresswoman Carolyn Maloney proudly informed the House Banking Committee of a bill she introduced, the Holocaust Education Act, which "will provide grants through the Department of Education to Holocaust organizations for teacher training, and provide

the Holocaust industry's decision to earmark compensation monies for Holocaust education rather than "fritter away the funds" (Nahum Goldmann) on survivors of Nazi death camps?[89]

In January 2000 officials from nearly fifty states, including Prime Minister Ehud Barak of Israel, attended a major Holocaust education conference in Stockholm. The conference's final declaration underlined the international community's "solemn responsibility" to fight the evils of genocide, ethnic cleansing, racism and xenophobia. A Swedish reporter afterward asked Barak about the Palestinian refugees. On principle, Barak replied, he was against even one refugee coming to Israel: "We cannot accept moral, legal, or other responsibility for refugees." Plainly the conference was a huge success.[90]

The Jewish Claims Conference's official *Guide to Compensation and Restitution for Holocaust Survivors* lists scores of organizational affiliates. A vast, well-heeled bureaucracy has sprung up. Insurance companies, banks, art museums, private industry, tenants and farmers in nearly

---

materials to schools and communities that increase Holocaust education." Representing a city with a public school system notoriously lacking basic teachers and textbooks, Maloney might have set different priorities for scarce Department of Education funds. (Hearings before the Committee on Banking and Financial Services, House of Representatives, 9 February 2000)

[89] Zweig, *German Reparations and the Jewish World*, 118. Goldmann was founder of the World Jewish Congress and the first president of the Claims Conference.

[90] Marilyn Henry, "International Holocaust Education Conference Begins," in *Jerusalem Post* (26 January 2000). Marilyn Henry, "PM: We Have No Moral Obligation to Refugees," in *Jerusalem Post* (27 January 2000). Marilyn Henry, "Holocaust 'Must Be Seared in Collective Memory,'" in *Jerusalem Post* (30 January 2000).

every European country are under the Holocaust industry gun. But the "needy Holocaust victims" in whose name the Holocaust industry acts complain that it is "just perpetuating the expropriation." Many have filed suit against the Claims Conference. The Holocaust may yet turn out to be the "greatest robbery in the history of mankind."[91]

When Israel first entered into negotiations with Germany for reparations after the war, historian Ilan Pappé reports, Foreign Minister Moshe Sharett proposed transferring a part to Palestinian refugees, "in order to rectify what has been called the small injustice (the Palestinian tragedy), caused by the more terrible one (the Holocaust)."[92] Nothing ever came of the proposal. A prominent Israeli academic has suggested using some of the funds from the Swiss banks and German firms for the "compensation of Palestinian Arab refugees."[93] Given that almost all survivors of the Nazi holocaust have already passed away, this would seem to be a sensible proposal.

[91] Claims Conference, *Guide to Compensation and Restitution of Holocaust Survivors* (New York: n.d.). Vincent, *Hitler's Silent Partners*, 302 ("expropriation"); cf. 308–9. Ralf Eibl, "Die Jewish Claims Conference ringt um ihren Leumund. Nachkommen jüdischer Sklaven. . . .," in *Die Welt* (8 March 2000) (lawsuits). The Holocaust compensation industry is a taboo subject in the United States. The H-Holocaust web site (*www2.h-net.msu.edu*), for example, barred critical postings even if fully supported with documentary evidence (personal correspondence with board member Richard S. Levy, 19–21 November 1999).

[92] Ilan Pappé, *The Making of the Arab–Israeli Conflict, 1947–51* (London: 1992), 268.

[93] Clinton Bailey, "Holocaust Funds to Palestinians May Meet Some Cost of Compensation," in *International Herald Tribune*; reprinted in *Jordan Times* (20 June 1999).

In vintage WJC style, Israel Singer made the "startling announce-ment" on 13 March 2000 that a newly declassified US document revealed that Austria was holding heirless Holocaust-era assets of Jews worth yet another $10 billion. Singer also charged that "fifty percent of America's total art is looted Jewish art."[94] The Holocaust industry has clearly gone berserk.

[94] Elli Wohlgelernter, "WJC: Austria Holding $10b. In Holocaust Victims' Assets," in *Jerusalem Post* (14 March 2000). In his subsequent Congressional testimony, Singer highlighted the allegation against Austria but – typically – maintained a discreet silence on the charges against the US. (Hearings before the Foreign Relations Committee, United States Senate, 6 April 2000)

CONCLUSION

CONCLUSION

It remains to consider the impact of The Holocaust in the United States. In doing so, I also want to engage Peter Novick's own critical remarks on the topic.

Apart from Holocaust memorials, fully seventeen states mandate or recommend Holocaust programs in their schools, and many colleges and universities have endowed chairs in Holocaust studies. Hardly a week passes without a major Holocaust-related story in the *New York Times*. The number of scholarly studies devoted to the Nazi Final Solution is conservatively estimated at over 10,000. Consider by comparison scholarship on the hecatomb in the Congo. Between 1891 and 1911, some 10 million Africans perished in the course of Europe's exploitation of Congolese ivory and rubber resources. Yet, the first and only scholarly volume in English directly devoted to this topic was published two years ago.[1]

Given the vast number of institutions and professionals dedicated

---

[1] Adam Hochschild, *King Leopold's Ghost* (Boston: 1998).

to preserving its memory, The Holocaust is by now firmly entrenched in American life. Novick expresses misgivings, however, whether this is a good thing. In the first place, he cites numerous instances of its sheer vulgarization. Indeed, one is hard-pressed to name a single political cause, whether it be pro-life or pro-choice, animal rights or states' rights, that hasn't conscripted The Holocaust. Decrying the tawdry purposes to which The Holocaust is put, Elie Wiesel declared, "I swear to avoid . . . vulgar spectacles."[2] Yet Novick reports that "the most imaginative and subtle Holocaust photo op came in 1996 when Hillary Clinton, then under heavy fire for various alleged misdeeds, appeared in the gallery of the House during her husband's (much televised) State of the Union Address, flanked by their daughter, Chelsea, and Elie Wiesel."[3] For Hillary Clinton, Kosovo refugees put to flight by Serbia during the NATO bombing recalled Holocaust scenes in *Schindler's List*. "People who learn history from Spielberg movies," a Serbian dissident tartly rejoined, "should not tell us how to live our lives."[4]

The "pretense that the Holocaust is an American memory," Novick further argues, is a moral evasion. It "leads to the shirking of those responsibilities that *do* belong to Americans as they confront their past, their present, and their future." (emphasis in original)[5] He makes an important point. It is much easier to deplore the crimes of others than to look at ourselves. It is also true, however, that were the will

[2] Wiesel, *Against Silence*, v. iii, 190; cf. v. i, 186, v. ii, 82, v. iii, 242, and Wiesel, *And the Sea*, 18.

[3] Novick, *The Holocaust*, 230–1.

[4] *New York Times* (25 May 1999).

[5] Novick, *The Holocaust*, 15.

there we could learn much about ourselves from the Nazi experience. Manifest Destiny anticipated nearly all the ideological and programmatic elements of Hitler's *Lebensraum* policy. In fact, Hitler modeled his conquest of the East on the American conquest of the West.[6] During the first half of this century, a majority of American states enacted sterilization laws and tens of thousands of Americans were involuntarily sterilized. The Nazis explicitly invoked this US precedent when they enacted their own sterilization laws.[7] The notorious 1935 Nuremberg Laws stripped Jews of the franchise and forbade miscegenation between Jews and non-Jews. Blacks in the American South suffered the same legal disabilities and were the object of much greater spontaneous and sanctioned popular violence than the Jews in prewar Germany.[8]

To highlight unfolding crimes abroad, the US often summons memories of The Holocaust. The more revealing point, however, is

---

[6] John Toland, *Adolf Hitler* (New York: 1976), 702. Joachim Fest, *Hitler* (New York: 1975), 214, 650. See also Finkelstein, *Image and Reality*, chap. 4.

[7] See, for example, Stefan Kühl, *The Nazi Connection* (Oxford: 1994).

[8] See, for example, Leon F. Litwack, *Trouble in Mind* (New York: 1998), esp. chaps 5–6. The vaunted Western tradition is deeply implicated in Nazism as well. To justify the extermination of the handicapped – the precursor of the Final Solution – Nazi doctors deployed the concept "life unworthy of life" (*lebensunwertes Leben*). In *Gorgias*, Plato wrote: "I can't see that life is worth living if a person's body is in a terrible state." In *The Republic*, Plato sanctioned the murder of defective children. On a related point, Hitler's opposition in *Mein Kampf* to birth control on the ground that it preempts natural selection was prefigured by Rousseau in his *Discourse on the Origins of Inequality*. Shortly after World War II, Hannah Arendt reflected that "the subterranean stream of Western history has finally come to the surface and usurped the dignity of our tradition" (*Origins of Totalitarianism*, ix).

when the US invokes The Holocaust. Crimes of official enemies such as the Khmer Rouge bloodbath in Cambodia, the Soviet invasion of Afghanistan, the Iraqi invasion of Kuwait, and Serbian ethnic cleansing in Kosovo recall The Holocaust; crimes in which the US is complicit do not.

Just as the Khmer Rouge atrocities were unfolding in Cambodia, the US-backed Indonesian government was slaughtering one-third of the population in East Timor. Yet unlike Cambodia, the East Timor genocide did not rate comparison with The Holocaust; it didn't even rate news coverage.[9] Just as the Soviet Union was committing what the Simon Wiesenthal Center called "another genocide" in Afghanistan, the US-backed regime in Guatemala was perpetrating what the Guatemalan Truth Commission recently called a "genocide" against the indigenous Mayan population. President Reagan dismissed the charges against the Guatemalan government as a "bum rap." To honor Jeane Kirkpatrick's achievement as chief Reagan Administration apologist for the unfolding crimes in Central America, the Simon Wiesenthal Center awarded her the Humanitarian of the Year Award.[10] Simon Wiesenthal was privately beseeched before the award ceremony to reconsider. He refused. Elie Wiesel was privately asked to intercede with the Israeli government, a main weapons supplier for the Guatemalan butchers. He too refused. The Carter Administration invoked the memory of The

[9] See, for example, Edward Herman and Noam Chomsky, *The Political Economy of Human Rights*, v. i: *The Washington Connection and Third World Fascism* (Boston: 1979), 129–204.

[10] *Response* (March 1983 and January 1986).

Holocaust as it sought haven for Vietnamese "boat people" fleeing the Communist regime. The Clinton Administration forgot The Holocaust as it forced back Haitian "boat people" fleeing US-supported death squads.[11]

Holocaust memory loomed large as the US-led NATO bombing of Serbia commenced in the spring of 1999. As we have seen, Daniel Goldhagen compared Serbian crimes against Kosovo with the Final Solution and, at President Clinton's bidding, Elie Wiesel journeyed to Kosovar refugee camps in Macedonia and Albania. Already before Wiesel went to shed tears on cue for the Kosovars, however, the US-backed Indonesian regime had resumed where it left off in the late 1970s, perpetrating new massacres in East Timor. The Holocaust vanished from memory, however, as the Clinton Administration acquiesced in the bloodletting. "Indonesia matters," a Western diplomat explained, "and East Timor doesn't."[12]

Novick points to passive US complicity in human disasters dissimilar in other respects yet comparable in scale to the Nazi extermination. Recalling, for example, the million children killed in the Final Solution, he observes that American presidents do little more than utter pieties as, worldwide, many times that number of children "die of malnutrition and preventable diseases" every year.[13] One might also consider a pertinent case of *active* US complicity. After the United States-led coalition devastated Iraq in 1991 to punish

---

[11] Noam Chomsky, *Turning the Tide* (Boston: 1985), 36 (Wiesel cited from interview in the Hebrew press). Berenbaum, *World Must Know*, 3.

[12] *Financial Times* (8 September 1999).

[13] Novick, *The Holocaust*, 255.

"Saddam-Hitler," the United States and Britain forced murderous UN sanctions on that hapless country in an attempt to depose him. As in the Nazi holocaust, a million children have likely perished.[14] Questioned on national television about the grisly death toll in Iraq, Secretary of State Madeleine Albright replied that "the price is worth it."

"The very extremity of the Holocaust," Novick argues, "seriously limit[s] its capacity to provide lessons applicable to our everyday world." As the "benchmark of oppression and atrocity," it tends to "trivializ[e] crimes of lesser magnitude."[15] Yet the Nazi holocaust can also sensitize us to these injustices. Seen through the lens of Auschwitz, what previously was taken for granted – for example, bigotry – no longer can be.[16] In fact, it was the Nazi holocaust that discredited the scientific racism that was so pervasive a feature of American intellectual life before World War II.[17]

For those committed to human betterment, a touchstone of evil does not preclude but rather invites comparisons. Slavery occupied roughly the same place in the moral universe of the late nineteenth century as the Nazi holocaust does today. Accordingly, it was often invoked to illuminate evils not fully appreciated. John Stuart Mill compared the condition of women in that most hallowed Victorian institution, the family, to slavery. He even ventured that in crucial respects it was worse. "I am far from pretending that wives are in

[14] See, for example, Geoff Simons, *The Scourging of Iraq* (New York: 1998).

[15] Novick, *The Holocaust*, 244, 14.

[16] On this point, see esp. Chaumont, *La concurrence*, 316–18.

[17] See, for example, Carl N. Degler, *In Search of Human Nature* (Oxford: 1991), 202ff.

general no better treated than slaves; but no slave is a slave to the same lengths, and in so full a sense of the word as a wife."[18] Only those using a benchmark evil not as a moral compass but rather as an ideological club recoil at such analogies. "Do not compare" is the mantra of moral blackmailers.[19]

Organized American Jewry has exploited the Nazi holocaust to deflect criticism of Israel's and its own morally indefensible policies. Pursuit of these policies has put Israel and American Jewry in a structurally congruent position: the fates of both now dangle from a slender thread running to American ruling elites. Should these elites ever decide that Israel is a liability or American Jewry expendable, the thread may be cut. No doubt this is speculation – perhaps unduly alarmist, perhaps not.

Predicting the posture of American Jewish elites should these eventualities come to pass, however, is child's play. If Israel fell out of favor with the United States, many of those leaders who now stoutly defend Israel would courageously divulge their disaffection from the Jewish state and would excoriate American Jews for turning Israel into a religion. And if US ruling circles decided to scapegoat Jews, we should not be surprised if American Jewish leaders acted exactly as their predecessors did during the Nazi holocaust. "We didn't figure that the Germans would put in the Jewish element,"

---

[18] John Stuart Mill, *On the Subjection of Women* (Cambridge: 1991), 148.

[19] It is no less repugnant to compare the Nazi holocaust, as Michael Berenbaum proposes, only in order to "demonstrate the claim of uniqueness" (*After Tragedy*, 29).

Yitzhak Zuckerman, an organizer of the Warsaw Ghetto Uprising, recalled, "that Jews would lead Jews to death."[20]

~

During a series of public exchanges in the 1980s, many prominent German and non-German scholars argued against "normalizing" the infamies of Nazism. The fear was that normalization would induce moral complacency.[21] However valid the argument may have been then, it no longer carries conviction. The staggering dimensions of Hitler's Final Solution are by now well known. And isn't the "normal" history of humankind replete with horrifying chapters of inhumanity? A crime need not be aberrant to warrant atonement. The challenge today is to restore the Nazi holocaust as a rational subject of inquiry. Only then can we really learn from it. The abnormality of the Nazi holocaust springs not from the event itself but from the exploitive industry that has grown up around it. The Holocaust industry has always been bankrupt. What remains is to openly declare it so. The time is long past to put it out of business. The noblest gesture for those who perished is to preserve their memory, learn from their suffering and let them, finally, rest in peace.

[20] Zuckerman, A Surplus of Memory, 210.

[21] I refer here both to the Historikerstreit and to the published correspondence between Saul Friedländer and Martin Broszat. In both instances, the debate largely turned on the absolute versus relative nature of Nazi crimes; for example, the validity of comparisons with the Gulag. See Peter Baldwin (ed.), Reworking the Past, Richard J. Evans, In Hitler's Shadow (New York: 1989), James Knowlton and Truett Cates, Forever in the Shadow of Hitler? (Atlantic Highlands, NJ: 1993), and Aharon Weiss (ed.), Yad Vashem Studies XIX (Jerusalem: 1988).

POSTSCRIPT TO THE FIRST
PAPERBACK EDITION

I.

In chapter three of this book I documented the Holocaust industry's "double shakedown" of European countries as well as Jewish survivors of the Nazi genocide. Recent developments confirm this analysis. Indeed, for confirmation of my argument, one need merely place documents readily available in the public domain under critical and close scrutiny.

In late August 2000 the World Jewish Congress (WJC) announced that it stood to amass fully $9 billion in Holocaust compensation monies.[1] They were extracted in the name of "needy Holocaust

---

[1] For this and the next paragraph, see Joan Gralla, "Holocaust Foundation Set for Restitution Funds," in *Reuters* (22 August 2000); Michael J. Jordan, "Spending Restitution Money Pits Survivors Against Groups," in *Jewish Telegraphic Agency* (29 August 2000); *NAHOS* (The Newsletter of the National Association of Jewish Child Holocaust Survivors) (1 September 2000, 6 October 2000, and 6 November 2000); Marilyn Henry, "Proposed 'Foundation

victims" but the WJC now maintained that the monies belonged to the "Jewish people as a whole" (WJC executive director, Elan Steinberg). Conveniently, the WJC is the self-anointed representative of the "Jewish people as a whole." Meanwhile, a black-tie Holocaust reparations banquet sponsored by WJC president Edgar Bronfman at New York's Pierre Hotel celebrated the creation of a "Foundation of the Jewish People" to subsidize Jewish organizations and "Holocaust education." (One Jewish critic of the "Holocaust-themed dinner" conjured this scenario: "Mass murder. Horrible plunder. Slave labor. Let's eat.") The Foundation's endowment would come from "residual" Holocaust compensation monies amounting to "probably billions of dollars" (Steinberg). How the WJC already knew that "probably billions" would be left over when none of the compensation monies had yet been distributed to Holocaust victims was anyone's guess. Indeed, it was not yet even known how many would qualify. Or, did the Holocaust industry extract compensation monies in the name of "needy Holocaust victims" knowing all along that "probably billions" would be left over? The Holocaust industry bitterly complained that the German and Swiss settlements allotted only meager sums for

for Jewish People' Has No Cash," in *Jerusalem Post* (8 September 2000); Joan Gralla, "Battle Brews Over Holocaust Compensation," in *Reuters* (11 September 2000); Shlomo Shamir, "Government to Set Up New Fund for Holocaust Payments," in *Haaretz* (12 September 2000); Yair Sheleg, "Burg Honored at Controversial NY Dinner," in *Haaretz* (12 September 2000); E.J. Kessler, "Hillary the Holocaust Heroine?" in *New York Post* (12 September 2000); Melissa Radler, "Survivors Get Most of Cash in Shoah Fund," in *Forward* (17 September 2000); "The WJC Defends Event Panned by *Commentary*," in *Jewish Post* (20 September 2000).

survivors. It is unclear why the "probably billions" couldn't be used to supplement these allocations.

Predictably, Holocaust survivors reacted with rage. (None was present at the Foundation's creation.) "Who authorized these organizations to decide," a survivor newsletter angrily editorialized, "that the 'leftovers' (in the billions), obtained in the name of Shoah victims, should be used for their pet projects instead of helping ALL holocaust survivors with their mounting health-care expenses?" Confronted with this barrage of negative publicity, the WJC did an abrupt about-face. The $9 billion figure was "a bit misleading," Steinberg subsequently protested. He also claimed that the Foundation had "no cash and no plan for allocating funds," and that the purpose of the Holocaust banquet was not to celebrate the Foundation's endowment from Holocaust compensation monies but rather to raise funds for it. Elderly Jewish survivors, not consulted in advance of, let alone invited to, the "star-studded gala" at the Pierre Hotel, picketed outside.

Among those honored inside the Pierre was President Clinton, who movingly recalled that the United States stood in the forefront of "facing up to an ugly past": "I have been to Native American reservations and acknowledged that the treaties we signed were neither fair nor honorably kept in many cases. I went to Africa . . . and acknowledged the responsibility of the United States in buying people into slavery. This is a hard business, struggling to find our core of humanity." Notably absent in all these instances of "hard business" were reparations in hard currency.[2]

---

[2] "Remarks by The President During Bronfman Gala," Office of The Press

On 11 September 2000 the "Special Master's Proposed Plan of Allocation and Distribution of Settlement Proceeds" from the Swiss banks litigation was finally released. (Hereafter: Gribetz Plan)[3] Publication of the Plan – more than two years in the making – was timed not for the "needy Holocaust victims dying every day" but for the Holocaust gala that same night. Burt Neuborne, lead counsel for the Holocaust industry in the Swiss banks affair and "the most vocal supporter of the distribution plan" (*New York Times*), praised the document as "meticulously researched . . . painstaking and sensitive."[4] Indeed, it seemed to belie pervasive fears that the

---

Secretary, The White House. Distributed by the Office of International Information Programs, US Department of State (http://usinfo.state.gov).

[3] The Plan was formulated by Judah Gribetz, past president of the Jewish Community Relations Council of New York, and currently member of the board of New York's Museum of Jewish Heritage – A Living Memorial to the Holocaust. He was appointed "Special Master" by Judge Edward Korman of New York's Eastern District Court, who presided over the class-action litigation in the Swiss case. The full Plan is posted on http://www.Swissbankclaims.com, and is referred to here as the *Gribetz Plan*. On 22 November 2000 Judge Korman issued a "memorandum and order" that "adopt[s] the Proposed Plan in its entirety." (*In re Holocaust Victim Assets Litigation* [United States District Court for Eastern District of New York: 22 November 2000], 7)

[4] Alan Feuer, "Bitter Fight Is Reignited On Splitting Of Reparations" (*New York Times*, 21 November 2000). "Statement of Burt Neuborne" appended to *Gribetz Plan*. Judge Korman's "memorandum and order" (see note 3 above) points up the crucial role of Neuborne in deflecting criticism of the Plan (4, 6). Prior to publication I forwarded my analysis of the Plan to Neuborne for his critical input. He replied: "I will leave to Judah Gribetz the pleasure of demolishing your effort to mischaracterize his remarkable work as a 'shake down' of holocaust victims." Reminding Neuborne that he played the crucial role in

monies would be misappropriated by Jewish organizations. The *Forward* typically reported that "the distribution plan . . . proposes that more than 90% of the Swiss monies be paid directly to survivors and their heirs." Protesting that "the World Jewish Congress has never asked for a penny, will never take a penny and does not accept restitution funds," Elan Steinberg piously acclaimed the Gribetz Plan as an "extraordinarily intelligent and compassionate document."[5] Intelligent it surely was, but hardly compassionate. For hidden in the details of the Gribetz Plan is the devilish reality that probably but a small fraction of the Swiss monies will be paid directly to Holocaust survivors and their heirs. Before considering this, however, it bears notice that the Plan conclusively, if unwittingly, demonstrates that the Holocaust industry blackmailed Switzerland.[6]

---

promoting the Plan and responding to criticism, I rejoined: "If demolishing my analysis promises such pleasure, why don't you do it yourself?" Despite repeated requests, Gribetz never replied.

[5]   Radler, "Survivors Get Most of Cash in Shoah Fund."

[6]   Significantly, Raul Hilberg, the world's leading authority on the Nazi holocaust, has explicitly charged that the World Jewish Congress blackmailed the Swiss: "It was the first time in history that Jews made use of a weapon that can only be described as blackmail." In a declaration supporting the motion to approve the Swiss settlement, Burt Neuborne, clearly worried by the blackmail allegation ("certain persons may be tempted to mischaracterize legitimate settlement payments as a form of blackmail"), called on Judge Korman to repudiate it, which the Judge dutifully did. ("Holocaust Expert Says Swiss Banks Are Paying Too Much," in *Deutsche Presse-Agentur*, 28 January 1999; *Declaration of Burt Neuborne, Esq.* (5 November 1999), para. 8; Edward R.Korman, *In re Holocaust Victim Assets Litigation* [United States District Court for Eastern District of New York: 26 July 2000], 23–4)

Readers will recall that in May 1996 the Swiss banks formally consented to a comprehensive, external audit – "the most extensive audit in history" (Judge Korman) – in order to settle all outstanding claims by Holocaust survivors and their heirs.[7] Before the audit committee (chaired by Paul Volcker) even had an opportunity to meet, however, the Holocaust industry pressed for a financial settlement. Two pretexts were adduced to preempt the Volcker Committee: (1) the Committee couldn't be trusted, (2) needy Holocaust victims couldn't wait for the Committee's findings. The Gribetz Plan demolishes both pretexts.

In June 1997, Burt Neuborne submitted a "Memorandum of Law" justifying preemption of the Volcker Committee. Against all evidence and with remarkable effrontery, Neuborne dismissed the Committee as a *Swiss* initiative to deflect criticism into a "private mediation effort that is sponsored, paid for and designed by the defendants."[8] It bears notice that Neuborne even held against the Swiss bankers that they footed the $500 million bill for the unprecedented audit imposed on them. In August 1998 the Holocaust industry successfully forced a *non-recoupable* $1.25 billion settlement on the Swiss before the Volcker Committee completed its work.[9] Although the pretext for this

---

[7] *In re Holocaust Victim Assets Litigation*, 19 (Korman).

[8] Burt Neuborne, "Memorandum of Law Submitted by Plaintiffs in Response to Expert Submissions Filed By Legal Academics Retained by Defendants" (United States District Court for Eastern District of New York: 16 June 1997), 68 (compare 62–4). Hereafter: *Neuborne Memorandum*.

[9] For non-recoverability of the final settlement, see *Gribetz Plan*, 12n18: "It should be noted that no part of the $1.25 billion settlement amount will revert to the defendant banks or to any other Swiss entities."

settlement was that the Volcker Committee couldn't be trusted, the Gribetz Plan heaps praise on the Committee and emphasizes that the Committee's findings and mechanism for processing claims ("Claims Resolution Tribunal" – "CRT") were and continue to be of "vital significance" in distributing the Swiss monies.[10] The Holocaust industry's enthusiastic reliance on the Committee for distributing the Swiss monies confutes its main pretext for preempting the Committee with a non-recoupable settlement.

In their settlement with the Holocaust industry, the Swiss were compelled not only to pay for Holocaust-era dormant Jewish accounts, but also to "disgorge the profits" they "knowingly" reaped from Jewish assets looted, and Jewish slave labor exploited, by the Nazis.[11] The Gribetz Plan reveals the flimsiness of these charges as well. It admits that "very few if any" direct links – let alone direct *profitable* links or *knowingly* profitable links – could be established between the Swiss, on the one hand, and looted Jewish assets and Jewish slave labor on the other. Indeed, the Plan makes clear that the entire indictment in these classes was built on what was "likely" or "presumed" or "potentially" to be the case.[12] Finally, Switzerland was

---

[10] *Gribetz Plan*, 11 ("vital significance"), 13–14, 93, 101–4.

[11] *Neuborne Memorandum*, 3, 6–7, 11–12, 28–31, 34–5, 43, 47–8. The memorandum concedes that the Swiss banks would be legally liable only if they "knowingly" profited from the ill-gotten gains of the Nazis: "If one assumes lack of notice on the part of defendant banks, defendants' actions would not give rise to a claim for equitable disgorgement of unjust profits" (34).

[12] *Gribetz Plan*, 23, 29, 113–14, 118n345, 128–9n371, 145–8, Annex G ("The Looted Assets Class"), G–3, G–43, G–57, Annex H ("Slave Labor Class I"), H–52, H–57–8.

compelled to provide restitution to Jews fleeing Nazism who were denied refuge. The Gribetz Plan explicitly concedes – if only in a footnote – the "questionable legal validity" of this claim.[13] Despite all these admissions, however, the Plan still approvingly quotes that "in a perfectly just world, plaintiffs should have received a far greater sum" than the $1.25 billion extracted from the Swiss.[14]

Apart from the Volcker Committee's alleged partisanship, the Holocaust industry gestured to the mortality of Holocaust survivors to force a non-recoupable settlement on the Swiss. Time was supposedly of the essence because "needy Holocaust victims" had only a short time left to live. With the money in hand, however, the Holocaust industry has suddenly discovered that "needy Holocaust victims" aren't dying so rapidly. Citing a study commissioned by the Jewish Claims Conference, the Gribetz Plan reports that "the population of Nazi victims is declining more slowly than previously

---

[13] *Gribetz Plan*, Annex J ("The Refugee Class"), J–26n85. Buried in a footnote we also learn that, according to a leading authority, Seymour J. Rubin, "Switzerland did admit many more refugees, in proportion to its population, than any other nation. This is in contrast to a United States that not only denied entry to the desperate St. Louis refugees, but systematically failed to fill even the limited immigration quota that was available" (J–5). Noting that refugees barred from entering Switzerland during World War II would now receive compensation, Burt Neuborne, in a letter to the *Nation* magazine, rued: "I only wish that a similar sanction could be imposed on the United States for its identical refusal to accept desperate refugees from Nazi persecution" (5 October 2000). Apart from hypocrisy and cowardice, what prevented the Holocaust industry's lead counsel from pressing this claim?

[14] *Gribetz Plan*, 89. The quote is cited from Judge Korman's court order granting final approval to the Settlement Agreement.

believed." Indeed, the Plan purports that "a fairly substantial number of Jewish Nazi victims may live for at least another 20 years and that 30–35 years from now" – that is, some *ninety* years after the end of World War II – "tens of thousands of Jewish Nazi victims are likely to be alive."[15] Given the Holocaust industry's track record, it should surprise no one if this revelation is eventually adduced to press yet new compensation demands on Europe. In the mean time it is already being used to slow the allocation of compensation monies. Thus the Gribetz Plan recommends that the monies be allocated in small increments over time because "building expectations among needy survivors, only to remove the funding and thus the assistance, would be a great disservice."[16]

During the Swiss banks affair, the Holocaust industry maintained that the average age of a survivor was 73 in Israel and 80 in the rest of the world. Life expectancy in the three countries where most Holocaust survivors currently reside ranges from 60 (former Soviet Union) to 77 (the United States and Israel).[17] One might be excused for wondering how it is possible for "tens of thousands" of Holocaust survivors to be alive 35 years from now. A partial answer is that the Holocaust industry has yet again revised the definition of a Holocaust survivor. "One of the reasons for this relatively slower decline in the size of the population," the above-mentioned Claims Conference study reports, "is the finding that, *using the broad definition*, there are many more relatively younger Nazi victims than

---

[15] *Gribetz Plan*, Annex C ("Demographics of 'Victim or Target' Groups"), C–13.

[16] *Gribetz Plan*, 135–6.

[17] *Gribetz Plan*, Annex C, C-12, Annex F ("Social Safety Nets"), F–15.

previously believed" (emphasis added).[18] Indeed, in a Weimar-like inflation, the Gribetz Plan puts the number of living Holocaust survivors at nearly a million – a four-fold increase from the already extraordinary figure of 250,000 Holocaust survivors reported during the Swiss shakedown.[19]

To manage this actuarial and demographic feat, the Gribetz Plan now deems every Russian Jew who survived World War II to be a Holocaust survivor.[20] Thus, Russian Jews who fled in advance of the Nazis or served in the Red Army now qualify as Holocaust survivors because they faced torture and death if captured.[21] Even accepting for argument's sake this truly novel definition of Holocaust survivor, it is unclear why Soviet functionaries who fled in advance of the Nazis or non-Jewish conscripts in the Red Army don't also qualify as Holocaust survivors. They too faced torture and death if captured. Indeed, the Plan reports that a Jewish–American serviceman captured by the Nazis was interned in a concentration camp.[22] Shouldn't every Jewish–American GI from World War II count as a Holocaust survivor? Possibilities abound. Defending the Gribetz Plan mortality

---

[18] Ukeles Associates Inc., Paper #3 (revised), *Projection of the Population of Victims of Nazi Persecution*, 2000–2040 (31 May 2000).

[19] *Gribetz Plan*, p. 9, Annex C, C–8, Annex E ("Holocaust Compensation"), E–89 and E–90n282. The 250,000 figure was used to distribute the monies from the "Special Fund for Needy Victims of the Holocaust" established by the Swiss in February 1997.

[20] *Gribetz Plan*, Annex C, C–7, Table 3. The Plan concedes in a footnote that "in the former Soviet Union, there are relatively few survivors of the concentration camps, ghettos, or work camps" (Annex E, E–56n150).

[21] *Gribetz Plan*, 122–3, 125, Annex E, E–138, Annex F, F–4n13.

[22] *Gribetz Plan*, Annex E, E–56.

projections for Holocaust survivors, a senior historian for the Holocaust wing of the British Imperial War Museum explained that in a
"still broader sense . . . second and even third generation can be
considered" Holocaust victims because "they may suffer from psychi-
atric disturbances."[23] It's only a matter of time before the Holocaust
industry restores Wilkomirski to grace as a Holocaust survivor since
– to quote Yad Vashem Director Israel Gutman – his "pain is
authentic."

For the Holocaust industry, this redefinition and upward revision
of the figure for Holocaust survivors serves multiple purposes. Not
only does it justify the shakedown of European countries, but it
justifies the shakedown of actual Holocaust victims as well. For years
these Holocaust victims have begged the Claims Conference to
allocate compensation monies for a health insurance program. Noting
this "thoughtful" proposal in a footnote, the Gribetz Plan laments that
the Swiss settlement "would be insufficient" to provide medical
insurance for "well over 800,000" Holocaust survivors.[24]

~

[23] Steve Paulsson, "Re: Survivor Article," posted on http://H-Holocaust@
N-Net.MSU.EDU (28 September 2000).

[24] *Gribetz Plan*, 135. It bears notice that the figure for Holocaust survivors in the
original sense also undergoes a radical revision upward in the Gribetz Plan.
The Plan states that roughly 170,000 former Jewish slave-laborers currently
receive pensions from Germany. (*Gribetz Plan*, Annex H ["Slave Labor Class
I"], H–5–6) It is estimated that only one in four former Jewish slave laborers
received a German pension. This would put the total figure for former Jewish
slave laborers still alive today at nearly 700,000, and the total for Jewish slave
laborers alive at war's end at 2,800,000. The standard scholarly figure for

Apart from a trivial sum, the Gribetz Plan earmarks the Swiss monies only for Jewish victims of the Nazi holocaust. The settlement technically covered every "Victim or Target of Nazi Persecution." In fact, this seemingly inclusive, "politically correct" designation is a linguistic subterfuge to *exclude* most non-Jewish victims. It arbitrarily defines "Victim or Target of Nazi Persecution" to include only Jews, Gypsies, Jehovah's Witnesses, homosexuals and the disabled or handicapped. For reasons never explained, other political (for instance Communists and Socialists) and ethnic (Poles and Belorussians, for example) persecutees are left out. These are numerically the larger victim groups; except for Jews, the groups designated "Victim or Target of Nazi Persecution" in the Gribetz Plan are numerically much less significant. The practical upshot is that almost all the compensation monies will go to Jews. Thus, the Plan covers 170,000 former Jewish slave laborers; of fully 1,000,000 non-Jewish former slave laborers, however, only 30,000 of these are deemed to qualify as a "Victim or Target of Nazi Persecution." Likewise, the Plan allocates $90 million for Jewish victims of Nazi plunder but only $10 million for non-Jewish victims. This division is partly justified on the ground that prior compensation agreements used such a ratio. Yet the Plan suggests that non-Jewish victims received a disproportionately smaller share of compensation monies in the past. Shouldn't a just allocation plan redress, not perpetuate, past inequities?[25]

Jewish slave laborers alive at war's end is about 100,000, with perhaps several tens of thousands still alive.

[25] *Gribetz Plan*, 7, 25–7, 83–4, 118–19, 138–9, 149, 154, and "Summary of Major Holocaust Compensation Programs." Apart from precedent, the Plan tautologically justifies this distribution "by current demographics, as Jewish

The Gribetz Plan sets aside fully $800 million of the $1.25 billion Swiss settlement to cover valid claims on Holocaust-era dormant accounts. The Plan's text, annexes and charts run to many hundreds of pages with well over a thousand footnotes. *The singular oddity of the Plan is that it makes no attempt to credibly justify this − the crucial − allocation.* It merely states that, "Based upon his analysis of the Volcker Report and the Final Approval Order, and upon consultation with representatives of the Volcker Committee, the Special Master estimates that the value of all bank accounts that will be repaid is within the range of $800 million."[26] In fact, this estimate appears wildly inflated. The actual sum paid out on dormant accounts will probably not come to more than a tiny fraction of the $800 million.[27] The

---

victims now constitute the overwhelming proportion of surviving 'Victims or Targets of Nazi Persecution' as defined under the Settlement Agreement" (119). Jews only constitute the "overwhelming proportion" because of how the category "Victims or Targets . . ." was defined. For Gypsy reservations to the Plan, see *Romani Comments and Objections to the Special Master's Proposed Plan of Allocation and Distribution* (Ramsey Clark et al., *In re Holocaust Victim Assets Litigation* [United States District Court for Eastern District of New York: November 2000]).

[26] *Gribetz Plan*, 15. The same statement is repeated verbatim on 98–9.

[27] The Volcker Committee recommended publication of the names of some 25,000 accounts having the highest probability of a relationship to victims of Nazi persecution. The total "fair current value" of 10,000 of these accounts for which some information is available runs to $150–$230 million. Projecting these estimates on the 25,000 accounts yields $375–$575 million. To judge by the Claims Resolution Tribunal's prior processing experience, valid claims will be filed against only one half of the 25,000 accounts and one half of the monies in these accounts for a total value of $188-$288 million. In addition, however, the 25,000 list overwhelmingly comprises not dormant but *closed*

"residual" monies – that is, what remains of the $800 million after all legitimate claims have been processed – are supposed to be distributed either directly to Holocaust survivors *or to Jewish organizations* engaged in Holocaust-related activities.[28] In fact, the residual monies will almost certainly go to Jewish organizations, not only because the Holocaust industry will have the final say, but because they won't be distributed until many years from now, when few actual Holocaust survivors will be alive.[29]

---

accounts bearing names that match a Holocaust victim. The Volcker Committee concluded that there is "no evidence of . . . concerted efforts to divert the funds of victims of Nazi persecution to improper purposes." Accordingly, the safe assumption is that almost all the closed accounts on the 25,000 list were properly closed by the actual account holders, rightful heirs, or those with a legitimate and credible power of attorney, and that the CRT will validate only a few claims against these closed accounts. The total value of validated claims against the 25,000 accounts will thus likely fall well below even the $188–$288 million estimate that assumed all the accounts were dormant and the claims on half legitimate. (*Gribetz Plan*, 94n298, 96–7, 105–6n326; Independent Committee of Eminent Persons, *Report on Dormant Accounts of Victims of Nazi Persecution in Swiss Banks* [Bern: 1999], 13, para. 41[a])

[28] *Gribetz Plan*, 12, 19–20. The Plan states on page 12 that the "remainder of the Settlement Fund is to be distributed among the other . . . settlement classes"– i.e., "looted assets," "refugees," and "slave laborers." As shown below, the monies allocated for the "looted assets" class will be paid not to Holocaust survivors directly but rather to Jewish organizations involved in Holocaust work. The Plan further states on pages 19–20 that "it also may be possible to allocate a portion of the remaining Settlement Fund to some of the proposed cultural, memorial or educational projects that have been submitted to the Special Master."

[29] The Plan specifies that distribution of residuals from the $800 million cannot

Besides the $800 million for Holocaust-era accounts, the Gribetz Plan allocates some $400 million mainly for the "looted assets," "slave labor," and "refugees" classes. The Plan enters the crucial caveat, however, that none of these monies will be released until "all appeals in this litigation have been exhausted." Conceding that the "proposed payments may not commence for some time," the Plan cites a crucial precedent in which the appeals process lasted three and a half years.[30] For elderly Holocaust survivors this is a no-win situation and for the Holocaust industry a no-lose one. Many Holocaust survivors, appalled by the Gribetz Plan, will undoubtedly want to appeal, but doing so means that few will be around to benefit even if an appeal is sustained. The Holocaust industry, already the main beneficiary of the Gribetz Plan, can only gain from an appeals process in which more monies will by default flow into its coffers as survivors die out.

Once the appeals process is completed, the Gribetz Plan provides for these allocations of the $400 million:

1. In the "looted assets" class, $90 million is earmarked not for direct

---

begin until all claims on the 25,000 accounts have been processed. It took the CRT fully three years to process 10,000 claims on a prior, separate list of 5,600 Swiss accounts. The Plan reports that many more than 80,000 claims will likely be filed against the list of 25,000. In addition, the Plan provides that all claims must be checked not only against the published list of 25,000 accounts but against millions of other Swiss accounts bearing no apparent relationship to Holocaust victims. Thus even if the CRT process is stream-lined, it will surely take many years to complete. (*Gribetz Plan*, 91, 94n299, 105–6n126) Apart from Holocaust victims holding dormant accounts, the Plan makes only vague and narrow provision for heirs. (18–19, and Annex D ["Heirs"])

[30] *Gribetz Plan*, 16–17.

payments to Holocaust survivors but for Jewish organizations servicing Holocaust communities "broadly defined." The largest allocation will go to the Claims Conference, which the Gribetz Plan repeatedly acclaims for its "unmatched expertise in serving the needs of Nazi victims."[31] The Plan sets aside $10 million for a "Victim List Foundation, the objective of which is to compile and make widely accessible, for research and remembrance, the names of all Victims or Targets of Nazi Persecution." It recommends that the Foundation start from the "irreplaceable data contained in the Initial Question-naires" for Holocaust victims. A typical response in this "irreplaceable data" is that fully one of every six Jewish victims (71,000/430,000) claimed title to a Swiss bank account before World War II. Did one in six also own a Mercedes and a Swiss chalet?[32]

2. In the "slave labor" class, each of 170,000 Jewish former slave laborers supposedly still alive will receive a token payment in two installments: $500 after the appeals process is completed, and "up to" an additional $500 after all claims on dormant accounts are pro-cessed.[33] In fact, the 170,000 figure is grossly inflated, and it is unlikely that many of the Jewish former slave laborers really still alive

[31] *Gribetz Plan*, 25–6, 120–1, 119–38.

[32] *Gribetz Plan*, 18, 27, 116, Annex C, C–10, Exhibit 3 to Annex C, 1. (The "Initial Questionnaires" were distributed to "Victims and Targets of Nazi Persecution" after Judge Korman approved the Swiss settlement.) Dismissing the extravagant claims of the Holocaust industry against the Swiss banks, Raul Hilberg, who fled Austria as a child with his parents, recalled in a recent interview: "In the 1930s, Jews were poor. My family belonged to the middle class, but we did not have a bank account in Austria, let alone in Switzerland." (*Berliner Zeitung*, 4 September 2000)

[33] *Gribetz Plan*, 29–31, 154–6.

will yet be around to collect the first, let alone the second, token payment. Applications will be processed by the Claims Conference, which – as the main beneficiary of residual compensation monies – will profit from every rejection.

3. In the "refugee" class, legitimate claimants will receive payments ranging from $250–$2500 in the same two installments as the "slave labor" class.[34] Based on the "irreplaceable data contained in the Initial Questionnaire," some 17,000 Jews have claimed membership in this class. It is likely that only a small fraction of these 17,000 will demonstrate a valid claim (the Conference processes applications), and that even fewer will still be around to collect the payments.

A close analysis of the Gribetz Plan thus confirms the main arguments in chapter 3 of this book. It demonstrates that the pretexts invoked by the Holocaust industry to force a non-recoupable settlement on the Swiss banks were false, and that few actual survivors of the Nazi holocaust will directly – or, for that matter, indirectly – benefit from the Swiss monies. A comparable analysis of other Holocaust industry settlements would presumably yield comparable results. Indeed, buried in the details of the Gribetz Plan is a nest egg for the Holocaust industry. Most of the Swiss monies probably won't be distributed until after all but a handful of survivors are dead. With the survivors gone, the monies will pour into the coffers of Jewish organizations. Small wonder that the Holocaust industry was unanimous in its praise of the Gribetz Plan.

~

---

[34] *Gribetz Plan*, 35–9, 172–5.

Soon after publication of the Allocation and Distribution Plan, I joined an exchange with Burt Neuborne in the pages of the *Nation* magazine. Deploring the cynicism of the Holocaust industry, I specifically pointed to the Plan's claim that nearly a million Jewish survivors of the Nazi holocaust are still alive today.[35] In his rejoinder, Neuborne flatly denied using this figure for surviving Jewish victims of the Nazi holocaust (even though he was the Gribetz Plan's "most vocal supporter" (*New York Times*), and his official statement specially appended to the Gribetz Plan praises its findings as "meticulously researched"). Rather, he claimed that the figure of nearly one million "was intended to include all surviving victims, not merely Jewish survivors," and that the breakdown he used was "about 130,000 Jewish survivors and about 900,000 non-Jewish survivors" still alive.[36] I reproduce opposite the relevant page from the Plan (box added by me). Can there be any question at all whether Neuborne accurately reported the figure?

As lead counsel for the Holocaust industry, Burt Neuborne contrived the "legal theories" used to shake down the Swiss banks. He figured as the main proponent of the Allocation and Distribution Plan used to shake down the victims of Nazi persecution. He flagrantly misrepresented a key document in published correspondence. Imagine if lawyers for the Swiss banks committed offenses of such magnitude. Wouldn't Neuborne be the first to call for their disbarment?[37]

---

[35] *Nation*, 18 December 2000.

[36] *Nation*, 25 December 2000.

[37] In addition to the Swiss shakedown, Neuborne figured centrally in the German slave-labor negotiations. For the latter travail, he raked in $5,000,000 – a "not particularly high" fee, Neuborne opined, especially as compared with

Gribetz Plan, Annex C, C–8

In Re HOLOCAUST VICTIM ASSETS LITIGATION (Swiss Banks)
SPECIAL MASTER'S PROPOSAL, September 11, 2000

C.   Jewish Survivors of Nazi Persecution

The Special Master has considered a variety of information concerning the

population of surviving Jewish Nazi victims, including estimates of the current Jewish survivor

population, their geographic distribution, their average ages and expected mortality rates, and the

number of Jewish survivors who have received payments from the Swiss Fund for Needy

Victims of the Holocaust/Shoa (the "Swiss Humanitarian Fund").[14]

1.   Number of Jewish Survivors

As stated by Ukeles, "[t]here are no reliable, agreed-upon, statistics on the

number of Jewish Nazi victims living in the world today."[15] The statistics reviewed by the

Special Master are estimates, based on the best available information. The estimates range from

a low of 832,000 Jewish survivors to a high of 960,000.

According to a report prepared by the Spanic Committee[16] and cited by the Notice

---

[14]   The Swiss Humanitarian Fund was established in March 1997 as a humanitarian gesture wholly
separate from the settlement of this action in order to provide assistance to "needy" victims of Nazi
persecution. Although the number of survivors who received payments from the Swiss
Humanitarian Fund is instructive to a demographic analysis, the number of survivors qualifying for
Swiss Humanitarian Fund payments may differ materially from the number of survivors qualifying
for benefits under the Settlement Agreement in this case because, among other reasons, (1) the Swiss
Humanitarian Fund used a narrower definition of "survivor" than that proposed herein; and (2)
certain groups targeted by the Nazis, such as Jehovah's Witnesses and other victims of political
persecution, could only qualify for the Swiss Humanitarian Fund if they had been interned in
"internationally recognized concentration camps" and had been born in 1921 or earlier. *See* Annex
K ("The Swiss Humanitarian Fund") for a more detailed discussion of the Swiss Humanitarian Fund.

[15]   Ukeles, at 2-2.

[16]   The Spanic Committee was organized by the Israeli Prime Minister's Office and consisted of E.
Spanic, Chair; H. Factor; and W. Struminsky. The Committee undertook a comprehensive effort to
estimate the number of surviving Jewish Nazi victims by geographic area between May and July
1997. These estimates were revised slightly in May 1998 by H. Factor and W. Struminsky. *See*
Ukeles, Appendix 1.1, at 2-13.

II.

In May 1998 a Presidential Advisory Commission on Holocaust Assets was charged by Congress with "conducting original research on the fate of assets taken from victims of the Holocaust that came into the possession of the U.S. Federal government" and "advising the President on policies that should be adopted to make restitution to the rightful owners of stolen property or their heirs."[38] In December 2000 the Commission, chaired by Edgar Bronfman (who orchestrated the assault on the Swiss banks), released the long-awaited report. Entitled *Plunder and Restitution: The U.S. and Holocaust Victims' Assets*,[39] it purports to demonstrate that "the United States has asked of itself no less than it has asked of the international community."[40] In fact, a close reading of the document points to the opposite conclusion: *although the United States was culpable of all the offenses it alleged against*

---

the German settlement's allocation of fully $7,500 to an Auschwitz survivor. (Jane Fritsch, "$52 Million for Lawyers' Fees in Nazi-Era Slave Labor Suits," in *New York Times* [15 June 2001]; Daniel Wise, "$60 Million in Fees Awarded To Lawyers Who Negotiated $5 Billion Holocaust Fund," in *New York Law Journal* [15 June 2001]; Gerald Locklin, "Lawyers Get Millions, Victims Get Thousands From Holocaust Deal," in *National Post* [18 June 2001])

[38] For background, see above 119. The commission was formed at the peak of US pressures on the Swiss banks and in the face of Swiss criticism that the US was itself not blameless in the matter of Holocaust compensation.

[39] Washington, DC. (Hereafter: *P&R*) It is divided into two parts: "Findings and Recommendations," and "Staff Report". Page numbers for the Staff Report are denoted "SR".

[40] *P&R*, 5.

the Swiss, no comparable demands have been imposed on the US for Holocaust restitution.[41]

The Presidential Commission juxtaposes the "intransigence of the Swiss banks" against the "extraordinary efforts" of the United States to return Holocaust-era assets.[42] I want first to compare the charges leveled against the Swiss with the American record as revealed in the Commission report.

Denial of access to Holocaust-era assets

The Holocaust industry alleged that the Swiss banks systematically denied Holocaust survivors and heirs access to their accounts after World War II. The Volcker Committee concluded that, apart from marginal exceptions, the charge lacked merit.[43] On the other hand, the Presidential Commission found that after the war "many" Holocaust survivors and heirs couldn't recover their assets in the United States due to the "expense and difficulty in filing" a claim. (From 1941 the Federal government had blocked or vested the assets of all nationals from Nazi-occupied countries.)[44] As with the Swiss banks,

---

[41] It bears passing notice that this report is replete with the hyperbole typical of Holocaust industry publications. Thus the Holocaust is deemed "the greatest mass theft in history." (*P&R*, SR–3) The entire United States was built on land stolen from the indigenous population, and US industrial development was fueled by centuries of unpaid labor of African–Americans in the cotton industry: Did the Commission reckon these thefts in its calculations?

[42] *P&R*, 4, 5.

[43] See above 111–12.

[44] *P&R*, 11–12; SR–167–8. The report also observes: "No noticeable relaxation of the rules or procedures facilitated victims' claims . . . Heirs faced more

in "some instances" the Federal government sought out rightful owners.[45]

Destruction of Holocaust-era asset records

The Holocaust industry alleged that, to cover their tracks, the Swiss banks systematically destroyed essential records. The Volcker Committee concluded that the charge lacked merit.[46]

On the other hand, the United States did destroy crucial "raw data." After the US declared war, the Treasury Department required American financial institutions to submit detailed descriptions of all foreign-owned assets on deposit. The Commission reports that these forms – fully 565,000 – "have been destroyed, and the staff's investigations have uncovered no duplicates. As a result, it is not possible to estimate the amount of victims' assets in the United States in 1941." The Commission is strangely silent on when or why these documents were destroyed.[47]

Misappropriation of Holocaust-era assets

The Holocaust industry justly accused Switzerland of using monies belonging to Holocaust victims from Poland and Hungary as com-

---

challenges than named account holders. Many case histories demonstrated that the initial claimant died during the claim process. In those cases, . . . further investigations . . . delayed cases."

[45] *P&R*, SR–170. See above 111–12.

[46] See above 112.

[47] *P&R*, SR–4, SR–213–14.

pensation for Swiss properties nationalized by these governments.[48] Yet, the Presidential Commission reports this happened in the United States as well: "[C]ompensation for U.S. assets lost in Europe took precedence over compensation for foreign-owned assets frozen in the United States. Congress regarded frozen German assets as a source from which to pay U.S. war claims for damages suffered by American businesses and individuals . . . Thus, U.S. war claims were paid in part by German assets that likely included victims' assets."[49]

Trading in looted Nazi gold

The Holocaust industry justly accused the Swiss of purchasing Nazi gold looted from the central treasuries of Europe.[50] Yet, the Presidential Commission reports that the United States did so as well. In fact, trading in looted Nazi gold was *official* US policy until Germany's declaration of war precluded the practice. The relevant passage from the Commission report merits extended quotation:

> The German invasion of France, Belgium and the Netherlands in May of 1940, prompted Mr. Pinsent, Financial Counselor at the British Embassy, to send a note to the Treasury Department to inquire of Mr Morgenthau [Treasury Secretary] "whether he would be prepared to scrutinize the gold imports with a view to rejecting those suspected of

---

[48] See above 97–8.

[49] *P&R*, 12; SR–6, SR–170.

[50] See above 96–7, 108–9.

German origin," as Pinsent explicitly feared that the private hoards of Dutch and Belgian gold might fall into German hands. In a June 4, 1940 memo, Harry Dexter White [head of the Division of Monetary Research] explained why the U.S. Treasury did not raise questions about the origin of "German" gold . . . The most effective contribution the United States could make to keep gold as an international exchange medium, White argued, "is to maintain its inviolability and the unquestioned acceptance of gold as a means of settling international balances." Indeed, six months later White would scornfully write of his "adamant opposition to give even serious consideration to proposals from those who know little of the subject that we stop purchasing gold, or that we stop buying the gold of any particular country, for this or for that or for any particular reason." In early 1941, White was asked again, through an internal Treasury memorandum, to consider the question "whose gold are we buying?" but from his memos it is clear that the answer was an "unquestioned acceptance of gold."[51]

The Holocaust industry also justly alleged that the Swiss purchased Nazi gold looted from Holocaust victims. (There was no evidence, however, that the Swiss *knowingly* purchased this "victim gold;" its total worth in current values was put at about a million dollars.)[52] The Presidential Commission similarly reports that "it is possible that gold bars and coins purchased by the Department of Treasury through the Federal Reserve Bank of New York, during and after the war,

[51] *P&R*, SR–51.
[52] See above 97, 110–11.

contained trace amounts of gold items looted from victims of Nazism."[53]

In sum, the Presidential Commission's report demonstrates that the United States was guilty of all the charges leveled by the Holocaust industry against Switzerland.

~

The Holocaust industry forced the Swiss banks to conduct an exhaustive, external audit costing a half billion dollars in order to locate all unclaimed Holocaust-era assets. Before this audit was even completed, the Holocaust industry forced a $1.25 billion settlement on the Swiss.[54] Yet, the Volcker Committee reported that, alongside Switzerland, the United States was also a primary safe haven for Jewish assets in Europe.[55] Compare now the demands imposed on the United States.

As noted above, the Presidential Commission claimed that its "work . . . demonstrates that the United States has asked of itself no less than it has asked of the international community." The Commission did not, however, undertake a comprehensive accounting of unclaimed Holocaust-era assets in the United States. The report maintains that it wasn't the Commission's mandate "to mechanistically quantify or assign dollar values to perceived historical shortcomings in U.S. policy making or implementation."[56] Indeed, it supposedly

---

[53] *P&R*, SR–214.

[54] For details, see above 89–120 *passim*.

[55] See above 114–15.

[56] *P&R*, 7.

couldn't do so due to the "necessary compromise between research goals and the time and resources available to complete them," and the "paucity and uneven quality of documentation at its disposal."[57] Inexplicably, Switzerland could, but the United States couldn't, finesse these obstacles. (What prevented a greater allocation of "time and resources," or a Swiss-style audit to fill the document gap?)[58] Likewise, an accurate reckoning of returned Holocaust-era assets would have required "systematic investigations that fell beyond the capacities"[59] of the Commission – but not beyond the capacities of the Swiss banks.

The Commission reports that the Jewish Restitution Successor Organization (JRSO) only "reluctantly accepted" the $500,000 com-

---

[57] *P&R*, 19; SR–212–13.

[58] The Commission merely conducted a "pilot project matching the names of a limited list of Holocaust victims with a list of escheated property maintained by the State of New York . . . This procedure . . . yielded 18 matches of names of victims with dormant bank accounts in the State of New York . . . the value of these accounts ranges from a few dollars to five thousand dollars." (Under the doctrine of escheat, American banks are supposed to transfer abandoned dormant accounts to the respective state government.) In addition, the Commission reached an agreement with major banks "defining suggested best practices to be used by banks when they search for Holocaust assets." Under this accord, banks volunteering to participate are supposed to conduct "their own investigations" of relevant records, and inform state officials of any Holocaust-era dormant accounts found. An abyss plainly separates these "suggested best practices" from the exhaustive, external audit imposed on the Swiss banks. Remarkably, the agreement even provides that cooperating banks don't have to publicly report "the identity of the account holder" for "any accounts identified." (*P&R*, 3, 15–17)

[59] *P&R*, SR–184n249.

pensation offered by the US government for unclaimed Holocaust-era assets.[60] Although the report findings support Seymour Rubin's contention that the $500,000 figure was "very low,"[61] the Commission

[60] *P&R*, SR–138. The JRSO was responsible for recovering heirless Holocaust-era assets after the war. Interestingly, the Commission reports that the JRSO claimed for itself property belonging to Holocaust survivors and their heirs:

> Individuals sometimes discovered that the JRSO had submitted a claim for their property and they then turned to the successor organization for restitution; the JRSO handled over 4,800 such claims by 1955. After internal discussion, the JRSO agreed to restitute property to such claimants even though it had obtained title to such assets . . . It did, however, assess a service charge to the late petitioners to cover its costs. The fees depended on the relationship of the claimant to the former owner and the appraisal of the property. If the JRSO had actually recovered a property, a surcharge of ten percent augmented these costs (although the organization reduced this to five percent if a claimant was indigent). One claimant sharply criticized US authorities for "awarding" her property to the JRSO. She argued that she had not heard about the filing deadline until after it had passed, and instead discovered that, "I shall be punished because the Occupation Army, for whom my husband and I pay plenty, deems it right to take my property and gives it to who knows whom." The frustration and anger expressed in this letter likely mirrored the sentiments of other claimants who missed the deadline; individuals hurled "demands" and "protests" at the JRSO for the immediate return of their property. (*P&R*, SR–156)

> A half century later the Jewish Claims Conference (successor to the JRSO) pursues the identical strategy to rob legitimate Jewish heirs of their properties in the former East Germany (see references cited above 87n11, and Netty Gross, "Time's Running Out," in *Jerusalem Report* [7 May 2001]).

[61] *P&R*, SR–171. The quoted phrase comes from a statement by Seymour Rubin in 1959 (for Rubin, see above 115–16). The JRSO ultimately acceded to this figure, according to Rubin, because Holocaust survivors were approaching death: "time is running out for these people." We have seen that the

predictably concludes that the measly compensation wasn't "attribut-
able to bad motives on the part of any official, agent or institution of
the United States."[62] The report never once proposes that the United
States should pay more compensation, let alone of a magnitude
comparable to the $1.25 billion extracted from the Swiss.

The Presidential Commission includes a list of noble recommendations.[63] At war's end, American GIs stationed in Europe engaged in
massive looting.[64] One recommendation calls on the Federal government "to develop, in concert with veterans' service organizations, a
program to promote the voluntary return of victims' assets that may
have been taken by former members of the armed forces as war
souvenirs." No doubt veterans are already queuing up to return the
booty. A final recommendation calls on the United States to "continue
its leadership to promote the international community's commitment
to addressing asset restitution issues." After this report, who can
question American leadership?

Norman G. Finkelstein
June 2001
New York City

Holocaust industry was still playing the "time is running out" tune during the
Swiss shakedown. One might have thought that a half-century later time had
already run out. For suggestive evidence that the total value of unclaimed
Holocaust-era assets ran much higher, see *P&R*: SR–6, SR–166–7, SR–172,
SR–214–15.

[62] *P&R*, 7.

[63] *P&R*, 21–6.

[64] *P&R*, SR–117ff.

POSTSCRIPT TO THE SECOND
PAPERBACK EDITION

Since publication of the first paperback edition of *The Holocaust Industry*, crucial new developments in the Swiss banks case have unfolded: (1) the completion of the Claims Resolution Tribunal-I (CRT-I) process, (2) the creation and subsequent total revamping of CRT-II, (3) the publication of the Bergier Commission *Final Report* and its use to discredit the Volcker Committee findings. In this postscript I will assess these developments.[1] To clarify what follows,

---

[1] This assessment is based in part on interviews with the principals in the case, several of whom requested anonymity. Jytte Kjaergaard of the Danish newspaper *B.T.* conducted the interviews with Michael Bradfield and Burt Neuborne, this writer interviewed Judge Edward R. Korman, and David Ridgen of the Canadian Broadcasting Corporation interviewed Raul Hilberg. Bradfield, Neuborne and Korman each received successive drafts of this assessment and were invited to identify for correction factual errors. None of the three reported any. All docket numbers refer to United States District Court, Eastern District of New York, Case Number 96-CV-4849.

I tabulate below the main differences between the accounts against which claims were filed in CRT-I versus CRT-II:

CRT-I	CRT-II
1. only dormant accounts	1. both dormant and closed accounts
2. all account names published	2. some account names published
3. both Holocaust-victim and non-Holocaust-victim accounts	3. only Holocaust-victim accounts

(Dormant accounts refer to accounts where the bank continued to hold the funds in the name and on behalf of the account-holder.)

1. Completion of CRT-I process

In September 2001, CRT-I, which processed claims from around the world against dormant Swiss bank accounts, completed its work. On 11 October 2001, the chair of CRT-I, Professor Hans Michael Riemer, issued a press release summarizing the Tribunal's main findings.[2] Upon issuing this press release Riemer was suspended effective immediately by Michael Bradfield, who supervised the Tribunal's administration. (Earlier Bradfield served as general counsel on the Volcker Committee, and was the de facto general manager of the audit.) Bradfield was reportedly livid because the press statement noted that, for claims filed under CRT-I, the Swiss banks owed

---

[2] "The Claims Resolution Tribunal has completed its initial mission" (press release, Zurich: 11 October 2001).

Holocaust victims only $10 million.[3] He maintains that Riemer was let go for not "adequately" signaling that CRT-I was only the first step of a two-step process.[4] A reading of the press release clearly belies Bradfield's claim. Professor Riemer also produced a detailed final report on the work of CRT-I.[5] The report earned the unstinting praise of CRT-I arbitrators. Keeping it under lock and key, Bradfield dismisses the report as "irrelevant" while pinning responsibility for withholding its publication on Paul Volcker and Rabbi Israel Singer. (They form the Board of Trustees of the Independent Claims Resolution Foundation, which oversaw CRT-I.) Judge Korman emphatically maintains that he never read the CRT-I final report whereas Bradfield maintains that Korman did read it.[6] In late July 2002, the Swiss Bankers Association (SBA) decided to post the Riemer report on its web site.

The key statistical data and final tallies from the CRT-I report are these:[7]

---

[3] This final tally received scant attention in the foreign media. The one notable exception was a London *Times* article by Adam Sage and Roger Boyes, "Swiss Holocaust cash revealed to be myth" (13 October 2001).

[4] Interview with Michael Bradfield on 22 July 2002. Unless otherwise indicated, all Bradfield quotes and paraphrases are from this interview. See also the exchange of letters between Paul Volcker and Prof. Riemer, dated 29 October 2001, and 7 November 2001 (docket numbers 1087 and 1092).

[5] *Final Report on the Work of the Claims Resolution Tribunal for Dormant Accounts in Switzerland* (5 October 2001).

[6] Interview with Judge Korman on 5 July 2002. Unless otherwise indicated, all Korman quotes and paraphrases are from this interview. (The CRT-I final report was never docketed.)

[7] All figures in this assessment are rounded off to nearest ten, hundred or thousand depending on order of magnitude.

CRT-I Statistical Data and Final Tallies

- 5,500 dormant account names published (including both Holocaust victims and non-Holocaust victims)
- 10,000 claims made against 2,300 of these accounts
- 6,000 claims (60 percent of all claims) rejected after initial screening and an additional 1,000 claims (10 percent of all claims) subsequently rejected
- 3,000 claims (30 percent of all claims) approved against 1,000 accounts, of which 200 were Holocaust-victim accounts
- total monies paid to the 3,000 approved claimants against 1,000 accounts = $40 million
- total monies paid against 200 Holocaust-victim accounts = $10 million

Consider now the available data for CRT-II and projections for CRT-II based on the CRT-I findings:

CRT-II Available Data

- 36,000 account names with probable or possible relationship to Holocaust victims (21,000 account names published, 15,000 account names unpublished)
- 32,000 claims made against the 36,000 published and unpublished accounts
- 12,000 claims match against names on published or unpublished accounts[8]

---

[8] See Burt Neuborne's letter to Judge Korman, dated 26 February 2002, and attached declaration (docket numbers 1171 and 1172).

These 12,000 matched-name claims are roughly equivalent to the initial 10,000 CRT-I claims — i.e., in both cases the claims are directed against specific account names.

CRT-II Projections Based on CRT-I

- 8,400 claims (70 percent of the 12,000 matched-name claims) will eventually be rejected
- 3,600 claims (30 percent of the 12,000 matched-name claims) will ultimately be approved
- monies paid to the 3,600 approved claimants will total $50 million[9]

Based on the available data for CRT-II and projections based on the statistical data and final tallies for CRT-I, the Swiss banks profited at the expense of Holocaust victims and heirs to the amount of $60 million ($10 million from CRT-I + $50 million from CRT-II). This sum falls dramatically short, however, of the $1.25 billion paid by the Swiss banks in the final settlement, let alone the $7–20 billion demanded during the campaign against the Swiss banks.

Even the $60 million projection perhaps goes well beyond the actual profits of the Swiss banks. CRT-I dealt only with dormant accounts, whereas CRT-II has processed claims on both dormant and — overwhelmingly — closed Holocaust-related accounts.[10] The

---

[9] Projection based on the $40 million paid out against the 3,000 approved claims in CRT-I (some $10 million would be paid out against an additional 600 approved claims).

[10] The decision to expand the audit of the Swiss banks to include closed accounts was made by Volcker, "tenaciously pushed" by Bradfield. See John Authers and Richard Wolffe, *The Victim's Fortune* (New York: 2002), 356.

Volcker Committee concluded, however, that there is "no evidence of . . . concerted efforts to divert funds of victims of Nazi persecution to improper purposes."[11] Thus, although the $50 million projection for CRT-II is based on claims made against both dormant and mostly closed accounts, there is no evidence that the Swiss banks significantly profited from the closed accounts. There remain a cluster of unresolved, and perhaps unresolvable, questions regarding how many Jewish account-holders in Nazi-occupied Europe closed their accounts due to Nazi threats, the value of these accounts closed under coercion, and the culpability of the Swiss banks for not taking proper precautions in processing the withdrawal orders. The Volcker Committee only found that the "banks transferred some 400 accounts to the Nazi authorities (in some cases where they knew or should have known that the transfer was ordered by the account holder under duress)."[12] In any event, all this is a separate matter from the

---

[11] Independent Committee of Eminent Persons, *Report on Dormant Accounts of Victims of Nazi Persecution in Swiss Banks* (Bern: 1999), p. 13, paragraph 41 (a).

[12] Ibid., p. 82, paragraph 4; cf. pp. 86–7, paragraphs 22–5. Regarding this complex matter, a former CRT senior judge observed: "I can recall at least one specific CRT-II case where an account holder was told by the Nazi authorities that he and his family could leave Germany only if they arranged for the prior transfer of their Swiss bank assets to a Nazi-controlled bank. In that case, obviously, the account owner affirmatively wanted the transfer to take place, and there has been no suggestion by anyone that in such circumstances the bank was 'culpable' for doing what the account owner wanted it to do. My recollection is that in that case, with New York approval, the heirs of the account owner were permitted to recover from the Settlement Fund" – i.e., the claim against the Swiss banks was nonetheless approved (private correspondence).

original allegation that, driven by greed (and anti-Semitism), the Swiss banks enriched *themselves* at the expense of Holocaust victims and heirs.

2. Creation and subsequent total revamping of CRT-II[13]

In accordance with the class-action settlement agreement, CRT-I reconvened, with some modifications, as CRT-II in November 2001, and began processing claims in earnest in January 2002.[14] CRT-II Special Masters Paul Volcker and Michael Bradfield proposed the governing rules of procedure and Judge Korman approved them. The relaxed evidentiary standards used in CRT-I were re-adopted, while the procedure was somewhat streamlined to expedite the processing of claims, and new rules for closed accounts granting the maximum presumptions in favor of the claimant were incorpo-

---

[13] A key source for this section is a 11 June 2002 letter by Roberts B. Owen running to nine single-spaced pages and originally addressed to his colleagues on CRT-II, which provides a careful overview and evaluation of the events narrated here. Owen, an American, served as Vice-Chairman of CRT-I and CRT-II and was the only active senior judge on CRT-II. On Paul Volcker's urging (he was shown an advanced copy), Owen did not distribute the letter to his colleagues but did send it to Messrs. Volcker, Bradfield, and Singer, and Judge Korman, from whom this writer obtained a copy. (This document was never docketed.) (Hereafter: *Owen Letter*.)

[14] Budgeting for CRT-II began already in February 2000, and the actual processing of claims for CRT-II commenced in May 2001, but this initial stage running to the end of the year proved abortive (former CRT-II employees put the blame for the false start on Bradfield).

rated.[15] Although technically CRT-I was an arbitral proceeding
(claimants versus banks), and CRT-II was not (having agreed to pay
a non-refundable sum of $1.25 billion in January 1999, the banks
were henceforth out of the picture), the fundamental mandate of
both was the same: to "make determinations regarding the rights of
claimants to accounts in Swiss banks" (*Rules*, 1). The essential conti-
nuity was pointed up in Article 11 of the *Rules* stating that the
"Chairperson and the Arbitrators" of CRT-I "may also act, respectively, as Tribunal Chairperson and as Senior Judges" of CRT-II. In
April 2002, two Swiss lawyers resigned from CRT-II, and soon
thereafter six foreign colleagues – three of whom were Jewish –
were asked to resign (they were given twenty-four hours to vacate
the premises). A distinguished CRT member from the US described
the six as "good hard-working lawyers who obey orders and do their
jobs . . . The most that can be said against these individuals is that
they had enough common sense and courage to ask tough questions
about the apparent weakness of the program being directed (indeed
micro-managed) by Bradfield." Another senior CRT member called
their firing "a shameful act." By June, one-third of the CRT-II staff,
including the Secretary-General, Veijo Heiskanen of Finland, was
gone. According to credible reports in the respected Swiss periodi-
cals *Weltwoche* and *NZZ am Sonntag*, the main source of dissension
was Bradfield's heavy-handed pressure on the staff to increase the
number of claim approvals by violating procedural rules and distorting facts. In addition, all sixteen senior judges either resigned or

[15] For the new rules regarding closed accounts, see Article 34 of "Rules
Governing the Claims Resolution Process." (Hereafter: *Rules*.)

were let go. Fully fifteen of these judges had already been completely sidelined from CRT-II, and many resented the use of their names and reputations as a fig leaf for an increasingly dubious process in which they had no involvement or influence.[16]

Of the 32,000 claims filed in CRT-II, 20,000 didn't match against a name on the list of possible or probable Holocaust-victim accounts. Before the personnel shake-up, the CRT-II staff had processed the first 2,800 of the remaining 12,000 claims. Even using relaxed standards of proof and maximum presumptions in favor of claimants, they could find sufficient evidence for an approval in just 400, or 15 percent, of the 2,800 claims. At this rate, only 1,800 of the total 32,000 claims in CRT-II would ultimately have been approved.[17] In CRT-I, the 3,000 approved claims yielded $40 million, which means

---

[16] See Hanspeter Born's articles, "Awarding the millions, eyes closed," in *Weltwoche* (23 May 2002), and "The Claims Resolution Tribunal without a Judge," in *Weltwoche* (6 June 2002), as well as "'Hitler had Switzerland in his pocket,'" in *NZZ am Sonntag* (9 June 2002), "$800 Million Dollars, Rough Justice," and "If Too Little is Known, Then Speculate," in *NZZ am Sonntag* (16 June 2002). The thrust of these articles was confirmed in numerous interviews and extensive correspondence with the parties involved. For "good hard-working lawyers . . ." and "shameful act" as well as further details, see *Owen Letter*.

[17] For the 15 percent approval rate, see *Owen Letter*, and "$800 Million Dollars, Rough Justice," in *NZZ am Sonntag* (9 June 2002). It merits notice that Bradfield's predictions for CRT-II proved wildly overblown. For example, in a 26 December 2000 memorandum to Judge Korman ("Draft Proposed Budget, January 2001-June 2003, for CRT"), he anticipated that 100,000 claims would be filed, of which (apparently) 85,000 would pass the initial screening, and 12,750 (15 percent of 85,000) would be approved (docket number 1064).

that the 1,800 approved claims in CRT-II would probably have yielded about $20 million. By this reckoning, the total profits of Swiss banks on Holocaust-victim accounts would come to $30 million in current values ($10 million from CRT-I + $20 million from CRT-II). Knowledgeable former CRT employees suggest that the actual final tally would probably have been somewhat higher.[18] Yet, even assuming that the figure came to double the projection, it would still have fallen within the vicinity of the $30 million that the Swiss bankers initially proposed as a basis for negotiations to compensate Holocaust-victim accounts. The calumnious campaign subsequently waged against the Swiss bankers forced on them a $500 million audit and a $1.25 billion settlement. *If CRT-II had been allowed to run its course, the outcome would likely have proven deeply embarrassing to the assailants of the Swiss banks.*

~

The key parties to the CRT-II process – Special Master Michael Bradfield,[19] Judge Edward Korman, and Lead Settlement Counsel Burt Neuborne – allege two main justifications for the staff shake-up:

(1) *The resolution process needed to be accelerated.* The consensus among former CRT personnel, however, is that the slow pace of CRT-I was primarily due to the long delay before Bradfield finally

---

[18] For instance, the computer program initially used to match claims against account names underestimated the number of name matches due to data-entry problems.

[19] Although Paul Volcker is officially also a Special Master, he is apparently not actively involved.

provided a procedural rule for appraising the current value of approved claims (a full year's time was lost) and that, overall, the slow pace of the CRT process has been due to the "cumbersome" rules he contrived for processing claims.[20] In any event, it's unclear how sacking the senior and most experienced personnel and replacing them with a questionable leadership presiding over a much demoralized staff will speed the process.[21] Korman and Bradfield claim that CRT-I dragged on for five years, whereas it actually took three and a half years from the first claim received in March 1998 to the last claim resolved in September 2001.[22] In its first seven months, CRT-II processed about one-quarter of the credible claims against Holocaust-victim accounts. At this rate, CRT-II would have required under two years to finish up. Yet, after the revamping of CRT-II it was reported that the new staff would take at least another two years to complete its work.[23] Judge Korman's avowed objective of improving on CRT-I is also hard to reconcile with his pretended

---

[20] For details, see *Owen Letter*. Owen observes that Bradfield had established a "cumbersome, overly elaborate arbitral mechanism" for CRT-I, and not only failed – despite the entreaties of the CRT-II leadership – to implement plainly needed reforms in CRT-II but "began to add additional cumbersome requirements."

[21] For this new leadership's dubious credentials, including "a young New York lawyer with only three years of law practice and no mass claims experience," and "a young Swedish lawyer who has not yet been admitted to the bar," see *Owen Letter*.

[22] "Notes from phone call from Judge Korman to CRT on 6 June 2002." For three and a half years, see *Owen Letter*.

[23] Yair Sheleg, "A long and winding road to compensation," in *Haaretz* (8 July 2002), quoting Rabbi Singer.

indifference to Professor Riemer's unique report analyzing the CRT-I experience. (Korman stated that he would only read the report if it were posted to him.) It further bears mention that – whether due to ignorance or disingenuousness – Bradfield, Korman and Neuborne aren't always the most accurate sources for even basic information about the CRT process. Bradfield has repeatedly asserted that there were six times more claimants in CRT-II than CRT-I, whereas there were three times more (30,000 versus 10,000). Judge Korman has stated that the procedure for calculating monetary awards in CRT-II is identical to CRT-I whereas a crucial revision was entered in early June. Neuborne stated in February 2002 that the number of "probable and possible" Holocaust-related accounts for CRT-II came to 46,000, whereas it was 36,000.[24]

---

[24] Neuborne letter to Judge Korman, dated 26 February 2002, and attached declaration (docket numbers 1171 and 1172). It's hard to find a public statement by this trio that's not either false or egregiously misleading. Consider Neuborne. He has repeatedly maintained that his services on behalf of Holocaust compensation are provided *pro bono*. Although this was true in the Swiss case (throughout he was still employed full time as a professor at New York University), it was emphatically not the case in the subsequent German settlement, where he raked in $5 million. See *The Victim's Fortune*, 250, 374, as well as the letter, dated 12 September 2002, of Sam Dubbin, an attorney enlisted by disgruntled Holocaust victims, to Burt Neuborne: "You tell my client . . . that you 'served without fee' [in the Swiss case]. You fail to inform . . . that you and the other attorneys who 'declined to seek fees in this case' collected $20 million in 'survivors money' for your roles in the German settlement, without public disclosure of your services (including whether you sought payment in that case for work you did in the Swiss case), time records, lodestar, or explanation of the value your work allegedly brought to that matter. Your statement gives my client the false impression

(2) *The CRT-II staff didn't understand its function.* Judge Korman maintains that senior judges "were never part of the CRT-II process, were never contemplated to be and their resignations were part of an effort to generate negative publicity."[25] Yet, the CRT-II *Rules* drafted by Bradfield and approved by Korman explicitly called for the CRT-I arbitrators to serve as senior judges and, in November 2001, Volcker and Bradfield invited (and the Settlement Fund paid for) all sixteen CRT-II senior judges to attend a "Convocation of Judges" in Zurich in the expectation that they would play a central role in CRT-II. Burt Neuborne maintains that the CRT-II senior judges "had a great deal of difficulty in shifting gears, in altering their sense of who they were, and what their mission was, that they were no longer judges, they were investigators . . . They were behaving as if they were judges." Yet, it was never suggested that senior judges would be "investigators" (all necessary factual

---

that you are representing survivors selflessly and at great personal sacrifice" (docket number 1379). Indeed, a "Memorandum" to Judge Korman pointedly observed: "As the Court is well aware, a group of counsel that Professor Neuborne subsequently aligned with attempted to hijack the [Swiss bank] litigation under the ruse that they would work *pro bono* . . . By gaining control of the Swiss Bank litigation, they hoped to control any other Holocaust litigation in which they would seek fees" (docket number 1197). As they did. Neuborne is also given to highlighting that the Swiss banks settlement "benefit[s] not only Jews but other victims or targets of Nazi persecution." See letter to *The Nation*, dated 5 October 2000. In fact, not only did the "other victims" receive barely a pittance, but it was Neuborne who strenuously fought to minimize disbursements to non-Jews. See 162 in this volume, and *The Victim's Fortune*, 354.

[25] "Notes from phone call from Judge Korman to CRT on 6 June 2002."

investigation was to be done by staff attorneys) and – apart from the American, Roberts B. Owen – senior judges couldn't have experienced adjustment "difficulty," let alone acted like judges, because none was asked to take any action at all during CRT-II. In fact, Neuborne's obscure distinctions are – wittingly or not – beside the point: Didn't CRT-I and CRT-II share the same fundamental mandate of verifying which claims on Swiss accounts were valid and which weren't? To justify eviscerating the standards of proof in CRT-II (i.e., using a yet lower "level of probability"), Neuborne juxtaposes CRT-I, which was "adjudicative" between claimants and banks, against CRT-II, which is confined to Holocaust victims who form a "family."[26] But wasn't the very point of the CRT process to determine who was and who wasn't a member of the "family"? Indeed, each claim wrongly approved means money subtracted from the residual fund for a Holocaust-victims health plan[27] – or, to quote Bradfield, "to the extent that you give it out to people who aren't entitled, you're being unfair to the members of the class." Echoing Neuborne, Bradfield states that "the departed employees had inherited various approaches and attitudes from CRT-I that needed to be changed," and emphasized that the revamped CRT-II would be based on what he called a "new cul-

---

[26] Interview with Burt Neuborne on 25 July 2002. Unless otherwise indicated, all Neuborne quotes and paraphrases are from this interview.

[27] Neuborne has recommended that residuals from the $800 million allocated for Holocaust-victim accounts be used for a health plan. See *NAHOS: The Newsletter of the National Association of Jewish Child Holocaust Survivors* (16 October 2001).

ture."[28] Exactly what this expression means was spelled out in a pep talk by Judge Korman to the newly reconstituted CRT-II. From the inception of CRT-I, Korman explained, "the people involved had a mindset of denying claims."[29] This remarkable assertion merits close scrutiny. The CRT-I Secretariat comprised 125 lawyers, paralegals, accountants, and so forth from twenty-five different countries. Board of Trustees members Paul Volcker and Rabbi Israel Singer (of the World Jewish Congress) had approved the seventeen eminent senior arbitrators hailing from seven different countries, including four each from Israel and the United States, while Bradfield managed the administration. The CRT-I rules of procedure explicitly provided for challenging an arbitrator's independence or integrity, and the arbitrators themselves established separate procedures to exclude the possibility and appearance of bias. The Tribunal received only one formal challenge of an arbitrator's impartiality, and claimants appealed only a tiny percentage of decisions. Riemer's final report is replete with illustrations pointing up the Tribunal's irreproachable treatment of claimants (cf. 31, 51–3). It further bears recalling that Korman himself approved extending the life of CRT-I into CRT-II based on the positive experience of CRT-I, and that the generous "plausibility" standard of proof used in CRT-I was – by all accounts – scrupulously adhered to in CRT-II as well. To listen to Korman now, however, Tribunal personnel have been engaged in a grand conspiracy of "denying claims." Bettering Korman, Neuborne alleges that lurking behind

---

[28] Born, "Awarding the millions, eyes closed."
[29] "Notes from phone call from Judge Korman to CRT on 6 June 2002."

the CRT claim denials are the Swiss bankers playing a "public relations game. They don't want the last sentence in the chapter to be
that they gave away $800 million to bank account holders; they
want to say that they found only a few [legitimate claimants]," and
were "blackmailed."[30] Yet, according to Riemer's final report on
CRT-I, "after initial misunderstandings were overcome, the Banks'
participation was generally cooperative and communication with
them constructive," while Bradfield categorically states that the
Swiss banks haven't played – indeed, according to Neuborne himself, *elected* not to play – any role whatsoever in CRT-II.

The real "public relations game" is perhaps the one being played by
Bradfield, Korman and Neuborne. Apparently dreading that the last
word will be that the Swiss banks were blackmailed, they have seized
total control of the new CRT-II. Korman acclaims Neuborne as "a
brilliant scholar and advocate," while Neuborne acclaims Korman as
"one of the most respected and fairest of American judges. He's a
really wonderful man, extraordinary."[31] The reciprocal esteem
touches, but where are the checks and balances? The procedural rules
for CRT-II have been amended to eliminate all independent judges
from the claims process, while the staff now consists mainly of young

---

[30] John Authers and William Hall, "Judge angers Swiss on Holocaust cash," in
Financial Times (12 June 2002).

[31] "Final Approval Order" (26 July 2000) in *In re Holocaust Victim Assets Litigation*
96 Civ. 4849 (ERK) (MDG). Judge Korman never misses an occasion to
publicly praise Neuborne's "brilliance." See, for instance, his "Memorandum"
dated 29 July 2002 (docket number 1308). Recall, incidentally, that during
the Swiss banks litigation, these two members of the mutual admiration
society served, respectively, as presiding judge and chief plaintiff counsel.

American lawyers handpicked by Bradfield. Korman justifies the latter on the grounds that "it's because of young Americans that every mess in Europe was cleaned up by this country."[32]

Korman has the final say on all rules of procedure and all claim decisions are subject to his final approval. To preempt the blackmail charge, nothing bars Judge Korman from revising these rules and approving claims until he reaches the desired number of claim approvals and the desired amount of award per approval. Indeed, the first order of business was to do precisely this. In a February 2002 letter to Judge Korman, Neuborne stated regarding CRT-II that "at the present rate, distributions will approach, if they do not exceed, the $800 million allocated to the deposited assets class." If Neuborne truly believed this, one wonders why he urged Judge Korman in late April 2002 to further relax the relaxed standards of proof. As it happened Neuborne's zeal proved in this instance gratuitous – the relaxation he proposed had already been incorporated in the CRT-II rules favoring claimants.[33] In early June, however, Bradfield did recommend and Korman approved a crucial revision: substantially larger sums than hitherto would be paid out on accounts with modest

---

[32] "Notes from phone call from Judge Korman to CRT on 6 June 2002."

[33] See Burt Neuborne's letter to Judge Korman, dated 26 February 2002, and attached declaration, and Neuborne's letter to Judge Korman, dated 11 April 2002 (docket numbers 1171, 1172 and 1205). For the CRT-II rules already incorporating Neuborne's recommendation, see Roger M. Witten's letter to Judge Korman, dated 16 May 2002. (This highly illuminating letter by Witten, a lawyer for the Swiss banks, was never docketed.) The presumptions on behalf of claimants that Neuborne proposed had already been incorporated in Article 34 of the *Rules*.

balances. (This increment is apart from the very generous compensation for interest and bank fees routinely paid on all approved claims.)
Bradfield justified this rule change on the grounds that a small
Holocaust-victim account must have been subject to "bank manipulation."[34] When he first proposed the rule change with this justification
in September 2001, the CRT staff, although willing to go along,
dismissed his hypothesis as "without any rational or factual basis (many
depositors deplete their accounts down to low levels)."[35] Indeed, as
noted above, the Volcker Committee found no evidence that the
Swiss banks systematically looted Holocaust-victim accounts. Under
CRT-I, the amount paid out per validated Holocaust-victim account
averaged $50,000. It now averages $115,000.[36] In addition, not a
single one of the 32,000 claims filed under CRT-II has to date been
officially rejected.

In a July 2002 letter to CRT-II staff members, Bradfield announced
that the Jewish Claims Conference (headed by Israel Singer) was being
brought in to help process claims.[37] Among its "important" responsibilities would be the re-examination of the 20,000 claims not
matching names on Holocaust-victim accounts, which even Neuborne

[34] Michael Bradfield "Memorandum" to Judge Korman, "Comparison of CRT-I
and CRT-II Rules," dated 16 July 2002 (not docketed). The new method of
calculation was incorporated in Article 35 of the *Rules*.

[35] *Owen Letter.*

[36] See Bradfield's official report filed with the Court on 28 November 2002
(docket number 1487). The "total of all the Awards to date amounts to
$50,352,616.14."

[37] Letter to "Claims Resolution Tribunal Staff Members," dated 12 July 2002
(not docketed). For the sordid record of the Jewish Claims Conference, see
chap. 3 in this volume.

assumed would "almost certainly" be rejected unless new information turned up. Neuborne states that the Claims Conference was enlisted because of the "brilliant job" it has done thus far in identifying and providing compensation for 105,000 Jewish former slave-laborers, with 40–45,000 more claims likely to be approved soon.[38] In fact, it has performed a veritable miracle. According to the world's leading authority on the Nazi holocaust, Raul Hilberg, the total number of Jewish former slave-laborers still alive in May 1945 was "well under 100,000."[39] Even the World Jewish Congress acknowledges that no more than 20 percent of the Holocaust survivors from May 1945 are still alive today[40] – or a maximum of 20,000 still living Jewish former slave laborers. If the Claims Conference can find 150,000 still living Jewish former slave laborers, who can doubt that it can turn the 20,000 claims "almost certainly" headed for rejection into approvals? (The names of these 150,000 alleged Jewish former slave laborers are "submitted under seal to the Court by the Claims Conference" – which means no one will ever know who they are, or if they even exist.[41])

[38] As of its "Report and Recommendations," dated 22 August 2002, the Claims Conference asserts it has paid 115,199 Jewish slave laborers (docket number 1353).

[39] Interview with Raul Hilberg on 22 April 2002. Respected scholars like Henry Friedlander reach the same figure (see 81 in this volume).

[40] *The Victim's Fortune*, 368.

[41] The quoted phrase "submitted under seal . . ." is standard in every request by the Claims Conference to the Court for monies from the Swiss settlement fund to compensate Jewish slave laborers. See, for instance, "Report and Recommendations of the Conference on Jewish Material Claims Against Germany, Inc. for the Fifth Group of Slave Labor Class I Claims" in *In re*

According to Neuborne, Judge Korman "will only scan in a quick way and in batches the approvals." The wonder will be if he does even that much. To date, Korman has rubber-stamped all of Bradfield's approval recommendations, however implausibly argued.[42]

Holocaust Victims Assets Litigations (Swiss Banks), dated 11 March 2002 (docket number 1180). The Claims Conference has estimated that ultimately 170,000–180,000 Jewish slave laborers will be identified. See Greg Schneider's letter to Judge Korman, dated 18 January 2002 (docket number 1140). This last figure technically includes 30,000 Jewish former forced laborers classified as Jewish slave laborers in the distribution plan for the Swiss monies.

[42] Korman has also rubber-stamped all of Bradfield's requests to cover CRT administrative expenses – recently averaging more than *one million dollars per month* – which are deducted from the $1.25 billion settlement fund. For these expenses, see Greg Schneider's letter to Judge Korman dated 17 September 2002 (docket number 1402). Serious allegations have been leveled about administrative waste, but this writer cannot independently assess them. Apparently in only one instance did a counsel for plaintiffs explicitly question administrative costs. Concerned about a supplemental request by the Claims Conference for nearly a million dollars, attorney Robert Swift wrote Judge Korman on 2 November 2001: "I think it is time to test the basis for the . . . application and determine whether past expenditures were appropriately distributed and whether future requested expenditures are prudent" (docket number 1096). The Claims Conference denied Swift's charges, and Korman sustained the Claims Conference, granting its request. See Jean M. Geoppinger's letter to Judge Korman, dated 20 November 2001, and Judge Korman's "Order," dated 28 November 2001 (docket numbers 1099 and 1098). In a prior letter to Judge Korman regarding a $2 million allocation to the Claims Conference, Swift had recommended the "employment of an accountant . . . to assure . . . that the settlement fund is being spent wisely and the work is being done productively" (9 March 2001; not docketed) – which the Claims Conference promptly shot down: "There is absolutely no foundation for Mr. Swift's thinly-veiled accusations" (letter dated 4 April 2001; docket number 982).

Against all available evidence in each respective case, one approved claim maintained that Swiss banks denied a Holocaust victim access to an open account, a second approved claim maintained that the original account holder hadn't already collected his proceeds, while a third approved claim maintained that the Swiss banks looted the account.[43]

---

[43] See *www.crt-ii.org*, under "Awards," respectively, in re Account of Hedwig Wetzlar (claim number 205408), in re Accounts of Ivo Herman (claim number 207328/HM), and in re Account of Illes Fillenz (claim number 206733/MBC). In his *Letter*, Owen recalled: "After Bradfield had identified some practices engaged in by some Swiss Banks during World War II, he demanded that I include, in every Award, a description of the practices and then to *presume* that the particular bank in the particular case had subjected the particular account owner to those practices, even if there was no evidence of such behaviour by the particular bank, and even if the point was not necessary to make an Award" (emphasis in original). Owen refused, and eventually Bradfield "backed down." Regarding Bradfield's repeated assertion that "Account Owners and their heirs would not have been able to access accounts after the War" (see, for instance, his letter to Judge Korman, dated 1 October 2002, docket number 1416), a CRT attorney with impeccable credentials commented: "This is based on nothing. It is true that banks often (too often) stonewalled heirs (often by interpreting the secrecy laws too rigidly – but those were the laws). It is also true that banks often refused to help Account Owners themselves who had their accounts confiscated by the Nazis . . ., thus blocking former Account Owners from claiming restitution from Germany. But there is no evidence that, when the account was still open after the war and the account owner survived, the banks refused to recognize the account owner himself" (private communication). The Volcker Committee also reached this conclusion (see below).

3. Publication of the Bergier Commission *Final Report* and its use to discredit the Volcker Committee findings

In early 2002, an international commission mandated by a 1996 Swiss government decree and chaired by the Swiss historian Jean-François Bergier released its *Final Report*, *Switzerland, National Socialism and the Second World War*.[44] The 600-page document summarizes and places in broader historical context specialized research studies filling twenty-five volumes. Polemical in tone and thrust, the *Final Report* of the Bergier Commission holds Swiss political and business elites to an impressively high standard of ethical and legal accountability – although it must be said that, notwithstanding their pretenses, it requires precious little moral courage and reaps considerable institutional rewards for Swiss academics to flog Swiss banks. (The moral courage required of an American academic sitting on the commission is even less and the institutional rewards are even greater.) Like many polemics, the *Final Report* is cast in overheated rhetoric – Switzerland's wartime record is said to "beggar the imagination" (493) – and is replete with exaggerations, omissions and distortions. The report rightly condemns Swiss elites for refusing entry to "several thousand" Jews fleeing the Nazi death machine but then overreaches in its conclusion that Swiss refugee policy played an "instrumental" role in the Final Solution (168). It highlights the fact that Swiss banks purchased gold looted by the Nazis from Holocaust victims – "the clearest material link between Swiss banking and Nazi genocide"

[44] Zurich: 2002.

(249–50) – but omits mention of the key finding from the Bergier Commission's specialized study on gold transactions that the Swiss banks didn't *knowingly* purchase the "victim gold."[45] The report rightly deplores the fact that after the war Switzerland occasionally served as a hiding place or staging post for fleeing Nazis, yet it further maintains that this policy went "against the post-war strategies of the victorious Allies" (387) – managing to ignore the US's deliberate and massive recruitment of segments of the Nazi elites (including senior SS officers) deemed useful for US projects.[46] It rightly scores the pervasive anti-Semitism in prewar Switzerland, but then claims that because this hostility was "mainly verbal" and "non-violent," it was "all the more dangerous for not causing any feelings of guilt amongst the population" (496–7). Would it really have been better if the Swiss murdered Jews? Finally, the report's conclusion enumerates multiple reasons for the renewed interest in Switzerland's wartime record and post-war record on Holocaust compensation but never once mentions the massive campaign of American Jewish organizations and the Clinton administration targeting Switzerland (493–8).[47] Truly, this is *Hamlet* without the Prince of Denmark.

The Volcker Committee concluded regarding the charges against the Swiss banks that there was "no evidence of systematic discrimina-

---

[45] Independent Commission of Experts, Switzerland – Second World War, *Switzerland and Gold Transactions in the Second World War, Interim Report* (Bern: 1998), IV.

[46] See, for instance, Tom Bower, *The Paperclip Conspiracy* (London: 1987), as well as Christopher Simpson, *Blowback* (London: 1988), and *The Splendid Blond Beast* (New York: 1993).

[47] There is one passing, vague allusion to "recent international criticism" (494).

tion, obstruction of access, misappropriation, or violation of document retention requirements of Swiss law," and "no evidence of
systematic destruction of records for the purpose of concealing past
behavior."[48] It is now alleged by Korman and Neuborne that the
Bergier Commission *Final Report* disproves these central findings of
the Volcker Committee. According to Korman, "the only history
that's relevant . . . is in the Bergier report . . ., the history of how
the banks obstructed survivors," while Neuborne maintains that the
Final Report demonstrates "the systematic deception practiced by the
banks, and the conscious reliance on the destruction of documents to
cover up the wrongdoing."[49] In a novel twist, Bradfield argues both
that "the Bergier Report clearly demonstrates that the Swiss banks
actively maintained a multifaceted policy of resisting claims of Nazi
victims," and that the Volcker Committee reached "similar findings."[50]
Before considering these claims, two anomalies deserve mention:

(1) Before publication of the *Final Report*, Neuborne and Korman
maintained that the Volcker audit itself supported the charges leveled
against the Swiss banks. "The significance of the report of the Volcker
Committee," Korman told the Court, "is that it provided legal and
moral legitimacy to the claims asserted" by the plaintiffs.[51] Neuborne

---

[48] *Report on Dormant Accounts*, Annex 5, p. 81; Part I, p. 6.

[49] Neuborne's letter to Judge Korman, dated 11 April 2002 (docket number
1205).

[50] Bradfield's letter to Judge Korman, dated 10 May 2002 (docket number
1224). Bradfield adduces the Bergier Commission *Final Report* to justify
revision of the CRT-II *Rules*. Yet, if the Bergier Commission reached "similar
findings" to the Volcker Committee, why didn't Bradfield implement the
revision after publication of the Volcker Report?

[51] "Final Approval Order" (26 July 2000).

similarly stated that the "Volcker audit validated the core allegations underlying the Swiss bank litigation."[52] Depositing the Volcker report in Orwell's memory hole, Neuborne and Korman now brandish the *Final Report* to vindicate the assault on the Swiss banks.

(2) The Volcker Committee investigation was – in Korman's words – "the most extensive audit in history," costing $500 million.[53] The two main forces behind the audit were Paul Volcker and Michael Bradfield. If, as Korman claims, the Bergier Commission *Final Report* invalidates the key findings of the Volcker Committee, then Volcker and Bradfield must have colossally bungled the investigation. One can't but wonder why Korman still retains Volcker and Bradfield as Special Masters for CRT-II.

A central piece of evidence cited from the Bergier Commission *Final Report* is a May 1954 meeting at which – in Neuborne's words – "the Swiss banking industry adopted common practices designed to frustrate efforts to trace funds that had been improperly transferred to the Nazis."[54] The passage Neuborne gestures to in the *Final Report* is culled from the Bergier Commission's specialized study devoted to dormant Swiss accounts (volume 15) by Barbara Bonhage, Hanspeter Lussy and Marc Perrenoud.[55] The *Final Report* typically exaggerates: whereas the Bonhage et al. volume makes passing reference to a

---

[52] Letter to *The Nation* (19 February 2002).

[53] "Final Approval Order" (26 July 2000).

[54] Neuborne's letter to Judge Korman, dated 11 April 2002 (docket number 1205).

[55] *Nachrichtenlose Vermogen bei Schweizer Banken Depots, Konen und Safes von Opfen des nationalsozialistischen Regimes und Restitutionsprobleme in der Nachkriegszeit.* Veroffentlichunger der UEK Band 15 (Zurich: 2001).

meeting of "the legal representatives of some big banks" (288), the *Final Report* prominently features this meeting of "the legal representatives of *the* big banks" (446; my emphasis). Even worse, Neuborne mangles the passage from the *Final Report* – it refers not to "funds . . . improperly transferred to the Nazis" but rather to "unclaimed victims' assets." The specialized Bergier study by Bonhage et al. explicitly confirms the key findings of the Volcker Committee (33). Indeed, for all its hyperbole, the Bergier *Final Report* itself never repudiates the Volcker Committee. Quite the contrary. Although the *Final Report* frequently renders critical judgments on prior investigations of relevant topics (31, 246), nowhere does it even hint at a reservation regarding the Volcker findings. Rather, the *Final Report* stipulates that its more "general" assessment relies entirely on the Volcker audit (34), and that "all in all" its conclusions "are borne out by the findings of the Volcker Committee" (456). The *Final Report* specifically dismisses the claim that the Swiss banks "systematically and concertedly attempted to cover up their tracks" by destroying records as "an ill-conceived conspiracy theory" (40).[56] Pointing up her study's confirmation of the Volcker findings, Barbara Bonhage

[56] In multiple submissions to the Court, Bradfield has continued to maintain regarding closed accounts that Swiss banks were "responsible for maintaining complete records," and that they "did not maintain the appropriate records on account disposition." See, for instance, his letter to Judge Korman, dated 15 August 2002 (docket number 1358). Yet under Swiss law, banks were not required to keep records on closed accounts beyond ten years. It ought to be remembered that there were no computers back then, so preserving anything meant huge space dedicated to physical files. That the banks have preserved anything on closed accounts is beyond the requirements of the law.

observed that it was "a pity that the Bergier Report is exploited," and that the findings of the Volcker Committee and Bergier Commission "supplement each other – one should not play one off against the other."[57]

~

From early on Raul Hilberg repeatedly charged that the Swiss banks were being "blackmailed." Burt Neuborne, clearly shaken by the blackmail allegation, called on Judge Korman to repudiate it, which the Judge dutifully did.[58] When the processing of claims against the Swiss banks threatened to confirm Hilberg's charge (now echoed even by the mainstream media),[59] the CRT-I final report was suppressed, the CRT-II staff was sacked, and the findings of the Bergier Commission *Final Report* were misrepresented. Will Bradfield, Korman and Neuborne now squander Swiss monies earmarked for Holocaust victims on invalid claims in order to protect their reputations? It seems all bases are being covered. When a Swiss bank guard, Christopher Meilli, alleged that the Swiss banks were destroying key

---

[57] *Tages Anzeiger* (1 June 2002). For Bradfield's (mis)use of the Bonhage et al. study to justify rule changes, see his letter to Judge Korman, dated 23 May 2002 (docket number 1245).

[58] For references, see 154n5 in this volume, and Raul Hilberg interviews posted on *www.NormanFinkelstein.com* under "The Holocaust Industry." This writer independently reached the same conclusion as Hilberg (see chap. 3 in this volume).

[59] Sheleg ("A long and winding road . . .") observes that the few Holocaust-victim accounts found in the Swiss banks "could mean that the Jewish representatives will be seen as having waged an international battle over a sum far higher than deserves to be paid out."

documents, he was lauded in the US (his new home) as a martyr and hero. Quickly souring on his new benefactors, however, Meilli has repeatedly denounced the corruption of those assailing the Swiss banks.[60] Seven pages into a February 2002 letter to Judge Korman regarding lawyers' fees, Burt Neuborne suddenly recommended a *one million dollar* payment "as a special lawyers' disbursement" to Meilli "for the losses that he suffered in an effort to tell the truth," and in March 2002, Korman approved this disbursement.[61] In the settlement Neuborne negotiated with German industry, each Auschwitz survivor received a $7,500 payment.

---

[60] *The Victim's Fortune*, 32–6. The disgust was communicated in personal correspondence initiated by Meilli with this writer.

[61] Neuborne's letter to Judge Korman, dated 26 February 2002, and attached declaration, and Judge Korman, "Order," dated 15 March 2002 (docket numbers 1171, 1172 and 1186). In accordance with Neuborne's recommendation, Korman ordered that Meilli immediately be given an initial payment of $775,000.

APPENDIX TO THE SECOND PAPERBACK EDITION

PERFECT INJUSTICE
A reply to Stuart E. Eizenstat's *Imperfect Justice:*
Looted Assets, Slave Labor, and the Unfinished Business
of World War II [1]

I believe the most lasting legacy of the effort I led was simply the
emergence of the truth . . . (346)

I.

President Clinton's term of office coincided with a curious chapter in
the annals of US diplomacy: the campaign for Holocaust compensation. Acting in concert with an array of powerful American Jewish
organizations and individuals, the Clinton administration extracted
from European countries billions of dollars, which had allegedly been

---

[1] New York: Public Affairs, 2003. All parenthetical references in the body of
the text refer to Eizenstat's book.

stolen from Holocaust victims during and after World War II. A key
role in this Clinton initiative was played by Stuart Eizenstat, who held
multiple senior positions in the Clinton administration but apparently
devoted most of his tenure to Holocaust compensation. (Previously,
as chief White House domestic policy advisor to President Carter, he
recommended and mediated creation of the US Holocaust Museum to
allay Jewish fury over Carter's recognition of the "legitimate rights"
of Palestinians and the sale of weaponry to Saudi Arabia.)[2] In *Imperfect
Justice*, Eizenstat provides an authoritative insider account of the
negotiations with, and pressures exerted on, European governments
and private industry. Containing crucial revelations as well as crucial
omissions, his account confirms that the campaign for Holocaust
compensation actually constituted a "double shakedown" of European
countries and Holocaust victims; and that its most lasting legacy was
to pollute memory of the Nazi holocaust with yet more lies and
hypocrisy.

Making little pretense to impartiality and evidently practiced in the
art of currying favor with power, Eizenstat portrays the main players
in the Holocaust shakedown in glowing tones. Edgar Bronfman, the
multibillionaire heir to the Seagram's liquor fortune and president of
the World Jewish Congress (WJC), "cut a dashing figure – tall,
handsome and debonair" (52). In Congressional testimony this liquor
salesman turned megalomaniacal diplomat claimed to represent all of
world Jewry, the living as well as the dead.[3] Rabbi Israel Singer,
Bronfman's sidekick and the executive director of the WJC, was

[2] For the US Holocaust Museum, see 72–8 in this volume. (Hereafter: *HI*.)
[3] *HI*, 90.

"charming yet roguish . . . brilliant, fast-talking, a gifted speaker, magnetic" (53). Others recalled this cynical vulgarian with his trademark black knit yarmulke cocked at an angle less fondly. "The way he talks to us is unbelievable," the normally reserved Swiss bankers exclaimed, "his tone and his manner" (134). Even a leading Holocaust industry class-action attorney concluded that for Singer "truth is a random event" (226). Anti-Defamation League national director Abraham Foxman, who specializes in character defamation when not embroiled in yet another scandal,[4] is said to be "widely admired" (125); the notoriously corrupt former senator from New York, Alfonse D'Amato, wins praise for his "remarkable energy, gusto, and political instincts that come straight from the gut"; and Lawrence Eagleburger, raking in $360,000 annually (for an average of roughly one workday per week) as head of the International Commission on Holocaust-Era Insurance Claims, gets high marks for "his sense of duty" (62, 267). On the other hand, Eizenstat excoriates the president of Belarus, Aleksandr Lukashenko, as an "iron fist" dictator (37). In fact, Lukashenko's main sin for the likes of Eizenstat is that he "is not given to taking orders" from Washington – or from the Holocaust industry, which has sought unsuccessfully to blackmail Belarus for Holocaust compensation.[5]

Replete with half-truths and hyperbole, Eizenstat's book also bears the earmarks of a Holocaust industry publication. He points to the

---

[4] See *HI*, 22, 65–6, "Anti-Defamation League (ADL) Letter to Georgetown University," at *www.NormanFinkelstein.com* (under "The real 'Axis of Evil' "), and the Marc Rich scandal below.

[5] See John Laughland, "The Prague racket," in *Guardian* (22 November 2002), and *HI*, 133.

"1941 murder of 1,600 Jews in the [Polish] village of Jedwabne" (42), although the total figure (awful enough) was almost certainly closer to a few hundred,[6] and declares rhetorically that "like the Holocaust itself, the efficiency, brutality, and scale of the Nazi art theft was unprecedented in history" (187).[7] He also reports without demurral the unverified claims of Holocaust survivors to looted assets and Swiss bank accounts; for example, the allegation of a Slovak Jewish leader that "his mother, who was so anxious to put her shattering wartime experiences behind her that she threw away the receipt for her personal effects" (36), and the never-substantiated testimonies of key witnesses in the Swiss banks case like Greta Beer (4, 46–8; on 183 Eizenstat concedes that "the truth will never be known" regarding Beer's frankly ludicrous story). Finally, Eizenstat repeats commonplaces of the Holocaust industry such as "it is ironic that [Switzerland's] bank secrecy laws were invoked against the families seeking

---

[6] See "The final findings of the investigation regarding the events in Jedwabne on July 10, 1941" (9 July 2002) at *http://www.ipn.gov.pl*.

[7] In typical Holocaust industry style, Michael J. Bazyler begins his book on Holocaust reparations with the declaration – neither argued nor documented – that "The Holocaust was both the greatest murder and the greatest theft in history." Elsewhere he writes that "the Nazi art confiscation program" during the Holocaust was "the greatest displacement of art in human history," and Hitler "spent more on art then [sic] anybody in the history of the world" (quoting another Holocaust industry historian). (Michael J. Bazyler, *Holocaust Justice* [New York: 2003], xi, 202) In his insightful study, *The Language of the Third Reich* (New York: 2002), Victor Klemperer recalls the Nazis' chauvinist mania for "superlatives" and kindred qualifiers like "unique" (110, 214, 215–24). For analysis of the Holocaust industry's "inverted" linguistic chauvinism ("greatest crime," "unique crime"), see *HI*, 41–9.

their accounts, since these laws had been passed in 1934 to provide a safe haven from the Nazis" (48) – whereas in fact the main purpose of the 1934 law "was not . . . to protect the assets of Jewish customers from confiscation by the Nazi regime."[8]

To account for the sudden public concern in the mid-1990s for Holocaust compensation Eizenstat initially contends that "Holocaust survivors . . . began to tell long-suppressed stories and now sought a measure of justice for what had been stripped of them" (4). *"Began* to tell . . .": one wonders where Eizenstat has been during the boom years of the Holocaust industry the past quarter of a century. He goes on, however, to concede that "Edgar Bronfman, the billionaire head of the World Jewish Congress, was politically well connected and a strong supporter of the president and first lady. He urged them . . . to take a personal interest in providing belated justice to Holocaust survivors" (5); and that Bronfman was "one of the largest donors to Bill Clinton's presidential campaign" and the Clinton administration was "under political pressure from Edgar Bronfman" to "restor[e] confiscated Jewish property" (57, 25). Indeed, Bronfman was among the top five individual donors (and maybe number one) to the Democratic National Committee for the 1996 election cycle, while "'Jewish money' is widely believed to account for about half the funding of the Democratic National Committee" and "also accounts for about half of Democratic presidential campaign funding – slightly more in the case of a candidate highly popular with Jews, like Bill

---

[8] Independent Commission of Experts, *Final Report, Switzerland, National Socialism and the Second World War* (Zurich: 2002), 261. (Hereafter: Bergier *Final Report.*)

Clinton."[9] The campaign for Holocaust compensation was so closely linked with powerful American Jewish interests that one of the main conferences on looted Nazi gold was purposely convened in London "so it would not appear that the entire restitution effort was simply an American idea driven by the American Jewish community" (112).

Nonetheless, Eizenstat emphatically denies that the Clinton administration acted from strictly mercenary motives. Although "political and economic self-interest, realpolitik, is the primary force behind European foreign policy," he observes, "not so in the United States. Even the most sophisticated Europeans fail to appreciate that U.S. foreign policy is a unique and complicated mixture of morality and self-interest" (5; cf. 272). Who can suspect Clinton's ethical impulses? During his last hours in office, Clinton pardoned Marc Rich, a billionaire commodities trader who fled to Switzerland in 1983 before standing trial on an indictment for fifty-one counts of tax evasion, racketeering and violating trade sanctions with Iran. Building a multibillion-dollar business empire from his Swiss redoubt, Rich became a major benefactor of Jewish and Israeli organizations, while simultaneously – and with perfect consistency – cultivating lucrative ties with the Russian mafia. The recipients of Rich's largesse such as ADL head Abraham Foxman (who initiated the idea of a presidential pardon), as well as U.S. Holocaust Museum chairman Rabbi Irving Greenberg, Ehud Barak, Shimon Peres and possibly Elie Wiesel,

---

[9] Information on Bronfman obtained from Douglas Weber of the Center for Responsive Politics (*www.opensecrets.org*); for background on Bronfman's wealth, see *http://www.motherjones.com/coinop_congress/97mojo_400/profile5.html*. J.J. Goldberg, *Jewish Power* (Reading, MA: 1996), 275–6 ("Jewish money"). (Goldberg is editor of *The Forward*, the main national Jewish newspaper.)

subsequently lobbied Clinton on Rich's behalf. Only unsophisticated Europeans, however, would doubt that the impetus behind the presidential pardon – for which there was "almost no precedent in American history" (Clinton) – was clemency.[10]

II.

The centerpiece of Eizenstat's account is the Swiss banks case, which inaugurated and served as the template for the blackmail campaign. The Holocaust industry alleged that Swiss banks denied Holocaust victims and heirs access to their accounts after the war.[11] Eizenstat reports that at the first meeting in September 1995 between the main protagonists, Edgar Bronfman avowed that "he was not interested in a lump-sum settlement but in establishing a reliable process for finding out what was actually in the accounts and paying them to their rightful owners," and the Swiss bankers agreed in principle to this proposal (59); that in December 1995 the World Jewish Restitution Organization (WJRO, a spin-off of the WJC) and the Swiss Bankers Association

[10] Niles Latham, "Marc Rich Was 'A Mossad' Spy for Israel," in *New York Post* (5 February 2001) (multi-billion dollar). Mathew E. Berger, "Did Pollard Pay For Efforts to Pardon Rich?," in *Jewish Telegraphic Agency* (13 February 2001) (Wiesel). Melissa Radler, "Foxman: I 'Probably' Shouldn't Have Asked for Rich Pardon," in *Jerusalem Post* (22 March 2001). Alison Leigh Cowan, "Supporter of Pardon For Fugitive Has Regrets," in *New York Times* (24 March 2001). P.K. Semler, "Marc Rich Was 'A Mossad' Spy For Israel," in *Washington Times* (21 June 2002) (Russian mafia). Andrew Silow-Carroll, "The Featherman File," in *Forward* (24 August 2001) ("no precedent").

[11] For background, see *HI*, 89–120.

(SBA) "reached the bare-bones outline of a deal" in which "the banks would open their files for a review of the dormant accounts, and the Jewish side would inspect them in confidence" (63); that before Senator D'Amato's April 1996 Senate hearing on the Swiss banks the SBA "faxed Singer a proposal for an independent audit" and "wrote D'Amato offering an independent audit" (66); and that the SBA representative at the Senate hearings "did his best to indicate that the Swiss banks would try to search for more dormant accounts and announced the banks' willingness to accept an independent audit" (68).[12] In May 1996 the independent audit was formalized in a "Memorandum of Understanding" between the SBA and Jewish representatives and, despite escalating pressures by the Holocaust industry to abort it, the Swiss bankers steadfastly supported the audit "to restor[e] our honor and the confidence in the banks by disproving the allegations" (153; cf. 119). To demonstrate Swiss recalcitrance, however, Eizenstat repeatedly resorts to distorting the chronology and dynamic of these negotiations. He states that if the Swiss banks had initially been "forthcoming about . . . an independent audit, the whole affair might have ended right there" (59) – although they acquiesced in an audit from the first meeting with Bronfman; that D'Amato's hearing "propelled . . . the idea of a having the wartime accounts audited" (69) – although the Swiss banks already agreed to the terms of the audit before the hearing;

---

[12] This discussion will not treat the trivialities featured in the press as well as sensationalist book-length accounts such as the alleged failure of the Swiss bankers to offer Bronfman a chair at their first encounter in September 1995; for a rebuttal of this allegation, see the letter of Dr. Georg F. Krayer, chairman of the Swiss Bankers Association, to Edgar Bronfman (13 March 1997; private source).

that the support tendered by the Swiss banks at the Senate hearing for an audit "was seen simply as a reflection of the banks' party line" (68) – as if it were the banks and not the Holocaust industry that demanded the audit; and that the Swiss banks feared an audit "in light of their postwar stonewalling tactics and their treatment of dormant accounts" (65) – although they firmly backed the audit's completion notwith-standing the Holocaust industry's opposition.

~

"By the end of the summer of 1996," Eizenstat reports, "the Swiss banking controversy was contained. The Volcker Committee was off and running, and an independent audit of Swiss bank accounts would soon begin – the goal of the WJC and of the U.S. government" (74). The obvious question is, Why didn't matters end there? Eizenstat's answer is simple: "The lawyers hijacked the Swiss bank dispute" (75). Yet, this explanation strains credulity. In late 1996 several teams of class-action lawyers filed multibillion-dollar suits alleging that, besides profiting from dormant Jewish accounts, Swiss banks benefited finan-cially from Jewish slave labor and looted Jewish assets. Acknowledging that "the lawyers were not in it to find the historical truth" but rather "most were in it for the money" (77), Eizenstat repeatedly points up the flimsiness of these new allegations: "a legal stretch" (116), "no documentary evidence" (118), "to bolster the quicksand on which the bulk of his legal allegations rested, he [Weiss, one of the class-action attorneys] began organizing outside pressure against the Swiss" (122–3), "in fact, they had no evidence upon which to base their demands" (141), "Hausfeld [another of the class-action attorneys] admitted he could not supply a connection that would stand up in court" (143), "I warned the plaintiffs that . . . there had to be some plausible linkage to justify the banks' large payments; they could not simply seem to bend to pressure" (144), "Hausfeld knew the weakness of his legal argument and did not want to expose himself to Swiss inquiries" (168), and so on.[13] On the other side, the SBA "attacked the lawsuits as lacking any legal merit, arguing that Volcker's audit was justice enough" (117) – rightfully so, to judge by Eizenstat's own account. Indeed, he further reports that the Federal judge presiding over the lawsuits, Edward Korman, "had grave doubts about the class-action lawyers' allegations on looted assets and slave labor profits" (121; cf. 168). Finally, Paul Volcker, chairman of the committee auditing the Swiss banks, "considered the lawsuits frivolous and inflammatory in attempting to reach beyond actual dormant accounts to looting and slave labor profits" and "were not necessary to locate dormant accounts" (116). In a formal complaint to Judge Korman, Volcker wrote that the lawsuits were "impairing our work, potentially to the point of ineffectiveness" (121). Beyond their new allegations, class-action lawyers justified the suits on the grounds that "Volcker's audit was a device established by the Swiss banks." Yet, as Eizenstat observes, "This ignored the fact that the audit had been forced upon the banks by Bronfman and Singer" (117).[14] When the class-action

---

[13] In the perfervid imagination of Bazyler, *Holocaust Justice*, Hausfeld had discovered "historical documents [that] became important pieces of legal evidence that he would use later against the Swiss banks to push them into a settlement. If the Swiss banks did not settle, Hausfeld was ready to introduce these documents as prime exhibits during trial" (9).

[14] The lawyers also claimed that its financing by the Swiss compromised the audit, although this monetary burden – as Eizenstat makes clear (72) – was

lawyers "attacked the Volcker process" in court, Judge Korman replied, "Why would Israel Singer sit on Volcker's board if he was a liar" (167)? (Singer was an alternate member of the Volcker Committee.) It also couldn't be argued that the Volcker audit delayed justice because "the results of his committee's work would have to be part of any final settlement" (127), establishing which claimants to dormant Swiss accounts were actually owed money.[15]

If the novel allegations in the lawsuits lacked merit; if Swiss banks agreed to an international audit of dormant accounts (the only plausible allegation); if the audit's findings were vital to any settlement; and if the "class-action lawsuits . . . undercut the Volcker audit" (115), why didn't Judge Korman simply dismiss them? "For over a year, he cleverly sat on the Swiss motions to dismiss the cases," according to Eizenstat, "both to allow the Volcker audit to be completed and to give my negotiations a chance to succeed" (165; cf. 122). These contentions are transparently absurd. On the one hand, the lawsuits "undercut" the audit; and on the other, negotiations wouldn't have been necessary if the lawsuits were dismissed. In fact, despite Volcker's entreaties and much to his ire, Eizenstat himself balked at calling for dismissal of the lawsuits: "Volcker called and accused me of strengthening the plaintiffs' hands by not taking a position against them on behalf of the U.S. government" (122). In his defense, Eizenstat maintains that his arbiter's role precluded taking sides. Yet, did this

---

also imposed on the Swiss (cf. *HI*, 156). Echoing the Holocaust industry lawyers, Bazyler, *Holocaust Justice*, repeatedly asserts the fraudulent claim that creating the Volcker Committee was a "tactic that the Swiss had employed in the litigation filed against them" (132, 179).

[15] See also *HI*, 157.

alleged neutrality warrant effectively sustaining spurious lawsuits? Eizenstat elsewhere pleads impotence: "While I realized the cases would be a bone in the craw of the Swiss, I saw no way of removing it for them" (89). Yet sufficient governmental pressures were miraculously brought to bear later when a lawsuit supported by Federal Judge Shirley Kram and opposed by the US government put in jeopardy the German compensation settlement (she was ordered to dismiss the lawsuit); and sufficient government pressures were miraculously brought to bear later when a lawsuit against IBM filed by Michael Hausfeld and opposed by the US government put in jeopardy the German settlement (he dropped the lawsuit; the pressures exerted on Hausfeld perhaps also sprung from the fact that this time he was suing an *American* company).[16] In fact, as Eizenstat concedes, "the lawsuits

---

[16] For the Kram imbroglio, see Nacha Cattan, "Survivors, German Firms Join Hands To Blast Judge as Shoah Pact Stalls," in *Forward* (20 April 2001), Jane Fritsch, "Judge Clears Obstacles To Pay Slaves Of The Nazis," in *New York Times* (11 May 2001), "Germans Dispute Judge's Order on Pay To Victims of Nazis," in *New York Times* (12 May 2001), "Decision on Nazi Reparations Is Appealed," in *New York Times* (16 May 2001), Jane Fritsch, "One Step Closer To Reparations For Nazi Victims," in *New York Times* (18 May 2001), Nacha Cattan, "With Judge's Ruling, Shoah Pacts Clear 'Last Hurdle,'" in *Forward* (25 May 2001). For the Hausfeld lawsuit, see Betsy Schiffman, "IBM Gets An Ugly History Lesson," in *Forbes* (12 February 2001), Michelle Kessler, "Book links IBM to Holocaust," in *USA Today* (12 February 2001), "Lawyer to drop IBM Holocaust case," in *Reuters* (30 March 2001), Robyn Weisman, "IBM Holocaust Lawsuit Dropped" (*http://www.newsfactor.com/perl/story/8596.html*). In addition to IBM, which allegedly "provided the technology, products, and services that catalogued concentration camp victims and substantially aided the persecution, suffering and genocide experienced in the camps before and during World War II," Hausfeld apparently intended to sue "a further 100

were little more than a platform for a political solution to the conflict" (171), and "the class-action lawyers and Singer would never be able to quantify the losses for which they were demanding reparations, and this realization drove home yet again the unique, political dimension to our negotiations" (144). Put otherwise, the lawsuits served as another lever in the Holocaust industry's extortion campaign. With Eizenstat's backing Judge Korman deferred judgment to put pressure on the Swiss banks for an out-of-court settlement. In the words of Burt Neuborne, the lead Holocaust industry attorney, Judge Korman "played it beautifully" (122; cf. 165).[17] (One can only imagine the

---

American corporations – identified by records culled from the FBI and the United States Treasury Department – as having traded with the Nazi regime," including "leading industrial and chemical companies and some of the top names in US banking" ("Case Watch: Cohen, Milstein, Hausfeld & Toll, P.L.L.C. Files Class Action Lawsuit Against IBM" at http://www.cmht.com/casewatch/cases/cwibm.html; Robert L. Gleiser, "IBM sued, 100 U.S. firms are accused of Nazi links" at http://www.mugu.com/pipermail/upstream-list/2001-February/001393.html). A federal appeals court also struck down a California law enabling World War II slave laborers in mostly Japanese firms to sue for wages and injuries after the federal government filed a brief on behalf of the defendants (Adam Liptak, "Court Dismisses Claims of Slave Laborers," in New York Times (22 January 2003); for the US government's shameless double standard of supporting the Holocaust industry's claims against German industry but opposing comparable claims by its own American POWs against Japanese industry, see Bazyler, Holocaust Justice, 307–17.

[17] For Neuborne's sordid role in the Holocaust shakedown, see HI, 154ff., 168–9, and Postscript to the Second Paperback Edition in this volume. Incidentally, Neuborne himself effectively concedes that, apart from the dormant accounts (which were already subject to the Volcker audit), the claims against the Swiss banks lacked any legal merit. In the German case, Neuborne faults the US courts for dismissing the lawsuits before a settlement

Swiss bankers' aghast reaction to Eizenstat's claim that they respected Judge Korman because he stood for an "independent judiciary" (165–6).)

Holocaust industry lawyers privately acknowledged that the lawsuits served as a façade for extortion: "[Weiss] was up-front with his strategy, without nuances. He wanted to exert external political and economic pressure" (118), "If I needed any reminder that we were in a political, not a legal negotiation, Weiss tartly supplied it: 'Look, the question is going to be how hard we squeeze their balls or how hard they squeeze ours'" (143; cf. 83).[18] While the Holocaust industry's refrain during the Swiss campaign was that "this is about truth and justice, not about money," the reality was that "the plaintiffs' attorneys . . . wanted the certainty of a lump sum and did not want to wait for Volcker to conclude his audit" (155). Although publicly ridiculing the class-action lawyers and claiming only to want an audit to achieve justice, the WJC likewise "insisted" even before the D'Amato hearing "that the Swiss government impose a settlement on the banks" (67); sought from early on in Eizenstat's negotiations a lump-sum final settlement in lieu of awaiting the audit's results (153); vehemently

---

was reached: even if they lacked merit, Neuborne seems to suggest, the courts should have (as in the Swiss case) delayed deciding to pressure the defendants (Burt Neuborne, "Preliminary Reflections on Aspects of Holocaust-Era Litigation in American Courts," in *Washington University Law Quarterly* (Fall 2002), 805n23, 807n31, 816n73).

[18] Neuborne – who claims no less than Aristotle as his mentor on ethics in the Holocaust litigation – repeatedly defers to and heaps praise on "the extraordinary combination of the talents of Mel Weiss and Mike Hausfeld" (Neuborne, "Preliminary Reflections," 292n3, 805n26, 829).

opposed Volcker's letter to Judge Korman because "it would add the [Volcker] committee's prestige to the Swiss banks' motions to dismiss the suits" (121); and "distrusted the lawyers but favored anything that would get more money out of the Swiss banks" (122).

~

Apart from the courts, the Holocaust industry mobilized every level of the US government in its shakedown. In a letter to Bronfman deeming Holocaust compensation "a moral issue and a question of justice," President Clinton urged "the return of Jewish assets in Swiss banks" (68). Enumerating multiple diplomatic demarches, Eizenstat reports that his mediation constituted "an unprecedented involvement by a senior government official in purely private lawsuits" (115), and that "I fielded one of our heaviest guns: I persuaded Madeleine Albright to become the first U.S. secretary of state to visit Switzerland since 1961" (126). In another ground-breaking initiative ordered by Clinton, Eizenstat conscripted 11 federal agencies to produce a report on looted Nazi gold purchased by Swiss banks: "The project demonstrated the awesome resources the U.S. executive branch can muster when it receives presidential backing . . . In the end we made public close to 1 million documents, the largest single declassification in U.S. history" (99–100). (Another senior US official, J.D. Bindenagel, spent "an entire year" [193] preparing a Washington conference on looted Nazi art.) In his foreword to the report on looted Nazi gold, Eizenstat had sensationally asserted that Swiss "trading links with Germany . . . contributed to prolonging one of the bloodiest conflicts in history." He remains adamant in his memoir that "my own personal observations in the foreword are accurate and will withstand historical scrutiny"

(108; cf. 340–1) – although even Switzerland's harshly self-critical Bergier *Final Report* concluded that "the theory which maintains that . . . Switzerland influenced the course of the war to a significant degree could not be substantiated."[19]

While the Eizenstat *Report* (as it came to be called) "did not produce any sensational new revelations,"[20] his foreword along with his pretense of having unearthed scandalous findings still served a useful purpose: "As the facts became clear, the WJRO pressed me to push the Swiss to pay out more funds" (101). The Senate hearings performed a similar function: "Both D'Amato and the WJC wanted the hearings to be as sensational and provocative as possible" (63). In fact Eizenstat unabashedly admits that, as D'Amato's aides disseminated "sensational materials" – "some accurate and some not," with the accurate materials cast as revelations although old news – he (Eizenstat) "tried to help by encouraging the declassification of documents" (63–7). "Because almost all of the documents were already known, the WJC and D'Amato had to spin the information in a new way," a prominent Holocaust industry journalist recently explained. "The only way was to describe the collaborations of Switzerland with Nazi Germany, to move Switzerland from the status of a neutral country to the status of an ally of Germany during the war. Whether it's true or not is a marginal question."[21]

---

[19] Bergier *Final Report*, 518; for the *Final Report*'s penchant for hyperbolic criticism of Swiss policy, see Postscript to the Second Paperback Edition in this volume.

[20] Ibid., 31.

[21] Elli Wohlgelernter, "Media were key in resolving Holocaust restitution issues, reporters tell Yad Vashem conference," in *Jerusalem Post* (1 January 2003), quoting Itamar Levin, deputy editor of the Israeli business magazine *Globes*,

Eizenstat's main achievement was just that: to "move" Switzerland's status – "whether it's true or not."

Ultimately, the threat of US economic sanctions proved the decisive lever. Orchestrated by Alan Hevesi, "the comptroller, or chief financial officer of New York City, who controlled billions of dollars in pension fund investments and business deals with the city and who had visions of being mayor one day" (122–3), the campaign to financially cripple Switzerland spread to state and local governments across the country. "Trying to pollute our own regulatory system," the WJC also put "tremendous pressure" on the New York State banking superintendent to block a newly merged Swiss bank from operating in the US (145). Although publicly denouncing the resort to economic sanctions, Eizenstat makes plain that his opposition was more formal than real: "I was hardly oblivious to the hard fact that they had gotten the attention of the Swiss banks in ways I alone could not" (157; cf. 160). Finally, in a breath-taking analogy, Eizenstat compares the Holocaust industry's enlistment of every level of state power in a multi-pronged extortion campaign to "the days of the Montgomery bus boycott" (355).[22]

~

In August 1998 the Swiss banks finally capitulated and, in a settlement presided over by Judge Korman, agreed to pay $1.25 billion. According

---

and author of *The Last Deposit*, on the Swiss banks case; for Levin, see *HI*, esp. 89, 120.

[22] In Burt Neuborne's fantastical analogy, this massive mobilization of American power to extract money on unfounded claims was reminiscent of "when I boycotted grapes to support farm workers seeking a union contract" (Neuborne, "Preliminary Reflections," 828n117).

to Burt Neuborne, the fact that the Swiss "elected to pay $1.25 billion rather than face" a court trial proved the "validity" of the plaintiffs' case.[23] Yet, as Eizenstat repeatedly acknowledges, the settlement signaled a triumph not of justice but extortion: "Except for the Volcker audits, conducted independently from the lawsuits, the evidentiary essence of the legal process that could have lent legitimacy to the massive settlement was utterly lacking. Not one shred of traditional legal discovery was made. Instead, external pressures and intervention of the US government compensated for serious flaws in the legal case" (177); "The costs of fighting cases that [the Swiss banks] might have won in a court of law had become too steep to sustain in the court of public opinion and in the enormous, profitable U.S. marketplace, where they were operating and hoped to expand" (340; cf. 165). Nonetheless Eizenstat also speculates that the Swiss banks acquiesced in the $1.25 billion settlement for fear that "Volcker would be so thorough that the total would come to more than that and they wanted to cut their losses" (170–1; cf. 166). His own evidence, however, belies this claim. The Swiss banks "calculated that all of the Volcker accounts would still total only about $200 million even when adjusted for the passage of time" (147), and likewise Judge Korman "assumed from his contact with Volcker that the audit would find $200 million in dormant accounts" (170). (The subsequent findings of the Claims Resolution Tribunal demonstrated that in all likelihood even this figure greatly overestimated Swiss liability.)[24] The $200 million figure merits attention for another reason. Analyzing in the first postscript to *The*

---

[23] Letter to *The Nation* (18 February 2002).

[24] See Postscript to the Second Paperback Edition in this volume.

Holocaust Industry the distribution plan for the Swiss monies, I stated that the allocation of $800 million from the $1.25 billion for validated dormant account claims "appears wildly inflated"; and that the Holocaust industry's real motive for this allocation was to pocket the difference. (Had $200 million been allocated for dormant accounts holders, the residual $1.05 billion would have gone directly to Holocaust survivors.)[25] Eizenstat's account confirms that, before the distribution plan was drawn up, it was already known that the $800 million figure bore no relationship to reality, and also suggests who conjured the wildly inflated figure – against all evidence Singer maintained "that the Volcker audits would produce between $600 million and $750 million" (148). Singer's inflation served a double purpose: first, to shakedown the Swiss banks; then, to shakedown Holocaust survivors.

To justify the $1.25 billion settlement in spite of the estimate for Swiss liability from dormant accounts being $200 million and the other claims against the Swiss lacking "one shred" of evidence, Eizenstat proudly brandishes the "novel concept of 'rough justice'" (181), which "may have applicability in future mass violations of human rights" (353): "The whole concept of rough justice was itself a novelty, a new theory to accommodate what amounted to political negotiation, not a legal principle. In any traditional lawsuit, the injured parties must establish a clear nexus, a direct relationship, to the party from whom they seek to recover. This could be done with the bank accounts Volcker was auditing. It could not be done with looted assets and slave labor profits, which had been at expense of people who, if they

[25] *HI*, 163–4.

or their heirs were even alive, could not tie their losses to the three Swiss banks in the class action" (137–8; cf. 130, 353). Yet, using a baseless pretext and extra-legal means to extract money already has a name: it's called a shakedown.

Eizenstat reserves his "greatest wrath" for the Swiss Federal Council. Although he "wanted to get the Swiss government engaged in nego-tiations in order to collect money from them for the settlement pot" and "to share the financial load," the Swiss refused: "The Swiss government was perfectly willing for the U.S. government to bloody itself in trying to settle the cases, . . . but at no cost to themselves" (126, 138, 163). Such ingratitude. The US was "willing . . . to bloody itself" shaking down Swiss banks, but the Swiss government wouldn't allow itself to be shaken down as well. Indeed, Eizenstat reports that even now "the Swiss government has still not fully absorbed the hard lessons of what the country has gone through." For example, "in the spring of 2002, the Swiss government froze military and other government contracts with Israel, in protest against the Israeli govern-ment policies toward the Palestinians" (185). Truly, the Swiss are incorrigible.[26]

---

[26] By all indications, the Holocaust industry has been pursuing against European insurance companies a strategy identical to its Swiss blackmail campaign. Meanwhile the International Commission of Holocaust-Era Insurance Claims (ICHEIC) is embroiled in scandal as it has spent more than $30 million on administrative expenses – including multiple international conferences lasting no more than 24 hours with first-class accommodations and business-class flight arrangements – while distributing only $3 million to Holocaust claim-ants. Shrugging off the criticism, WJC executive director Elan Steinberg said that the "bill is footed by the insurance companies and banks" – i.e. "It's on the goyim" (Yair Sheleg, "Profits of doom," in *Haaretz* [29 June 2001], Henry

After the financial settlement, Eizenstat reports, the Swiss inexplicably soured on the Volcker Committee (178–9). Does this really surprise? Swiss banks had spent hundreds of millions of dollars on "the most extensive and expensive audit in history" (179), yet its findings were pre-empted and $1.25 billion exchanged hands due to "external pressures and intervention of the U.S. government." (Even after the settlement, the audit's "cost was skyrocketing.") Notwithstanding Swiss disenchantment, however, the audit proceeded smoothly and in December 1999 the Volcker Committee published the results of its investigation.[27] Eizenstat dispatches the Committee's conclusions in one lone paragraph (180) – unsurprisingly, since its central finding was that "for victims of Nazi persecution there was no evidence of systematic discrimination, obstruction of access, misappropriation, or

---

Weinstein, "Spending by Holocaust Claims Panel Criticized," in *Los Angeles Times* [17 May 2001]). Apart from its vulgarity, the statement is almost certainly untrue: under the German settlement's terms, administrative expenses are deducted from the $100 million total allotment to policyholders. Typically, the Holocaust industry is now demanding that the German insurers foot its vacation bills. In yet another ICHEIC scandal, Neil Sher, chief of staff of ICHEIC's Washington office, was "investigated for allegedly misappropriating commission funds for personal use before resigning" (Nacha Cattan, "Restitution Exec Was Probed on Spending," in *Forward* [1 November 2002]).

[27] Independent Committee of Eminent Persons, *Report on Dormant Accounts of Victims of Nazi Persecution in Swiss Banks* (Bern: 1999). The report observes that, although "after the settlement of the class action lawsuit in New York in 1998, Swiss banks collectively took a more critical view of the investigation[,] . . . these problems were worked out to the satisfaction of the Committee and almost all Swiss banks without compromising the integrity of the investigation" (Annex 3, p. 56, paras 65–6).

violation of document retention requirements of Swiss law."[28] Instead, Eizenstat leans on the "shocking discoveries" of the subsequent Bergier Commission *Final Report* which, according to Eizenstat, "exploded the myth, subscribed to by the Volcker Committee, that there was no conspiracy to deprive Holocaust-era account holders of their money" (180–1). Yet, the Bergier *Final Report* explicitly stipulates that its more "general" assessment relies entirely on the Volcker audit, and that "all in all" its conclusions "are borne out by the findings of the Volcker Committee."[29] Eizenstat prudently passes over in silence the recent findings of the Claims Resolution Tribunal, which both indisputably disproved the Holocaust industry's central allegation that Swiss banks stole "billions of dollars" belonging to Holocaust victims, and confirmed Raul Hilberg's initial assessment that the Holocaust industry conjured up "phenomenal figures" and then "blackmailed" the Swiss banks into submission.[30] With only the tiniest fraction of the $1.25 billion

---

[28] Ibid., Annex 5, p. 81, para. 1; for analysis of Volcker findings, cf. *HI*, 111ff.

[29] Bergier *Final Report*, 34, 456; for analysis, cf. Postscript to the Second Paperback Edition in this volume. Like Eizenstat, Bazyler, *Holocaust Justice*, devotes all of one sentence buried in an endnote to the Volcker Committee's findings (342n80), while giving over nearly three full pages (46–9) to what the Bergier Commission (allegedly) found.

[30] For the Claims Resolution Tribunal's findings, see Postscript to the Second Paperback Edition in this volume; for Hilberg, see "Comment s'écrira désormais l'histoire de l'Holocauste? Entretien avec l'auteur de 'La destruction des juifs d'Europe,'" in *Libération* (Paris, 15 September 2001) ("spectacular figures"), and "Holocaust Expert Says Swiss Banks Are Paying Too Much," in *Deutsche Presse-Agentur* (28 January 1999) ("blackmail"). In Bazyler's mathematical universe, the Claims Resolution Tribunal's award in a single instance of $5 million to a claimant "directly" proves that the $1.25 billion settlement was justified (*Holocaust Justice*, 43).

settlement being paid out to Holocaust victims and heirs, the battle among blackmailers has predictably begun over who gets to keep the Holocaust booty – and caught in the crossfire are the blackmailers' victims. Claiming that Israel is the rightful recipient and that "I don't trust the World Jewish Congress," Israel's Minister of Justice is demanding that "the deal with the Swiss banks . . . be renegotiated."[31]

~

It is instructive to juxtapose the fate of the Swiss banks against that of the French banks. In April 2002 a French commission investigating "the spoliation of Jews in France" during the Nazi holocaust "identified but did not publish, because of privacy concerns, approximately 64,000 names on 80,000 bank accounts that presumably belonged to Holocaust victims" (318) – a figure significantly higher than the 36,000 bank accounts "with a possible or probable relationship to Holocaust victims" in the Swiss case.[32] Subsequently, French banks agreed to compensate the validated claimants to Holocaust accounts (few were expected) and to contribute $100 million to a French-based Holocaust foundation to compensate for heirless Holocaust accounts (322, 331, 336–7). By comparison, before the audit (let alone the claims validation process) was completed, Swiss banks were forced to pay $1.25 billion into the coffers of the Holocaust industry. Moreover, the Holocaust industry relentlessly denounced Swiss banks, which invoked privacy laws, for

---

[31] Pierre Heumann, "Israel fordert neuen Bankenvergleich," in *Weltwoche* (10 January 2002).

[32] For the 36,000 figure, see Postscript to the Second Paperback Edition in this volume.

not publishing the names of all Holocaust accounts. "The Swiss Bankers' Association wanted only 5,000 accounts published," Eizenstat typically remonstrates. "The Swiss haggled to the last moment" (179–80). (They eventually published the names of 21,000 accounts with the highest probable relationship to Holocaust victims.) Yet French banks, invoking "privacy laws" (321), likewise refused to publish the names on Holocaust accounts. In the French case, however, Eizenstat didn't wax indignant (321).

The obvious question is, What accounts for the Holocaust industry's relatively benign treatment of the French banks? The short answer is *power*. Like Jews in Weimar Germany, the Swiss were economically prosperous but politically feeble. Indeed, except for dyed-in-the-wool Nazis, who would support "fat Swiss bankers" against "needy Holocaust victims"? In the French case, however, Eizenstat had to factor in "our relations with a close, if prickly, political and economic ally in Europe" (323). In addition, the powerful French Jewish community made "clear" that it "could handle things themselves, without American Jewish interference" (323–4), and backed the French government "to the hilt . . . [and] resented American intervention in . . . France's own business" (327; cf. 320). (French Jewish organizations even "agreed that the lists [of Holocaust accounts] should not be published" [328].) Fear of the unified French reaction neutralized the Holocaust industry's main weapons. "The landscape I faced in the French negotiations was far different from what I had experienced with the Swiss," Eizenstat recalls. "No pressure from Congress, from Israel Singer or from Alan Hevesi" (323). When the class-action lawyers treaded on French sovereignty, Eizenstat – unlike in the Swiss case – broke ranks, deferring to "French sensibilities" (335). With "no external pressure to help them" (324), the lawsuits collapsed. French banks walked away handing over barely a franc to the Holocaust industry.

The French case underscores the absurdity of Eizenstat's contention that "the lawyers hijacked the Swiss bank dispute." Without US government backing, the class-action lawsuits lacked teeth. The lawyers suffered no illusions on this score. As negotiations with the French unfolded into the last days of the Clinton administration, Hausfeld "wanted to settle the French case quickly and creatively," Eizenstat reports. He "realized the danger of leaving these negotiations unfinished when the Clinton administration left office . . . [W]ithout the government as a catalyst, the lawyers and their clients would face a long and uncertain course in the courts" (324).

~

Finally, Israel's record on compensation for Holocaust-era assets was subsequently shown to be no better than Switzerland's. Unlike in the Swiss case, however, this discovery sparked neither profound musings on the defects of the Jewish national character,[33] nor a concerted campaign for a cash settlement. Rather, Eizenstat reckons it merely as a curiosity: "But by far the most unexpected revelations came from Israel. In January 2000 Israel's largest bank, Bank Leumi, disclosed that it held some 13,000 dormant accounts" (347) – roughly the same number as the Volcker audit found in the Swiss banks.[34] Additionally,

[33] For the libelous campaign against the Swiss, see *HI*, 93–4.

[34] The Volcker Committee identified some 15,000 dormant accounts with a "probable or possible relationship" to Holocaust victims. Another 39,000 *closed* accounts with a "probable or possible relationship" were also identified. After vetting this list of 54,000 dormant and closed accounts for errors, the

"it is estimated that hundreds of millions of dollars worth of land and property in Israel, purchased by Jews who were killed in the Holocaust, has yet to be restored to its rightful heirs."[35] In fact, all the allegations leveled against the Swiss apply to Israel. "Like the Swiss, the Israeli banks had for years insisted that they held no assets of Holocaust victims in dormant accounts." They've just now begun to cooperate with independent auditors, and have yet "to grapple with the process of trying to track down heirs." Furthermore, not only has there been "no systematic effort by the state to assist survivors and heirs in claiming properties, let alone to locate heirs," but property of Holocaust victims has been illegally transferred, while would-be heirs have been denied access to archival information supporting their claims and have been challenged to produce the death certificates and property deeds of those killed in concentration camps. "They have put impossible obstacles in my path," an elderly Holocaust survivor complained to the *Jerusalem Report*. "All over Europe, relatives have been paid compensation for land that was owned by Holocaust victims. It's terrible that Israel refuses to come clean." Revealingly, "few" Knesset members, "even those with survivor backgrounds, have shown any interest in Israeli Holocaust restitution issues." Avraham Hirschson,

---

total was found to be 36,000 (it's not known how many of these were dormant and how many closed); cf. Volcker *Report*, 10, and Postscript to the Second Paperback Edition in this volume.

[35] Netty C. Gross, "Cheating Our Own," in *Jerusalem Report* (16 December 2002); cf. Netty C. Gross, "Up Front: Too Many Questions," in *Jerusalem Report* (13 January 2003). (All quotes in this paragraph are from Gross's articles.) A Knesset committee put the value of the dormant accounts at "more than \$20 million" (whether this total includes accumulated interest is unclear).

"who was very active in pursuing the Swiss banks," for example, "never bothered showing up for meetings" of a Knesset committee to "locate and restore Holocaust assets."[36]

III.

In his foreword to Eizenstat's book, Holocaust industry CEO Elie Wiesel wonders why the "economic dimension" of the Holocaust had been hitherto "utterly neglected" (x), while Eizenstat – referring directly to Germany – similarly ponders "why did it take more than fifty years to provide imperfect justice to the civilian victims of Nazi barbarism" (3; cf. 114)? The short answer is, it *wasn't* neglected. In his conclusion Eizenstat maintains that, on account of Clinton's diplomatic initiative, "for the first time in the annals of warfare, systematic compensation was sought and achieved for individual civilian victims for injuries sustained" (343). Yet, earlier on, he reports that since the 1950s Germany has paid out "more than $60 billion" to "500,000 Holocaust survivors around the world" (15), and this "payment of massive benefits to individual Holocaust victims has been without precedent in the annals of war" (210).[37] Beyond the unprecedented

---

[36] For Hirschson, see *HI*, 134–5.

[37] For background, see *HI*, 83ff. Eizenstat repeats the standard Holocaust industry claim that the German government only compensated Holocaust victims for "their general loss of liberty and damage to their health . . ., [b]ut they explicitly excluded payments for their slave and forced labor" (207) – as if the lifetime pensions Holocaust victims received for injuries incurred in the camps were totally unrelated to their coerced labor.

payments undertaken by the postwar German government, Eizenstat reports that "many" German companies – including Krupp, I.G. Farben, Daimler-Benz, Siemens, and Volkswagen – provided separate compensation beginning in the late 1950s to the Jewish Claims Conference (JCC)[38] for Holocaust victims. The JCC explicitly waived any future claims, promising to defend – even indemnify – German companies against any new claims by Holocaust victims in exchange for their many tens of millions of dollars in Holocaust compensation. Yet, German industry's pay-out didn't stop "the class-action lawyers from filing billion-dollar claims, nor did [it] prevent the Claims Conference from ignoring its earlier commitments and trying to exact more" (209–11). And, whereas the Holocaust industry publicly reviled "the Germans" for not compensating Holocaust victims, "the Claims Conference had carefully cultivated its relationship with the German government during almost half a century of massive reparations payments," and "Singer had once joshed" that the German government "was 'our friend who lays the golden eggs'" (241). During negotiations Eizenstat declared any consideration of past German compensation "totally unacceptable to the victims and to the U.S. government" (233) – although he never explains why. The Holocaust industry also boasted that its campaign against German industry was designed to benefit not just Jewish but exploited non-Jewish laborers from Eastern Europe.[39] Yet, Eizenstat reports that "public discussion in Germany about compensating these [East European] laborers had been going on since the early 1980s, and it had been part of the platform of the small

---

[38] For the Claims Conference, see *HI*, 85.
[39] See, for instance, Burt Neuborne's letter to *The Nation* (5 October 2002).

Green Party for most of the time"; that in the early 1990s the German government had paid out compensation (albeit modest) to East European governments for these Nazi victims; and that already before the Holocaust industry launched its assault on German companies the "Red-Green" coalition of Social Democrats and Greens had pledged in its September 1998 governing agreement "to provide justice" for exploited East European laborers (206–8).[40]

The assault on German industry duplicated the successful shakedown tactics of the Swiss campaign. "As my State Department team and I were working on the Swiss bank negotiations," Eizenstat recalls, "many of the same American class-action lawyers . . . saw an irresistibly vulnerable new target: German companies" (208). The potent threat of "economic sanctions, boycotts" (246) crucially supplemented the courtroom theatrics. Meanwhile, at each critical juncture in the negotiations, Eizenstat elicited support from Clinton to renew pressure on the Germans. He reports that "the speedy turnaround" of the first request for a letter "was a reflection of the president's personal interest" (243); that "obtaining a presidential letter to a foreign head of government is usually difficult on any topic," while "getting a second one is even more so . . ., but when I asked for another, [the] Chief of Staff . . . and the National Security Council quickly obtained it" (248); that "once again I would need my heaviest artillery, the president of the United States. I learned that Clinton, Schroeder, and Prime Minister Tony Blair of Britain were meeting

[40] See also Norman Finkelstein, "Reply to my Critics in Germany: Conjuring Conspiracies or Breaking Taboos?" at *www.NormanFinkelstein.com* under "The Holocaust Industry" (first published in 9 September 2000 issue of *Suddeutsche Zeitung*).

. . . Clinton told Schroeder that both sides were close but had to do a little more . . . Schroeder pleaded budget stringency. Undaunted, Clinton came back and pointed out what a success it would be for both sides to put the past behind them" (252–3); that "in effect we were negotiating in Germany simultaneously at both my level and that of the heads of government" as Clinton yet again "raise[d] the matter with Schroeder" (271). Finally, "there was no precedent in American history" (257), according to Eizenstat, for the legal commitments the US government entered into in order to seal the German settlement.

The German settlement, capped at $5 billion, covered both Jewish and non-Jewish slave laborers as well as forced laborers. (Although both slave and forced laborers were conscripted by the Nazis, forced laborers received nominal wages and generally worked under less onerous conditions than the slave laborers herded into concentration camps.) Eizenstat initially states that there were "200,000 concentration camp survivors" at the end of World War II (9), and that "slightly more than half the slave laborers were Jewish, the rest mostly Poles and Russians" (206). This would put his total figure for Jewish slave laborers alive in May 1945 at roughly 100,000 – which is in line with the estimates of serious scholars like Raul Hilberg and Henry Friedlander. Yet Eizenstat goes on to cite as authoritative the Holocaust industry's claim that, 50 years after the end of World War II, in "the mid-1990s, approximately 250,000 former slave laborers were still alive" (208; cf. 240), of which supposedly 140,000 were Jewish.[41] The motive behind the Holocaust industry's inflation was

[41] For the Friedlander and Hilberg figures, see *HI*, 125–6, and Postscript to the

straightforward: more living Holocaust survivors meant a larger share of the capped German settlement. Eizenstat recalls chiding the East European representatives for submitting "inflated numbers" of survivors and that "Singer was also livid" that these numbers were "jacked up" (239–40). He utters not a word, however, about Singer's "jacked up" number for Jewish slave laborers, but rather maintains that "the Claims Conference had good records of Jewish survivors" – which no doubt can explain how the figure of 100,000 former Jewish slave laborers alive in 1945 grew to 140,000 former Jewish slave laborers still living fifty years later.

In fact, the Claims Conference itself has effectively conceded the fraudulence of the 140,000 figure. Yehuda Bauer, former director of Yad Vashem (Israel's main Holocaust research institute), currently serves as the Claims Conference's advisor on Holocaust education. In a recent study, Bauer "estimate[s] that at the end of World War II about 200,000 Jews emerged from the Nazi concentration and slave labor camps and had survived the death marches." Although double the standard scholarly estimates, Bauer's figure is still impossible to reconcile with the Holocaust industry's claim during the German negotiations that 700,000 Jewish slave laborers survived the war and

Second Paperback Edition in this volume. (Hilberg has kindly provided this writer with a breakdown and explanation of his calculations.) For the Holocaust industry's numbers game on Holocaust survivors, and Eizenstat's part in it, see *HI*, 126ff., 158ff., 168–9. Judging from the context it's conceivable that Eizenstat meant the 200,000 figure to designate only Jewish slave laborers alive at war's end but, as argued below, this figure still can't be reconciled with 140,000 former Jewish slave laborers among the living 50 years later.

140,000 remain among the living 50 years later.[42] Even Holocaust survivor organizations decry that the Holocaust industry inflated the number of survivors during negotiations only to deflate the number once it had the compensation monies earmarked for Holocaust survivors in hand: "Why during the negotiations were the numbers of actual Shoah survivors so vastly exaggerated and why were the negotiators so fearful that the press and the German and Swiss opponents might challenge their proclaimed survivors' statistics?"[43]

[42] Yehuda Bauer, *Rethinking the Holocaust* (New Haven: 2001), 246. Before the Holocaust compensation campaign, Bauer estimated that, referring to the camps, "the number of Jewish survivors who remained alive . . . was 100,000" at war's end (*Yad Vashem Studies*, vol. 8 [1970], 127–8n3). The likelihood is that only about 10–20 percent of the Jewish slave-laborers alive at war's end still remain among the living. This percentage is supported by recent estimates that during the war Germany's Roman Catholic Church "used 10,000 forced laborers and about 1,000 are still alive" (*New York Times*, 8 November 2000). On this and related matters, see esp. Gunnar Heinsohn, *Juedische Sklavenarbeiter Hitlerdeutschlands – Wie viele ueberlebten 1945 den Genozid und wie viele konnten im Jahr 2000 noch leben?*, Schriftenreihe des Raphael-Lemkin-Instituts Nr. 9 (Bremen: 2001); revealingly, Heinsohn reports that the German media suppressed serious discussion of the slave-labor numbers (67). The exact figure for former Jewish slave-laborers still alive will probably never be known, however, since the German government has elected to only spot-check the applications for compensation submitted by the Claims Conference (see Ministry of Finance's response to query of Martin Hohmann [CDU], 9 October 2001).

[43] *NAHOS*, The Newsletter of the National Association of Jewish Child Holocaust Survivors, vol. 7, no. 18 (14 August 2001); cf. *NAHOS*, vol. 7, no. 15 (11 May 2001), which upbraids the Claims Conference for manipulating survivor numbers "depending on political exigencies" – for instance, to expedite negotiations the Holocaust industry has lamented from the mid-1990s that

This inflation now exceeds that of the Weimar years with the US State Department's Special Envoy for Holocaust Issues, J.D. Bindenagel, proclaiming that "in the postwar years many millions of Holocaust victims were caught behind the Iron Curtain."[44]

The Holocaust industry also conjured other schemes to swindle a bigger chunk of the German settlement. In this regard Eizenstat's account merits extended quotation. Singer and Gideon Taylor of the Claims Conference

> argued that there were some 8,000 Jewish slave laborers who lived in other parts of the world not represented in our talks and they wanted the Claims Conference to control the money for them. They also wanted to be given enough money to pay the 28,000 Jewish forced laborers in this category the full 5,000 DM each. It meant that a third of the fund we had set aside for this group – we called it "Rest of the World" – would go to them. Gentz and Lambsdorff [the German representatives] were appalled. So was I, telling Singer bluntly that his position threatened the talks and could create the very anti-Semitic backlash he had been trying to avert. Singer responded angrily that he could not compromise further. With the visibly reluctant consent of the Germans, I agreed to a secret footnote in the German legislation to give these Jewish laborers an additional amount of 260 million DM, or $130 million. This effectively meant less for non-Jewish forced

---

"Holocaust survivors are dying every day" and "ten percent" are dying annually, yet to justify ever-escalating demands the number it sets forth for living Holocaust survivors increases from one year to the next.

[44] "Nun bitte auch zahlen," in *Die Zeit* (12/2001).

laborers, primarily in Western Europe and the United States. I reluctantly gave in to this demand because I believed Singer might have aborted the deal on the spot. It was too risky at this stage to call his bluff. But I remain embarrassed at the concession. (265–6)

"I concluded my negotiations holding a firm conviction," Eizenstat recalls, "that postwar Germany is entitled to full acceptance as a 'normal' nation, with a well-ingrained set of democratic values" (278). In other words, it passed the crucial test of submitting to US blackmail. On the eve of the US attack on Iraq, however, the German government's normality and democratic commitment were again called into question after it refused to submit to US blackmail and bowed to popular anti-war sentiment. Meanwhile those Germans who believed that paying the extortion money and publicly heaping praise on the Holocaust industry's moral righteousness would finally close the chapter on Holocaust compensation have been in for a rude awakening. The Holocaust industry started greedily eyeing $350 million in the settlement set aside for a German foundation promoting tolerance ("Fund for the Future"). Maintaining that "it is the job of the Jewish community to challenge parts of the settlement it does not agree with," Singer opined, "I don't believe we should play by the rules of the Germans" – although the settlement's "rules" were overwhelmingly imposed not by the Germans but the Holocaust industry. Small wonder that even fellow Jews, according to Singer, "describe me as a gangster."[45] Indeed,

[45] Nacha Cattan, "Shoah 'People' Fund Attacked," in *Forward* (28 December 2001) ("rules"). Yair Sheleg, "Only he knows what needs to be done," in *Haaretz* (9 November 2001) ("gangster").

after embarrassing even Eizenstat with his conjuring of Holocaust victims, this shameless Holocaust huckster returned to Germany less than two years after the settlement was signed to demand "a few dozen millions" more ("bread crumbs") for Jewish labor conscripts "whose existence has only now become known." "This is my last visit regarding this matter," Singer promised. "One will not see my face again."[46] Rather unlikely, unless he is finally put where he belongs, behind bars.

~

Like Germany, the Austrian government enacted legislation right after the war to compensate Holocaust victims, and in the early 1990s allocated substantial supplementary funds for Holocaust victims as well as for Holocaust education (281–3, 302).[47] Although both the US government and the Claims Conference explicitly "forswore further claims" against Austria, Eizenstat acknowledges, "my team and I were doing just the opposite" (302). Meanwhile, "the same cast of

---

[46] Wolfgang Koydl, "'Berlin sollte nicht schachern'. Israel Singer sieht die Bundesregierung trotz Etat-Problemen zu Zahlungen an alle Zwangsarbeiter verpflichtet," in *Suddeutsche Zeitung* (3 February 2003) ("dozen millions," "existence," "last visit," "face"), and "Singer sieht Deutschland in der Pflicht," in *Frankfurter Allgemeine Zeitung* (13 February 2003) ("bread crumbs").

[47] Criticizing these postwar compensation laws, Eizenstat writes: "Perhaps most egregious were the judgments of some Austrian courts in deciding property claims after the war. They required the original Jewish owners to repay the current occupant the forced sales price he had been required to take, adjusted upward for inflation, thus enriching the Aryanizers twice" (302). Why "twice"? The original Jewish owners were simply called upon to return the payment (adjusted for inflation) that they received from the current occupant before reclaiming the property.

characters, the 'usual suspects' I dealt with on Switzerland and Germany" (283) filed suits against Austria for Holocaust compensation; Hausfeld demanded $800 million for looted property, although "he admitted that this was simply an arbitrary figure" (305). Singer threatened to give Austria the "Waldheim treatment" again unless they paid up (294), while Eizenstat "had Secretary of State Albright call Chancellor Schuessel in Vienna" to "ratchet[] up the political pressure" (296), and brought her in again later to deliver another "warning" (305). The novelty of these negotiations was that they unfolded just as Austria was being ostracized after Joerg Haider's rightist Freedom Party joined the governing coalition. The US, downgrading its contact with Austria, declared that the new coalition "might be a step back into a very dark past" and that "there will not be business as usual," while Israel, recalling its ambassador, similarly proclaimed that "Israel cannot remain silent in the face of the rise of extremist right-wing parties . . . in those countries which played a role . . . in the Holocaust," and that "the Jewish people . . . will never allow the world to conduct business as usual in light of the events in Austria."[48]

Unless, of course, it's Shoah business. Eizenstat reports that

---

[48] Mathew Lee, "US vows to keep an eye on new government in Vienna," in *Agence France Presse* (5 February 2000) ("step back"), David E. Sanger, "U.S. Is Facing Wider Issues In Its Actions Over Austria," in *New York Times* (6 February 2000) ("never allow"), Joel Greenberg, "Israel Plans to Recall Envoy Over Right-Wingers in Austria" in *New York Times* (3 February 2000) ("not be business"), "Austrian far-right enters government," in *BBC News* ("cannot remain"). The European Union applied stiff diplomatic sanctions on Austria but lifted them several months later.

"Secretary Albright permitted me to have unfettered negotiations with the Schuessel government, even including Freedom Party ministers, if necessary to my success" (285), and that "Singer and Gideon Taylor pleaded with me for some kind of political figleaf to cover their participation" (289) – which he dutifully provided, enabling them to become full parties to the negotiations (298). Eizenstat excuses negotiating with an Austrian government including Haider on the grounds that "I had been in politics long enough to know that the thirst for power at the top often produces unpalatable relationships" (291). Without gainsaying Eizenstat's expertise on hatching dirty deals from a lust for power, one wonders why everyone else was expected to ostracize Austria – and suffer chastisement if they didn't?[49] On 13 March 2000 Singer announced that a newly declassified document would prove that Austria owed no less than $10 billion in Holocaust compensation, and just two days later (15 March) he spoke at "the first public demonstration in Israel Against Haiderism."[50] Was this sheer coincidence or was the Holocaust industry manipulating the campaign to ostracize Austria as a bargaining chip to extract Holocaust compensation? In fact, both sides played the same game. Upon coming to power and confronted with international censure, the right-wing Austrian coalition immediately declared its intention to pay Holocaust compensation, while the US government declared that it was "particu-

[49] See, for instance, the WJC's critical coverage of the Pope's meeting with Haider in *Dialogues* (newsletter of the Institute of the World Jewish Congress in Jerusalem) (June 2001).

[50] For Singer's $10 billion document, see *HI*, 139; for the demonstration, see "Say No to Haiderism" (press release), in *JAFI* (The Jewish Agency for Israel).

larly concerned about Austria's attitude to reparations."[51] Restoring
Austria's diplomatic bona fides was the quid pro quo for paying off
the Holocaust industry (297).

After the November 2000 presidential election the US re-estab-
lished normal relations with Austria and Austria offered to increase
the total amount of Holocaust compensation for looted property
(305). Holding out for yet more money, Eizenstat "offered the
sweetener of a public statement of praise by President Clinton, along
with a warning that, if the talks failed, the victims' side had told me
they would try to isolate Austria . . . Singer could create such a cloud
over Austria that American investors might shy away" (308–9).
Extracting one concession after another from Austria before finally
reaching agreement, Eizenstat recalls, "was like pulling teeth until
there were none left . . . The chancellor had walked the last mile to
achieve a deal" (310). Earlier on, after cutting a separate deal with
Austria on Jewish slave laborers, Eizenstat heaped praised on the
Austrian government for having "shown leadership not just in Austria,
but leadership to the rest of Europe and to the world about how one
can reconcile with one's past, and how one can heal wounds even
many decades later." The very same government that marked a "step
back into the dark past" miraculously metamorphosed – after payment
of the protection money – into the harbinger of a bright future.
Indeed, the negotiations with Austria pointed up an important "lesson

---

[51] Donald G. McNeil, "Chancellor Proposes to Compensate Austria's Wartime
Slaves," in *New York Times* (10 February 2000), Sue Masterman, "Not United:
U.S., Israel Reject EU's Lifting of Sanctions Against Austria," in *ABCNews.com*
(13 September 2000) ("particularly concerned").

of the Holocaust": posturing against anti-Semitism can pay rich dividends.[52]

IV.

Eizenstat touchingly reports that attorneys Melvyn Weiss and Michael Hausfeld worked on the Swiss case pro bono because "neither wanted the many impoverished survivors to have what might be their meager portions diluted even further by the legal fees," while Burt Neuborne – with a "sadness to his demeanor, a pall over his face" – conceived "his work as a living memorial to his lost daughter" (a rabbinical student, she died prematurely of a heart attack) (83, 85–6). Eizenstat says not a word, however, about their nobility of soul in the German case. Total attorney fees in the German settlement came to $60 million. Weiss and Hausfeld led the pack with, respectively, $7.3 million and $5.8 million, while at least 10 others clocked in at more than $1 million. Understandably Weiss, for example, could not litigate yet another Holocaust compensation case pro bono: his annual earnings have averaged only $12 million. Neuborne reflected that his

---

[52] For Eizenstat's remarks, see "Unofficial Transcript: Schaumayer, Eizenstat on Nazi Slave Labor Fund" (17 May 2000). Never passing up an opportunity to make a buck, the WJC also called on Jews to "stop Austria's Joerg Haider and other extremists by making an emergency contribution to the World Jewish Congress" (mail solicitation). A top American Jewish philanthropist and financier, Michael Steinhardt, noting that "anti-Semitism sells," told the *Jerusalem Post* that organized Jewry "vastly exaggerated" anti-Semitism for fundraising purposes (*Jerusalem Post Internet Staff*, 5 January 2003).

$5 million fee was "not particularly high" – especially as compared with the German settlement's allocation of $7,500 for an Auschwitz survivor. Lagging behind with a piddling $4.3 million, Robert Swift waxed philosophical about his "minimal by any standard" payment: "Not everything you do in life can be measured in dollars and cents." Looking elsewhere for solace, one enterprising attorney sold the story of his client to Hollywood's Mike Ovitz, former president of Disney. When the lawyers' fees were first announced Eizenstat rose to defend them as "exceedingly modest." Holocaust survivors thought otherwise. "If only half the amount, or about $30 million, could have been saved on attorneys' fees," a survivor organization editorialized, "it could have been used to establish one or several health-care centers for ailing Survivors. Shame on these unconscionable fees!"[53]

It would be a mistake, however, to focus exclusively on the misdeeds of the class-action lawyers. This has been the Holocaust industry's main strategy for diverting attention from itself as ugly

[53] Jane Fritsch, "$52 Million for Lawyers' Fees in Nazi-Era Slave-Labor Suits," in *New York Times* (15 June 2001) (Neuborne), Daniel Wise, "$60 Million in Fees Awarded to Lawyers Who Negotiated $5 Billion Holocaust Fund," in *New York Law Journal* (15 June 2001), Larry Neumeister, "Millions in legal fees awarded in slave labor cases," in *Associated Press* (18 June 2001) (Eizenstat, Swift), Jonathan Goddard, "Holocaust lawyers make millions as the survivors wait," in *London Jewish News* (22 June 2001), Jonathan Goddard, "Nazi Story Sold," in *London Jewish News* (6 July 2001) (Hollywood). "The Survivors Belong At The Head Of The Table," in *NAHOS* (1 November 2001), reprint of article originally published in *Aufbau* (28 March 2001) (survivors). For Weiss's annual earnings, see Bazyler, *Holocaust Justice*, 338n25. For Hausfeld, Weiss and Neuborne litigating the Swiss case pro bono as a "ruse" in order to "control any other Holocaust litigation in which they would seek fees," see *HI*, 191n24.

truths seep out. (Beyond scapegoating the lawyers, the Holocaust industry was also at odds with them over "the fundamental issue of who at the end of the day would control the bulk" [132] of the compensation monies.) In fact, the class-action lawyers together have pocketed only a tiny percentage of the various Holocaust settlements. The real thieves are Holocaust hucksters like Bronfman and Singer who control the "interlocking" directorates of the WJC, WJRO and the Claims Conference (57). Although the Holocaust industry put the spotlight on allegedly cheated "needy Holocaust victims" and heirs, Eizenstat emphasizes that the "WJC's priority was control of the 'heirless' assets" (119; cf. 61) – i.e., compensation monies on which Holocaust victims couldn't stake a direct claim. According to Eizenstat, the Holocaust industry, "representing the interests" of Holocaust survivors "the world over" (41), has earmarked these heirless monies for "aging Holocaust survivors" (119), "to help Holocaust victims in general" (262), "to recompense . . . elderly" Holocaust survivors "before they died" (304), and so on. In the first edition of this book, however, I documented the Holocaust industry's history of systematically misusing compensation monies. Although emphatically denying the existence of a "'Holocaust industry' of lawyers and Jewish organizations profiting at the expense of victims" (339; cf. 345), Eizenstat never refutes the allegations. (Nor, for that matter, has anyone else.)[54] In fact, he never confronts an obvious question begging

[54] For the Claims Conference's squandering of compensation monies earmarked by the German government and German private industry for Holocaust victims, see *HI*, 84ff., and esp. Auschwitz survivor Gerhard Maschkowski's "Correspondence with Claims Conference and others," at *www.jewishcompensation.com*. My original conclusions relied heavily on Prof.

for an answer: if Germany has paid out "more than $60 billion" to "500,000 Holocaust survivors around the world" since the 1950s, why have so many Holocaust survivors complained that they received little or no compensation? Eizenstat notes that compensation monies paid out by Germany to Eastern Europe "often merely lined the pockets of corrupt government bureaucrats" (232; cf. 263), yet blithely ignores the comparable record of the Holocaust industry.

Recent developments fit this sordid pattern. In November 2001 the WJC announced that it had collected $11 billion in Holocaust compensation and expected the figure eventually to reach some $14 billion. (It's unclear whether these figures include the tens of thousands of properties worth billions of dollars that the Claims Conference is still contesting in Germany.) The Holocaust industry is now "debating not whether, but how," to use the "probably billions" in "leftovers" after needy Holocaust victims "pass from the scene." Declaring that Holocaust survivors alone should not decide "how to use monies that will not be needed after they die," Singer proposes devoting the "probably billions" to "rebuild the Jewish soul and spirit."[55] Leaving aside Singer's unseemly haste to divide up the

Ronald Zweig's study commissioned by the Claims Conference, *German Reparations and the Jewish World*. After publication of *The Holocaust Industry*, Zweig repeatedly charged that I "misused" and "distorted" his research, yet – despite ample space and time to present his case – cited not a single example (cf. Zweig's review on *www.Amazon.com* for *The Holocaust Industry*, and p. 10 of his introduction to the second edition of *German Reparations and the Jewish World* (London: 2001), as well as our "Democracy Now" radio debate at *www.webactive.com/pacifica/demnow/dn20000713.html*).

[55] Jon Greenberg, "Jewish leaders say Holocaust reparations are nearly complete," in *Associated Press* (2 November 2001) ("11 billion"), Yair Sheleg,

inheritance, and even acknowledging the need to "rebuild the Jewish soul and spirit" especially after the battering they suffered the past few years from the likes of Singer, it's nonetheless hard to figure how the Holocaust industry already knows that there will be "probably billions" in residuals if – as it also maintains – nearly a million indigent Holocaust survivors are still alive and "tens of thousands" are "likely to be alive" in 2035.[56] The Holocaust industry forecasts billions in residuals while simultaneously avowing that it can't even afford health care for elderly Holocaust victims.

"Why are we talking about excess riches," a Holocaust writer wonders, "when there is no money to pay for survivors' basic necessities?" In a staggering display of chutzpah, the Holocaust industry is now demanding that "the German government, with the participation of German industry" yet again foot the bill because the poor Claims Conference can't afford to. On the other hand, twenty thousand Holocaust victims, decrying the Holocaust industry's misuse of their compensation monies, formed a new organization in June 2001, Holocaust Survivors Foundation – USA, "to ensure that billions of dollars raised for survivors are paid to survivors." The Foundation's secretary, Leo Rechter, charged that Holocaust survivors, as well as "foreign governments," had been "duped for decades into believing" that the Claims Conference "had OUR interests at heart." The

---

"Conflicting claims," in *Haaretz* (10 December 2001) (German properties), Cattan, "Shoah 'People' Fund Attacked" ("debating"), Nacha Cattan, "Clash Looming Over Uses of Shoah Funds," in *Forward* (9 November 2001) ("scene"), Israel Singer, "Transparency, Truth, and Restitution," in *Sh'ma* (June 2002) ("soul and spirit").

[56] For these figures, see *HI*, 152, 159–60.

Foundation's president, David Schaecter, deplored that many aging Holocaust survivors live in "desperate conditions" while "the Claims Conference has allocated only a minuscule fraction of the billions it has acquired in the name of Holocaust survivors." It's "not right" for Holocaust survivors to lack health care, said the Foundation's chairman, Joe Sachs, "when millions are spent building institutions in remote locations such as Siberia and hundreds of millions are spent on dubious purpose projects around the world." These doubtful undertakings have included "$20.7 million to a subsidiary of the Jewish Agency," "$3 million to the World Zionist Organization," "$1.4 million to the 'Yiddish Theater' in Tel Aviv," "$1 million to the 'Mordechai Anielevich Memorial' in Israel," "hundreds of thousands of dollars for a study of the history of pre-war yeshivot," and "over a half million dollars for a 'Memorial Foundation for Jewish Culture' in New York, which is twice as much as the recent allocation to all needy survivors in Florida." Scoring the Holocaust industry for "moving in and trying to get money for their favorite charities rather than giving money to people in whose name they obtained it," Rechter rhetorically asked whether negotiators for the Holocaust industry informed their German opposites that a "sizable chunk" of the compensation monies would be spent not on survivors but "pet projects"? "Representatives of the Jewish organizations, which ostensibly conducted the worthy campaign to set up the compensation funds, did not do this out of deep concern for Holocaust survivors or their heirs," Knesset member Michael Kleiner told the Israeli parliament amid Jewish infighting for the Holocaust booty. "The real aim was not to restore Jewish property to its legal owners. The representatives of the organizations did everything possible to ensure that the money that was taken and the Jewish property would come into their own coffers instead of going to their lawful owners. In this way, the representatives of the Jewish bodies hoped to breathe new life into their organizations and the lives of luxury to which they have become accustomed." While elderly Holocaust survivors languish without medical coverage, the current annual salary and benefits of Gideon Taylor, executive vice-president of the Claims Conference, total $275,000. Additionally, Taylor informed Judge Korman that Claims Conference "administrative expenses" – running to fully *thirty million dollars* – "may require there be a reduction" in the $7,500 awarded former Jewish slave laborers under the German settlement. "At times it seems that the Holocaust has become a tool in the hands of the large Jewish organizations," the eminent Israeli newspaper *Haaretz* observed, "to obtain funds for the favorite projects of the organizations' leaders."[57]

---

[57] Eva Fogelman, "Our Task: To Dignify the Lives of Survivors," in *Sh'ma* (June 2002) ("basic necessities"), Menachem Rosensaft, "For Aging Survivors, a Prescription for Disaster," in *Forward* (31 January 2003) ("German government . . . German industry"). *PRNewswire* (4 June 2001) ("ensure," Sachs, Schaecter), *NAHOS*, vol. 7, no. 15 (11 May 2001) (Rechter), *NAHOS*, vol. 7, no. 17 (16 July 2001), *NAHOS*, vol. 8, no. 2 (20 December 2001), *NAHOS*, vol. 8, no. 13 (6 February 2003), and David Schaecter, "Use Restituted Funds for Urgent Survivors' Needs," in *Sh'ma* (June 2002) (doubtful undertakings). *NAHOS*, vol. 7, no. 13 (9 March 2001) ("sizable chunk"), Cattan, "Shoah 'People' Fund Attacked" ("favorite charities"). Yair Sheleg, "Future imperfect, tense," in *Haaretz* (1 February 2002) (Michael Kleiner). Eliahu Salpeter, "Time is running out for compensation," in *Haaretz* (13 February 2002) ("tool"). Taylor's salary and benefits from the Claims Conference's 2001 Tax Return provided by the Internal Revenue Service; although the Claims Conference web site stipulates "full" disclosure of "Financial Statements," its Director of

To account for the "intensity, at times belligerency" of "the Bronfmans, Singers" during the Holocaust compensation campaign, Eizenstat explains that they had a "twofold motivation": "It was both a just retribution for what was done by their corporate predecessors to European Jewry, and an expiation of the American Jewish community's own collective guilt for doing so little to stop it six decades before" (354). Indeed, the "Bronfmans, Singers" suffered such pangs of expiation that they kept the fruits of retribution for personal aggrandizement.

~

Apart from managing to extract monies, Eizenstat lauds the Holocaust compensation campaign for having "helped further marginalize revi-

---

Communications, Hillary Kessler-Godin, refused to supply financial data. "Conference on Jewish Material Claims Against Germany, Inc.": *Memorandum* to Hon. Edward R. Korman (1 August 2002) ("reduction"). See also Amy Dockser Marcus, "As Survivors Age, Debate Breaks Out on Holocaust Funds," in *Wall Street Journal* (15 January 2003), and Eric J. Greenberg, "Shoah Money Debate Intensifies," in *Jewish Week* (21 February 2003). Rechter wondered why the constituent organizations of the Holocaust industry are "fighting so ferociously" for a cut of the compensation monies if there supposedly isn't even enough to cover a health-care program (*NAHOS*, vol. 8, no. 3 [8 February 2002]). Denouncing the Holocaust industry's fraudulent use of the term "Holocaust survivor" to deny actual survivors their due, Rechter also observed: "Giving aid to needy Jews is certainly a worthy cause, but it must be remembered that this money was demanded on behalf of Holocaust survivors and it should go to their welfare. Russia was not under Nazi occupation. Many of its Jews did flee eastward for fear of the Nazis, and therefore they constitute 'war victims,' but they are not Holocaust survivors." The term was similarly falsified to inflate the number of survivors during compensation negotiations (Sheleg, "Conflicting claims," and *HI*, 160).

sionist historians who were denying the Holocaust had taken place" (114). It's unclear, however, how inflating the number of Holocaust survivors, thereby deflating the number of Holocaust deaths, or how Jewish leaders carrying on like caricatures straight from the pages of *Der Stuermer* and the *Protocols of the Elders of Zion*, helped marginalize Holocaust deniers. The Holocaust industry has designated as a main beneficiary of compensation monies "Holocaust education" – which, according to Eizenstat, constitutes the "greatest legacy of our efforts."[58] The purpose of this Holocaust education is naturally to "learn the lessons of the Holocaust." But what lessons does the Holocaust industry want us to learn? One important lesson is "do not compare" the Holocaust with other crimes – unless comparing is politically expedient. Thus, a Holocaust industry periodical compared the September 11 attack on the World Trade Center with "the ordeal of WWII and the suffering of the Shoah," while *Atlantic Monthly* pondered whether bin Laden or Hitler stood higher on the "hierarchy of evil," and *The New York Times Magazine* opined that Islamic fundamentalism was "a more formidable enemy than Nazism." A little over a year later, mainstream American Jewish organizations (as well as Israel) rallied behind the Bush administration's criminal aggression

---

[58] See *HI*, 135. One lucrative spin-off of Holocaust education for university academics is the "historical commission"; for one egregious example, see "Prof. Gerald Feldman – Another Holocaust huckster?" at *www.NormanFinkelstein.com* (under "The Holocaust Industry"), as well as Gerald Feldman, "Holocaust Assets and German Business History: Beginning or End?" in *German Studies Review* (February 2002), protesting rather too much that "I see no reason why historians should not be paid for their services in the manner of other professionals" (30).

against Iraq, with Elie Wiesel declaring that "the world faced a crisis similar to 1938" and "the choice is simple," and with self-promoting "Nazi hunter" Simon Wiesenthal proclaiming that "you cannot wait indefinitely on dictators. Adolf Hitler came to power in 1933, but for six years the world did not act." Critics of the war stood accused of everything from Chamberlain-style "appeasement" to "an anti-Semitism of a type long thought dead in the West," while even prominent American poets opposing the Iraqi war and Israel's occupation were chastised for playing "on the edges of 1930s-style anti-Semitism."[59]

---

[59] *Together: American Gathering of Jewish Holocaust Survivors* (November 2001), Ron Rosenbaum, "Degrees of Evil," in *Atlantic Monthly* (February 2000), Andrew Sullivan, "Who Says It's Not about Religion?" in *The New York Times Magazine* (7 October 2001). For mainstream American Jewish support for attacking Iraq, see, for instance, "ADL Commends President Bush's Message To International Community On Iraq Calling It 'Clear and Forceful'" (Anti-Defamation League, press release [12 September 2002]), and "AJC Lauds Bush on State of Union Message on Terrorism . . ." (American Jewish Committee, press release [7 February 2003]); for Israel's enthusiastic support, see Meron Benvenisti, "Hey ho, here comes the war," in *Haaretz* (13 February 2003), Uzi Benziman, "Corridors of Power/O What a lovely war," in *Haaretz* (14 February 2003), Gideon Levy, "A great silence over the land," in *Haaretz* (16 February 2003), Aluf Benn, "Background/Enthusiastic IDF awaits war in Iraq," in *Haaretz* (16 February 2003), and Aluf Benn, "The celebrations have already begun," in *Haaretz* (20 February 2003); for Wiesel, see "The Oprah Winfrey Show" (transcript for "Where Are We Now?," aired 9 October 2002), "War is the only option," in *Observer* (22 December 2002), and Randall Mikkelsen, "Nobel Laureate Wiesel backs Bush over Iraq," in *Reuters* (27 February 2003); for Wiesenthal, see Simon Wiesenthal Center, "Famed Nazi Hunter Simon Wiesenthal's Statement On Impending Iraq War," at *www.wiesenthal.com*; for "appeasement," see Brian Knowlton, "Top U.S. Official Urges U.N. to Maintain Pressure on Hussein" (quoting Condoleezza Rice) in

The wonder is that critics haven't been charged with Holocaust denial, yet. And, as the German people courageously refused being browbeaten into supporting Washington's criminal war, the German branch of the Holocaust industry, explicitly comparing Saddam Hussein to Hitler, used the occasion of Holocaust remembrance day to deplore German opposition to the Iraqi war, and later urged support for "necessary wars."[60]

Another important Holocaust lesson is to remember the Nazi genocide – but forget all other genocides. Thus Israeli Foreign Minister Shimon Peres dismissed Turkey's systematic extermination of Armenians as mere "allegations," and Armenian accounts of the mass slaughter as "meaningless."[61] And still another lesson is to keep

---

International Herald Tribune (16 February 2003); for "anti-Semitism," see Eliot A. Cohen, "The Reluctant Warrior," in *Wall Street Journal* (6 February 2003) and J. Bottum, "The Poets vs. The First Lady," in *Weekly Standard* (17 February 2002), as well as "ADL Says Organizers of Antiwar Protests in Washington and San Francisco Have History of Attacking Israel and Jews" (Anti-Defamation League, press release [15 January 2003]), "Blackballing Lerner" (editorial) and Max Gross, "Leftist Rabbi Claims He's Too Pro-Israel for Anti-War Group," in *Forward* (14 February 2003), and David Brooks, "It's Back: The socialism of fools has returned in vogue not just in the Middle East and France, but in the American left and Washington," in *Weekly Standard* (21 February 2003).

60 "Spiegel kritisiert Nein zum Irak-Krieg" in *Suddeutsche Zeitung* (26 January 2003), Helmut Breuer and Gernot Facius, " 'Es gibt notwendige Kriege.' Paul Spiegel, Zentralratsvorsitzender der Juden, sieht die Oeffentlichkeit in einem 'Dornroeschenschlaf,' " in *Die Welt* (13 February 2003) ("necessary wars").

61 Robert Fisk, "Peres stands accused over denial of 'meaningless' Armenian Holocaust," in *The Independent* (18 April 2001). Recoiling at any comparison between the Nazi and Turkish exterminations, Israel's ambassador to Georgia

vigilant for crimes against humanity – except those committed by your own government. Thus, while the US's uncontrollable power wreaks havoc on much of humanity, the US Holocaust Memorial Council "urged the United States to focus on 'the threat of genocide' in Sudan."[62] Finally, the Israeli military is learning a most instructive Holocaust lesson. To repress Palestinian resistance to the thirty-five-year-long occupation, a senior Israeli officer called on the army to "analyze and internalize the lessons of . . . how the German army fought in the Warsaw ghetto."[63]

One regrettable outcome of the blackmail campaign, Eizenstat concedes, was that "anti-Semitic sentiments increased" (340). The surprise would have been were it otherwise. Just as the Holocaust industry's falsification of history foments Holocaust denial, so its exploitation of Jewish suffering in a shakedown racket inexorably foments anti-Semitism. Nonetheless, Eizenstat's evidence of the "resurgence of anti-Semitic actions in Europe" merits scrutiny. For example, he cites the "threatened boycott of Israeli universities" and "treating Israel as a pariah state" in protest of Israel's brutal occupa-

---

and Armenia maintained that Jews suffered a "genocide" while what happened to the Armenians was merely a "tragedy" ("Armenia files complaint with Israel over comments on genocide," in *Associated Press* [16 February 2002]; for a bitter response, see "Armenian, Greek, and Kurdish Americans Voice Concern to Nine Jewish American Groups," in *Armenian Weekly* [April/May 2002], and see also Thomas O'Dwyer, "Nothing Personal/Among the deniers," in *Haaretz* [9 May 2003]).

62 "Bush Remembers Holocaust Victims, Pledges Defense of Israel," in *Reuters* (19 April 2001).

63 Amir Oren, "At the gates of Yassergrad," in *Haaretz* (25 January 2002), and Uzi Benziman, "Immoral Imperative," in *Haaretz* (1 February 2002).

tion; and reports that "the spate of anti-Semitic actions in Europe has coincided with the response by . . . Prime Minister Ariel Sharon to Palestinian terrorism" – but apparently hasn't coincided with *Sharon's* terrorism (348–9). On a related matter, he cautions against any comparison between Holocaust compensation and the "demands for restitution for the homes that many Palestinians lost" during the 1948 war, maintaining that it is "historically inaccurate" that Palestinians "were unjustly driven from their homes" (351). Finally, he does enter a "hope" that settlement of the Israel–Palestine conflict "will include an international fund, in lieu of actual property restitution" (351). Heaven forbid that Israel should itself pay compensation, let alone return stolen property.

V.

Eizenstat takes special pride in America's unique moral leadership during the Holocaust compensation campaign: "The United States was the only country that cared enough to take an interest" (4); "The world . . . had to understand that the U.S. took the matter of Holocaust assets very seriously" (92); "For those who doubted the capacity of the U.S. government to do things right, this was a shining example of a governmental success" (344); "Only the United States, of all the nations on the globe, cared enough" (355). Likewise, Eizenstat recalls that, in compiling the indictment of Switzerland's trafficking of looted gold with the Nazis, he took the "daring course" (108) of setting "forth the facts and conclusions, however harsh" (108), and that Clinton – lending his unique imprimatur – praised the report as "a landmark on morality" (110).[64] Finally, Eizenstat expresses the pious hope that "by helping nations face their responsibilities for the past," they will prove "more tolerant and self-confident in the future" (344). Gandhi once observed that "it is only when one sees one's own mistakes with a convex lens, and does just the reverse in the case of others, that one is at a just relative estimate of the two."[65] In other words, the only meaningful measure of morality is the claims one makes not on others but on one's self. A simple test of Eizenstat's moral claims is to look at how the US has faced its own "responsibilities for the past." In fact, the US has looked at itself with neither a convex nor even a concave lens, but rather with a black patch.

All the charges leveled by the Holocaust industry at European countries applied to the US. Although Eizenstat never mentions it, the Volcker Committee found that, alongside Switzerland, the US served as a primary safe haven for transferable Jewish assets in Europe before and during the Second World War.[66] Eizenstat does acknowl-

---

[64] According to Eizenstat, his wife also evinced rare moral rectitude during the compensation campaign. Standing in Auschwitz on a cold winter day while listening to stories of the inmates' suffering, "Fran said out loud that she felt guilty wearing her fur coat" (21). Truly she must have been moved.

[65] Mohandas K. Gandhi, *Autobiography* (New York: 1983), 424.

[66] See *HI*, 114ff. for background. Recalling a testy exchange with Roger Witten, a lawyer for the Swiss banks, Eizenstat writes: "Witten insisted that 'wealthy Jewish families sent their money to the U.S., Argentina, and the UK' rather than Switzerland. I found this an astonishing statement" (141). Eizenstat carefully evades, however, the crucial point that the US was *also* a major safe haven. For the record, when queried by this writer about the alleged quote, Witten replied: "The point I was making was that it was a

edge that the US only paid out the "pittance of $500,000" (112; cf. 15–16) on unclaimed Holocaust assets, but goes on to say that when the US contributed another $25 million for Holocaust compensation during his tenure "I have rarely been more proud of my country" (114). Yet, $25 million would seem to fall rather short of what was demanded of the Swiss (leaving aside the astronomical costs of the international audit, which the US was never subjected to). Eizenstat makes one passing allusion to the US Commission on Holocaust Assets chaired by Edgar Bronfman (200) – indeed, the less said the better about the embarrassingly apologetic recommendations and conclusions of its not exactly "daring" final report.[67] Nonetheless this report did contain crucial revelations predictably ignored by Eizenstat; for example, it turns out that trading in looted Nazi gold – the charge he famously leveled against the Swiss banks, and for which he repeatedly

---

mistake to indulge the over-general assumption that Jewish families who succeeded in getting their money out of Germany necessarily sent it to Switzerland. Rather, I said, if they were able to do so, they often sent funds to havens that then appeared to be safer than Switzerland (which was subject to Nazi invasion), particularly the U.K., the U.S., and Argentina (whose economy then was very strong). I also said that when some Jewish families sent money to Switzerland in the first instance, they intended Switzerland to be a way station for some or all of the money, i.e., they expected to be able to transfer it from Switzerland to some place like the U.S., U.K., or Argentina. I believe we had some capital flow data that tended to support these assertions, which certainly had anecdotal support. I certainly never said, nor could reasonably have been understood to say, that Jewish families hadn't sent funds to Switzerland for safekeeping" (private correspondence, 6 January 2003).

[67] See *HI*, 170ff.

chastises the Swiss in his book (49–50, 104, 114) – was *official* US policy until Germany's declaration of war preempted it.[68] Eizenstat acknowledges on multiple occasions that "on a per-capita basis, the Swiss took in far more refugees under more difficult circumstances than did the United States" (103; cf. 9–10, 184), but this begs the question – which he never confronts – of why the Holocaust industry called on the Swiss to pay compensation for Jewish refugees denied entry but put no such demands on the US.[69] Finally, Eizenstat's account of the US record on slave-labor compensation merits extended quotation. To boost the total German settlement, Eizenstat recalls, he proposed creating

[68] *HI*, 173–4. Eizenstat also repeatedly recalls that the Swiss purchased Nazi gold looted from Holocaust victims (50, 91, 101–2, 111, 114) – passing over in silence the fact that there's no evidence the Swiss *knowingly* purchased the "victim gold" and that the US was likely guilty of the same practice (*HI*, 174–5), as well as falsely implying that the value of this "victim gold" purchased by the Swiss came to $14.5 million (114) whereas it was valued at about $135,000 (or $1 million in current values) (*HI*, 110–11). Congratulating the Swiss for having finally reformed, Eizenstat reports that "they have been freezing secret accounts of dictators like the Nigerian strongman, Sani Abacha" (185) – yet skirting over that the Abachas also secreted their ill-gotten gains in US banks (*HI*, 110).

[69] In a letter to *The Nation* (18 February 2002), Burt Neuborne sought to defend this grotesque double standard on the grounds that "the Swiss asked that refugees be allowed to participate in the settlement, and we agreed." In fact, the initial indictment of the class-action lawyers included "the Swiss government in barring refugees" (76). Elsewhere Neuborne concedes that the Swiss settlement included Jewish refugees denied entry due to "the potential theories of liability asserted against various categories of Swiss defendants" (Neuborne, "Preliminary Reflections," 808n34).

a "mirror image" fund for the dozens of American companies whose big German subsidiaries had employed slave labor. According to a 1943 Treasury Department list, the more celebrated names included Ford, General Motors, Gillette, IBM, and Kodak, among many others. I got off to a fast start on December 3, when I met with John Rintanaki, Ford's group vice president and chief of staff. An energetic, upbeat person, he got right to the point. Strikingly frank, he volunteered that Henry Ford, the company's founder, was a notorious anti-Semite who had been publicly recognized by Hitler for his work in Germany. He made no attempt to deny that the Nazis had employed forced and slave laborers in Ford's plants and promised to help recruit American companies with a goal of raising half a billion dollars. He said his task would be easier if we could create a charitable organization so the corporate contributions would qualify as tax deductions. Craig Johnstone, head of the international division of the U.S. Chamber of Commerce and a former State Department colleague, made it easier for the companies to contribute without appearing to admit wartime guilt by persuading the Chamber of Commerce to approve a humanitarian fund that its corporate membership could use for everything from hurricane to Holocaust relief. We jointly launched it with fanfare at a news conference at the chamber's Washington, D.C., headquarters. But the money never arrived. Despite several more meetings with Rintanaki, who made a genuine effort to convince other firms to join, it was a dry hole. In December 2001, two years after my first meeting with Rintanaki and well after the end of the Clinton administration, one of Rintanaki's aides told me that the Ford Motor Company would contribute $2 million. No other American company ever gave a nickel to the chamber fund, relying on their

German subsidiaries to pay instead into the German Foundation. (254–5)

In his conclusion, Eizenstat observes that "one enduring message we sent was that, regardless of treaties and legal precedents, there is no effective statute of limitations on corporate accountability" (354) – unless, of course, it's an American corporation.[70]

~

[70] When Holocaust survivors from Hungary sued the US government for the return of assets looted by pro-Nazi Hungarian troops and subsequently misappropriated by American military personnel, Eizenstat (now in private practice) ridiculed the "legal basis" of the claim as "suspect," and called for merely "some token payment to the Hungarian Jewish community" (Stuart Eizenstat, "Justice Remains Beyond Grasp of Too Many Holocaust Victims," in *Forwards* [18 October 2002]). Even in his egregiously apologetic account of the compensation campaign, Bazyler, *Holocaust Justice*, concedes that "the U.S. Holocaust Assets Commission headed by Bronfman was . . . a failure. After spending $2.7 million, the commission failed to meet even its primary goal: assembling a database of Holocaust-era assets still in the United States. Moreover, given its limited mandate to look at only the activities of the federal government and thus not the activities of American industry during the war, the commission could not ask the same questions about American corporate complicity with the Nazis that similar government-created historical commissions had asked in Europe . . . Unfortunately, there seems to be a double standard here. The demands that we have made on European governments and corporations about honestly confronting and documenting their wartime financial dealings and other activities are not being followed in the United States" (305). Putting to one side the matter of compensation, simply compare the $2.7 million allocated by the US for its own commission with the "nearly $700 million" (300–1) Swiss banks have had to pay out to

"The Bible says that the sins of the father should not be visited upon the son," Eizenstat reflects. "But just how much do present generations owe the victims of the past when part of their prosperity is based on their country having enslaved and robbed them" (279)? In the case of the Nazi holocaust, the answer seems to be quite a lot; in the cases of American slavery and South African apartheid, the answer seems to be not much at all. Although the US's industrialization was crucially based on African slave labor, Eizenstat maintains that the only relevant monetary "lesson" from the Holocaust compensation campaign for the current "American slavery cases" is that "the companies sued might" provide "minority scholarships, or training and hiring programs" (353). Eizenstat mentions the "anti-apartheid class-action suits" filed against companies that profited from decades of racist exploitation (351), but inexplicably forgets to mention that – in a true profile in moral consistency – he himself is "now acting as the advocate" for the targeted companies.[71] "To the degree that property restitution becomes a regular process," Eizenstat surmises, "it will help the countries of Eastern Europe to become healthier democracies" (45). Making amends for ill-gotten gains no doubt strengthens a society's moral fabric. Yet, Eizenstat never thought to apply this insight to the US. Consider a multibillion-dollar class-action lawsuit filed by Native

---

auditors. In another testament to the double standard, Bazyler, while indignantly dilating on the fate of Holocaust-era Jewish assets deposited in Swiss banks, makes not a single direct reference to the fate of Holocaust-era Jewish assets deposited in US banks.

71 See Andreas Mink, "'Das Schlimmste steht uns noch bevor.' Der Ex-US-Staatssekretaer Stuart Eizenstat engagiert sich in der Auseinandersetzung um Menschenrechts-Klagen," in *Aufbau* (12 December 2002).

Americans against the Clinton administration that strikingly resembled the Swiss banks litigation – except that the allegations were true. Indeed, a main target of this lawsuit was the Treasury Department during Eizenstat's tenure as its Deputy Secretary.

VI.

In June 1996 the Native American Rights Fund filed the largest class-action lawsuit in US history on behalf of Elouise Pepion Cobell of Montana's Blackfeet tribe, and 300,000–500,000 other Native Americans. "Plaintiffs' class includes some of the poorest people in this nation," Judge Royce C. Lamberth later observed. "Human welfare and livelihood are at stake."[72] Per capita income among these impoverished descendants of the "American holocaust"[73] hovers at less than $10,000 per year and unemployment stands at nearly 70 percent, while more than 90 percent of the elderly lack long-term health care. The Clinton administration "ought to have been ashamed," Cobell rebuked a Justice Department official. "People are dying in all Indian communities. They don't have access to their own money."[74]

---

[72] United States District Court for the District of Columbia, Elouise Pepion Cobell et al., Plaintiffs, v. Bruce Babbitt, Secretary of the Interior, Lawrence Summers, Secretary of the Treasury, and Kevin Gover, Assistant Secretary of the Interior (Civil Action No. 96–1285) (RCL), *Memorandum Opinion: Findings of Fact and Conclusions of Law* (21 December 1999), 6. (Hereafter: *Memorandum Opinion – December 1999*.)

[73] See David Stannard's authoritative study, *American Holocaust* (Oxford: 1992).

[74] Jeffrey St. Clair, "Stolen Trust" in *CounterPunch* (5 September 2002).

At issue were Native American monies held in trust by the US government. The genesis of these Individual Indian Money (IIM) trust accounts reached back to the late nineteenth century when, under the General Allotment Act (1887), 140 million acres of communally-owned tribal lands were broken up into private plots. "As the government concedes," Judge Lamberth stated, "the purpose of the IIM trust was to deprive plaintiffs' ancestors of their native lands and rid the nation of their tribal identity."[75] Fully 90 million acres were deemed "surplus" and quickly opened to non-Indian settlement, while another 40 million acres "have *never* been accounted for."[76] Revenue from leases for grazing, mining, drilling and lumbering rights on these lands – now reduced to 10 million acres – was supposed to go into the IIM trust accounts. The class-action suit called on the US government to finally audit – "abide by its duty to render an accurate accounting of"[77] – these accounts. Designating their condition a "national disgrace," a 1992 Congressional report found that IIM accounts "look as though they had been handled with a pitchfork," and were the "equivalent of a bank that doesn't know how much money it has."[78] "For decades there have been dozens of government

---

[75] *Memorandum Opinion – December 1999*, 5.

[76] United States District Court for the District of Columbia, Elouise Pepion Cobell, et al. vs. Bruce Babbitt, Secretary of the Interior et al., Defendants, *Plaintiffs' Plan for Determining Accurate Balances in the Individual Indian Trust* (6 January 2003), 2–3 (emphasis in original). (Hereafter: *Plaintiffs' Plan – January 2003*.)

[77] *Memorandum Opinion – December 1999*, 6.

[78] Committee on Government Operations (102d Congress, House Rept. 102–499), *Misplaced Trust: The Bureau of Indian Affairs Mismanagement of the Indian Trust Fund* (1 April 1992), 12, 84–5. (Hereafter: *Misplaced Trust*.)

reports, congressional hearings and findings," Secretary of Interior Bruce Babbitt conceded during litigation, "that have criticized Department of Interior's management of its trust responsibilities," yet "few, if any of these proposals have ever been implemented."[79] "It would be difficult to find a more historically mismanaged federal program," Judge Lamberth concluded. "The United States . . . cannot say how much money is or should be in the trust . . . It is fiscal and governmental irresponsibility in its purest form."[80] And again: "The Department of Interior's administration of the Individual Indian Money trust has served as the gold standard for mismanagement by the federal government for more than a century . . . [T]he federal government regularly issues payments to beneficiaries – of their *own* money – in erroneous amounts."[81]

In 1994 Congress enacted the Indian Trust Fund Management Act, which formed the legal basis for the Cobell suit. It required the Department of Interior and Treasury Department to provide – in Judge Lamberth's words – "an accurate accounting of all money in the IIM trust . . ., without regard to when the funds were deposited."[82] The trial was eventually bifurcated into two phases: "fixing

---

[79] *Memorandum Opinion – December 1999*, 125; for details of the US government's long record of delinquency, cf. *Misplaced Trust*, 86ff.

[80] *Memorandum Opinion – December 1999*, 4–5.

[81] United States District Court for the District of Columbia, Elouise Pepion Cobell, et al., Plaintiffs, v. Gale A. Norton, Secretary of the Interior, et al., Defendants (Civil Action No. 96–1285) (RCL), *Memorandum Opinion* (17 September 2002), 1–2 (emphasis in original). (Hereafter: *Memorandum Opinion – September 2002*.)

[82] United States District Court for the District of Columbia, Elouise Pepion, et al., Plaintiffs, v. Bruce Babbitt, Secretary of the Interior, Lawrence Summers,

the system" or reforming the management and accounting practices of the IIM trust; and "correcting the accounts" or performing a comprehensive historical audit of the IIM trust with "the government bringing forward its proof . . . and then plaintiffs making exceptions to that proof." After successive court findings of contempt against the defendants (more on which presently), an intermediate 1.5 phase was created to further monitor government compliance.

In the course of the trial, the court repeatedly chastised the Department of Interior and Treasury Department for grossly mishandling documentation crucial to the audit. In a February 1999 trial, Judge Lamberth found defendants in civil contempt for having "failed to produce" a "substantial" "set of documents required by a court order," and – in the specific case of the Treasury Department, where Eizenstat served as Deputy Secretary – for "destroying" documents "it had promised to maintain." Noting that apparently "no sitting Secretary in modern times has been held in contempt of court," and that "I do not relish holding these cabinet officials in contempt," Lamberth charged defendants with "actions [that] can be characterized as nothing short of contumacious," a "behind-the-scenes cover-up," "campaign of stonewalling," and "shocking pattern of deception," "numerous illegitimate misrepresentations," "nothing short of a travesty," "reckless disregard for the orders of this court," "misconduct [that] rises above the level of 'reckless disregard'," "willful dereliction . . . perilously close to *criminal* contempt of court" and so on. "I have never seen," he concluded, "more egregious misconduct by the federal govern-

Secretary of the Treasury, and Kevin Gover, Assistant Secretary of the Interior (Civil Action No. 96–1285) (RCL), *Order* (21 December 1999).

ment." Eizenstat praises his boss, Robert Rubin, as "one of the most successful treasury secretaries since Alexander Hamilton" (227) but ignores that – for "destroying" documents in a compensation case – Rubin "has been tarnished with this contempt citation" (Lamberth).[83] In a December 1999 report the court-appointed Special Master disclosed the Treasury Department's renewed destruction of documents "potentially responsive or potentially relevant to the Cobell litigation . . . at the exact time the Secretary of the Treasury was held in contempt for violation of his discovery obligations," as well as its failure "to disclose the destruction . . . notwithstanding myriad opportunities to do so." "This is a system," the Special Master concluded, "clearly out of control."[84]

In his December 1999 opinion for Phase 1 of the trial, Judge Lamberth found that the Department of Interior had committed "four

---

[83] United States District Court for the District of Columbia, Elouise Pepion, et al., Plaintiffs, v. Bruce Babbitt, Secretary of the Interior, Robert Rubin, Secretary of the Treasury, and Kevin Gover, Assistant Secretary of the Interior (Civil Action No. 96–1285) (RCL), *Memorandum Opinion* (22 February 1999), 15 ("travesty"), 17 ("modern times," "relish"), 33 ("failed," "substantial"), 50–3 ("destroying"), 62 ("contumacious"), 67 ("cover-up," "campaign"), 70 ("illegitimate"), 71–2 ("reckless," "close to *criminal*" [emphasis in original]), 77 ("shocking," "egregious"), 79 ("tarnished"). (Hereafter: *Memorandum Opinion – February 1999*.)

[84] United States District Court For the District of Columbia, Elouise Pepion Cobell et al., Plaintiffs, v. Bruce Babbitt, Secretary of the Interior, et al., Defendants (Civil Action No. 96–1285) (RCL), *Recommendation and Report of the Special Master Regarding the Delayed Disclosure of the Uncurrent Check Records Maintained by the Department of the Treasury* (3 December 1999), 24ff. (renewed destruction), 56 ("myriad opportunities"), 117–18 ("potentially," "out of control").

statutory breaches" in mishandling documents and administrative procedures "necessary to render an accurate accounting." In particular, "Interior has no written plan to gather . . . necessary missing information required to render an accurate accounting. Indeed it does not even have a discernible intent to do so"; "The missing-data problem is undoubtedly the single biggest obstacle that Interior will face in rendering an accurate accounting"; "[I]t is clear that the longer Interior waits to retrieve missing information, the less of that information will be available and able to be located." Likewise, Lamberth found that the Treasury Department's systematic destruction of documents ("Treasury's documents pertaining to the [IIM] funds, including canceled checks, went to the shredder") was "a breach of plaintiffs' right to have retained the documents necessary to allow the United States to render an accounting"; and that Treasury still lacked a clear plan for retention of relevant documents.[85] Upholding Lamberth's opinion, the US Court of Appeals subsequently ruled that the Treasury Department's "destruction of potentially relevant IIM-related trust documents that may have been necessary for a complete accounting is clear evidence that the Department" breached its "fiduciary duty"; and that "given the history of destruction of documents and loss of information necessary to conduct an historical accounting, the failure of the government to act could place anything approaching an adequate accounting beyond plaintiffs' reach."[86]

---

[85] *Memorandum Opinion – December 1999*, 33 ("no written plan"), 49 ("shredder"), 90–1 ("four statutory breaches"), 97 ("missing-data problem"), 109 ("longer Interior waits"), 117 ("breach of plaintiffs' rights"); cf. 112, 118.

[86] United States Court of Appeals for the District of Columbia Circuit. Argued September 5, 2000; Decided 23 February 2001. No. 00–5081. Elouise

In a September 2002 contempt trial Judge Lamberth found that, in grossly misrepresenting the current state of the IIM trust, defendants had committed multiple "frauds" on the court: "It is now abundantly clear that the six week Phase I trial was nothing more than a dog and pony show put on by the Interior defendants . . . [T]he defendants deliberately allowed this Court to rule on a record that was replete with factual errors"; "In my fifteen years on the bench I have never seen a litigant make such a concerted effort to subvert the truth seeking function of the judicial process. I am immensely disappointed that I see such a litigant today and that the litigant is a Department of the United States government. The Department of Interior is truly an embarrassment to the federal government in general and the executive branch in particular"; "The egregious nature of the Department's conduct in this regard is exacerbated by the fact that attorneys in the Solicitor's Office actively participated"; "It is almost unfathomable that a federal agency would engage in such a pervasive scheme aimed at defrauding the Court and preventing the plaintiffs from learning the truth about the administration of their trust accounts."[87]

~

The U.S. government's handling of the actual audit has proven equally scandalous. With cost estimates ranging from $200 to $400 million, already in the early 1990s both Congress ("it makes little sense to

---

Pepion Cobell, et al., Appellees v. Gale A. Norton, Secretary of the Interior, et al., Appellants. Consolidated with 00–5084. Appeals from the United States District Court for the District of Columbia (No. 96cv01285).

[87] *Memorandum Opinion – September 2002*, 199 ("abundantly clear"), 202 ("fifteen years"), 204 ("egregious nature"), 206 ("almost unfathomable").

spend so much") and the Department of Interior ("a difficult task, perhaps costing over $200 million") questioned the financial wisdom of auditing the accounts. In 1996 Interior requested only a modest sum for the audit and even this amount was slashed by the Federal government.[88] In the September 2002 contempt trial Judge Lamberth found that, despite a court order, for more than a year and a half Interior "had not even taken the preliminary steps" toward conducting the audit. As of early 2002 (when the trial record closed) Interior "still only had . . . a plan for developing a plan" to conduct an audit. "The Court is both saddened and disgusted," Judge Lamberth observed, "by the Department's intransigence."[89] Additionally, the court found that Interior had "committed a fraud on the Court" regarding the audit's design. The basic options were a "transaction-by-transaction" versus a "statistical sampling" method. While pretending to solicit the preference of Native Americans ("numerous IIM beneficiaries, at their own expense, traveled to and provided comments at numerous meetings across the country") and knowing full well that they "overwhelmingly favored" the exhaustive audit, Interior had already decided beforehand on a very restricted statistical sampling. The main rationale was cost. Among "Department staff, Congress and outside third-parties," the consensus was that "a complete transaction-by-transaction accounting for every account would cost hundreds of millions of dollars," and "Congress has made it clear . . . that they are unlikely to fund such a process." Indeed, recalling

---

[88] *Misplaced Trust*, 38 ("little sense"); *Memorandum Opinion – December 1999*, 21 ("difficult task").

[89] *Memorandum Opinion – September 2002*, 64 ("only had"), 180–2 ("saddened").

that "the evidence presented and representations made at this contempt trial . . . prove just how deceitful and disingenuous the
defendants can be," Judge Lamberth found that the formal solicitation
of Native American opinion was "actually part of a scheme" hatched
by the Department of Interior. By pretending to act in good faith it
sought to overturn on appeal "this Court's Phase I trial ruling, delay
initiating a historical accounting project, and prevent more invasive
relief from this Court." He went on to question the commitment of
Clinton's Interior Department to *any* audit: "In light of the agency's
history of recalcitrance towards such an endeavor, the assumption is
dubious at best."[90]

Reviewing the entire court record, Judge Lamberth scathingly
observed that the Department of Interior "handled this litigation the
same way that it has managed the IIM trust – disgracefully"; that it
had engaged in "despicable conduct" and "disgraceful actions"; that
"the defendants' contention that the Court should consider their
'good-faith' efforts would be laughable if it were not so sad and
cynical"; that "the recalcitrance exhibited by the Department of
Interior in complying with the orders of this Court is only surpassed
by the incompetence that the agency has shown in administering the
IIM trust"; and so on. "I may have life tenure," he concluded, "but at
the rate the Department of Interior is progressing that is not a long

---

[90] *Memorandum Opinion – September 2002*, 41n30, 48–50, 54–55 ("hundreds of
millions," "unlikely to fund"), 190–4 ("numerous meetings," "overwhelmingly," "scheme," "trial ruling," "dubious"). Although sharply critical of Bush's
Department of Interior, Judge Lamberth did acknowledge that it was
"marginally more responsive" (212).

enough appointment."[91] In January 2003, Native American plaintiffs presented Judge Lamberth a "detailed court filing . . . based on private historical records asserting that the government had cheated them out of as much as $137.2 billion over the last 115 years."[92]

But who can doubt the US's authority to render moral judgment on the "perfidious Swiss"?[93]

---

[91] *Memorandum Opinion – September 2002*, 2 ("disgracefully"), 212 ("laughable"), 216 ("despicable"), 218 ("disgraceful actions"), 242 ("recalcitrance"), 267 ("life tenure").

[92] Joel Brinkley, "American Indians Say Documents Show Government Has Cheated Them Out of Billions," in *New York Times* (7 January 2003). This was one of only 6 articles the *Times* has devoted to the Cobell case, as against 359 articles to the Swiss banks case. For the court filing, see *Plaintiffs' Plan – January 2003*.

[93] Neuborne avows that the impetus behind Holocaust compensation was "a sense of the moral obligation of foreign defendants to live by American rules of fundamental fairness . . . if they wish to participate in the remarkable success of this economic, social, and political culture," and that "when a foreign corporation wishes to reap the benefits of our economic and social system, I am not the slightest bit embarrassed to insist that the foreign corporation agree to live by the legal rules that allowed the social and economic system to flourish." Indeed, why should he be embarrassed that, whenever its own liability is at stake, the US ignores these "rules of fundamental fairness": for, isn't the cardinal rule that enabled this system to flourish that none of the rules applies to itself? (Neuborne, "Preliminary Reflections," 831).

INDEX